BELCHING OUT THE DEVIL

To Jenny

BELCHING OUT THE DEVIL

MARK THOMAS

EBURY
PRESS

1 3 5 7 9 10 8 6 4 2

Published in 2009 by Ebury Press, an imprint of Ebury Publishing
A Random House Group Company
First Published in the UK in 2008

The Random House Group Limited Reg. No. 954009

Addresses for companies within the Random House Group can be found
at www.randomhouse.co.uk

A CIP catalogue record for this book is available from the British Library

The Random House Group Limited supports The Forest Stewardship
Council (FSC), the leading international forest certification organisation.
All our titles that are printed on Greenpeace approved FSC certified
paper carry the FSC logo. Our paper procurement policy can be found at
www.rbooks.co.uk/environment

Printed in the UK by CPI Cox & Wyman, Reading, RG1 8EX

ISBN 9780091927042

To buy books by your favourite authors and register for offers visit
www.rbooks.co.uk

Contents

An Admission

Globalisation can claim to have won on the day elderly grandparents started wearing trainers. Somehow it just seems wrong that a generation who fought and defeated the Nazis with sacrifice, ration books and allotments should endure the graceless experience of Footlocker. At that moment this very generation who had endured wars, created welfare states and could mend radios and bikes changed into consumers. It was around the same time that someone decided that instead of selling things with guarantees it was more profitable to sell the goods and then sell the guarantee too.

My own grandmother lived to ninety-eight and was no role model for sobriety or chastity. Her name was Margaret Isabel and she had more lovers than her family will ever know. She was small but got into fights because she hated bullies. And when I went to stay with her as a boy she would bounce me on her knee, sing Geordie folk songs and entrance me with the smoke rings she could blow. She could also flip the lit end of the cigarette into her mouth, blow smoke through the now protruding filter and then pop the lit end out again, using only her tongue. I utterly adored her. She was a unique woman, who took pride in her family's shoes being polished. I'm glad she never wore a trainer. But I cannot smell Coca-Cola without thinking of her. That is my admission. I used to love drinking Coca-Cola. Moreover, whenever I held a glass of just poured Coca-Cola to my lips and felt the bubbles popping under my nose, I would think of my nan. It was a Pavlovian response. When I stayed with her, every day began with the two of us making a trip to a coffee shop. She would have an Embassy and a coffee and I would have a Coca-Cola and a sticky bun. It is one of my favourite memories.

To this extent I was a classic Coke drinker. It was a treat when I was young. I'd drink Coke all the time in my twenties and Diet Coke in my thirties. I even dabbled with caffeine-free Diet Coke, which is about as pointless as consumerism can get. Coca-Cola is essentially sugar and caffeine and water, so take out two of the main ingredients and really I was just buying chemically treated water with a nice logo. But I fell into the ultimate Coca-Cola advertising trap when I started associating an intricate part of my life, the memory of my grandmother, with their product. Weaving their drink into our lives has been Coke's greatest advertising feat. Why am I telling you this? The fact is that before I looked into the Company I enjoyed their drink. Immensely. And Fanta, too. All I am saying really is: my name is Mark and I'm a recovering Coca-Cola drinker...one day at a time.

PROLOGUE

'The Coca-Cola Company is on a journey. It is a bold journey...fuelled by our deep conviction that collectively we can create anything we desire...Ultimately, this journey will be propelled by unleashing the collective genius of our organisation...it is our very nature to innovate, create and excel. It is who we are.'

The Coca-Cola Company, Manifesto for Growth[1]

am not that great a traveller. I may like to think of myself as a mix between Hunter S Thompson and Michael Palin, but in reality I am a middle-aged fat dad with asthma, trudging around the world with half-eaten bars of Kendal Mint Cake and a six-pack of Ventolin inhalers.

I'm fond of neither airplanes nor airports, believing them to be the secular limbo of the badly dressed. No one wears their best clothes to fly in and as a rule, the larger the flyer the more likely they are to be decked in sportswear. Thus creatures the size of sea mammals trawl departure lounges in clinging tracksuit bottoms that serve only to highlight the disparity between sporting aspiration and achievement. I know: I'm one of them. I'm a man who has seen too many airports in too few hours; my eyes are glazed, my pallor is pasty and I'm starting to look like my police picture. Atlanta is my seventh airport in five days. I have been propelled to 36,000 foot in metal tubes so many times that my ears pop if I walk up a flight of stairs, and after 4,207 miles of recycled air and microwaved food my breath tastes like someone else's fart.

There is no greater reminder of the reasons, need and urgency for reducing air travel than airports and spending time in them. I wince at the carbon footprint I am going to leave, though it occurs to me that no one pointed the carbon footprint finger at the United Nations Climate Change Conference and that was in Bali – an island in the Indian Ocean, a location which enabled only Balinese delegates to reduce emissions by walking or getting the bus. Everyone else had to fly. I decide there is a corrupt UN official in charge of such conferences who collects air miles.

Such is the mental state of my meanderings. I have stood in too many queues with my shoes in my hands over the past few days. Only half an hour ago I saw an elderly couple, with cardigans and travel sweets, shuffle to the front of the line at the metal detectors. They respectfully asked, 'Do we have to take our shoes off?'

'Yes, ma'am. Shoes off and into the tray,' said the member of staff who had obviously excelled at brusqueness training school.

'Shoes...' They looked at each other and shrug.

'Shoes and belts please,' he barked

'Belts...'

'Belts and jackets, please into the tray.'

A large young black woman turned to them confidently and said, 'It's the same all over, you wanna go anywhere these days you gotta get half-naked, honey. That's the truth.' Then, staring directly at the security guard, she yelped, 'Come on. Let's get them off.' And she begins to disrobe in a manner that can only be described as hostile.

I smile at the memory and traipse through a row of the terminal gift shops looking for something to read and a present to take home for my children. This isn't shopping, this is Groundhog Day. Another airport, another baseball cap; same cap, different city, just a matter of changing place names and animals. And so the Chicago Bears become the Miami Dolphins, who become the Washington Pandas, who in turn morph into the Georgia Head Lice or some other sporting mascot. The hats are on stands placed strategically around the newsagent's cash register and sweet display, while the walls are packed with magazines ranging from *Home & Garden* to *Guns & Ammo*, shelf loads of glossy front covers featuring cars, bridal dresses, computers and Britney Spears. There are hundreds of magazines here. To paraphrase Sir Winston Churchill: never in the history of consumerism have so many been offered so much of so little.

On one display stand alongside the hats is a pyramid of shot glasses, little tumblers for downing spirits in a gulp. These glasses have I ? OUR TROOPS over a khaki background so while the troops are living under fire some patriotic stay-at-home is getting drunk on their behalf. Next to the glasses is a pile of teddy bears, little soft toys full of Styrofoam beans or some such stuff. Each is decorated in the US army desert camouflage kit, complete with Stars and Stripes on its chest and a plaintive stare on its little face. It is as if the bear is saying 'I've seen some things out there man. Things a bear shouldn't see.'

'Who buys this crap?' I think. Tired idiots with a misfiring sense of kitsch value, I conclude, slouching into a moulded plastic seat, sweaty and glazed with a soldier teddy bear on my lap.
I sit, pale and tired, watching the display boards and listening for flight information on Colombia, my next destination being Bogota. My journey is seven airports, five days and four cities old and now I'm heading off to the cocaine capitol of the world with a teddy bear dressed like a US marine...

Oh God, what have I done...

* * *

At this moment in time you may well be asking yourself three questions: 'Where has Mark been, why is he going to Colombia and more importantly, have I kept the receipt for this book?'

To which the short answers are: the Coca-Cola museum, to meet a Coca-Cola deliveryman and I don't know.

You find me at the midway point of a trip to the US and Colombia. This is the first of a series of journeys to try and find the reality behind the PR image of the world's most famous brand, Coca-Cola. Quite why I set myself this task needs some explanation and to fully understand you need to grasp one fact: I have been a paid egotist all my working life. I started out as a comedian in the mid-1980s in London. Back then you didn't have to fuck a footballer or eat kangaroo penis on a reality show to appear on TV. No, back then any half-decent comic could get their own series on Channel 4, and being half-decent, I did. The shows ran from 1996–2002, 45 episodes over six series and a string of one-off documentaries. Some of the shows were crap, so bad I have not been able to watch them and I never will. Some of them were good and actually worked – the government tightened up tax laws on the back of two shows I did. A large company changed their policies and practices, some of the stories I covered made the front pages of the national press and Amnesty commended my work. By this stage my ego was robust enough to shield entire towns from most forms of attack (with the possible exception of kryptonite to which I have always been vulnerable). If I were to do a graph of my ego's peaks and troughs you would find the high spikes of my vanity and self-belief coincided with the decision to take on Coca-Cola. At the pinnacle of my narcissistic faith in my abilities, a series of events conspired that led to me being here.

Back in 2001 I was writing a column for the *New Statesman* magazine, a left-of-centre weekly with circulation figures that were the envy of every other British left-wing journal. It is sold in many cities and was once spotted in a petrol station rack. It is a crotchety old rag that is owned by a New Labour millionaire, runs adverts for the arms dealers BAE Systems and gives out Tesco gift vouchers as prizes for its competitions, but somehow it manages to host really good columnists from John Pilger to Shazia Mirza. I loved working for it and after one column was left a message from a chap called Professor Eric Herring, offering to help me by providing academic research and data. After the initial shock of realising that some academics have social skills and can conduct a conversation without the need for footnotes and peer review, a world of wonderfully brainy folk opened up to me. It is not that the academic world is closed to outsiders; it is just insular, very insular. So it is essential to have a guide through this world, someone like Professor Eric Herring. If he was unable to help with an issue, he would invariably pass me on to another academic who could. It was like Mensa meets the Masons but without the aprons and David Icke pointing the finger.

One day Professor Eric Herring left a message saying, 'Really good column, nice analysis but you need up-to-date examples, you need to talk to Doug, one of my research students. He'll tell you about Colombia.' And what he told me about Colombia was the shocking figures and facts about the number of trade union organisers and leaders killed by paramilitary death squads. Thousands killed for the audacity of challenging sackings, wage cuts, intimidation, coercion to work longer hours, unsafe conditions and trying to halt the wave of casualised jobs – temporary jobs with no security or protection – that has swept over Colombia.

As one of the academics was connected to the Colombia Solidarity Campaign it was only a matter of time before I came into contact with them and their campaign on Coca-Cola, as trade union leaders working for the Coke bottlers had been killed by death squads: one of those was killed inside the bottling plant.

Misfortunes seemed to rain upon the Company around this time. Coca-Cola were getting some considerable attention on the issue of obesity from the Parliamentary Select Committee on Health[2] and the story of Plachimada in Kerala hit the international airwaves after the Coca-Cola bottlers there faced massive protests accusing the Company of exploiting the communal water resources. So depleted was the water supply that the Company was forced to bus in two tankers of water a day for the villagers.[3]

Then one afternoon I was talking to the man who used to produce my TV work, Geoff Atkinson. He is a quirky British chap, a large man with curly blond hair and a habit of wiggling his thumbs to signify excitement and contentment. In effect he has shrugged off years of evolution and relegated his prehensile thumb to the role of a dog's tail. Geoff was drinking a bottle of Coca-Cola and as we started to discuss New Labour I had pointed at the bottle and said , 'That is New Labour. Good packaging, lots of sugar and otherwise worthless.' Half an hour later I had formalised my obsession with the Company. There followed two months of internet trawls, late-night phone calls to anyone who was still awake and long meetings with non-governmental organisations and journalists, all of which culminated at the start of 2004 with me standing outside the Coke bottling plant in Southern India clutching a borrowed camera from Geoff pondering the subjects of globalisation, democracy, and wet wipes.

Over the next year I wrote and toured a stage show about the company, had numerous columns about Coke in the *New Statesman* (to the extent of the editor telling me 'You really can't do them three weeks running') and I co-curated an exhibition, with artist and friend Tracey Moberly, that invited anyone to submit drawings, pictures and Photoshopped images mocking the company's adverts.

All of us have psychological ticks and mine is that I find enemies easier to work with than friends. Broadly speaking you know where you are with an enemy and there is always the faint possibility of redemption; friends are altogether more complex and require much more attention. In the voyeuristic car-crash TV world of agony aunts and life coaches we are often told of the value of 'moving on', of walking away from trouble and getting on with our lives. But there is little joy to be had in avoiding trouble and people who don't bear grudges frankly have not got the emotional stamina for the job.

Friends who still wanted to speak to me asked, 'Why Coca-Cola, why are you going after them?' And the answer I most frequently gave was that The Coca-Cola Company is a relatively small company that makes syrup – they don't actually make much pop themselves. They franchise out the pop production, getting other companies to make it. Admittedly they own some of those companies, they have major shareholdings in others and some are what are called 'independent bottlers' –but they are all franchisees. They operate under what the company calls 'the Coca-Cola system'. The Coca-Cola Company (or TCCC) controls who gets the franchise, they control the distribution of concentrate (the syrup with which to make Coke), the production method, the packaging and they even coordinate marketing and advertising with the local bottlers. They have an enormous level of control over the bottlers yet will often claim they have no legal or moral responsibility for the actions of their bottlers if it involves labour rights or environmental abuses.

The one thing The Coca-Cola Company does have is a whopping great enormous brand and that is what they sell. Coke epitomises globalisation: a transnational worth billions that actually produces very little and yet is known the world over.

And that is truly part of the reason. But it is not the whole answer. There are two other reasons why I wanted to look at Coca-Cola and the first is simple: I don't like Pepsi. I never have and I never will. Coca-Cola is what I used to drink every day and, like many everyday things, I never really questioned it. In a similar way, I look at my watch but I have never wondered who first quantified units of time. Then one day sitting with Geoff I just looked at the bottle and thought, 'What actually is it I am drinking?' And I wasn't looking at just the physical ingredients, but the ingredients of the brand and the company. Like many, I did not buy South African goods while Mandela was jailed, as they were contaminated by the apartheid system; so what battles were going on in a bottle of Coke? I just wanted to know – and considering that every year they spend billions of dollars on advertising, I reckon a few of those dollars were spent on me. As far as I'm concerned they came after my custom, so they started it.

The first reason is specific to me; the second is global. When George Mallory was asked why he wanted to climb Mount Everest he said 'Because it's there.' Why do I want to write about Coke? 'Because it's everywhere.' You can't escape it.

And sitting here in Atlanta airport the impact of that statement was just beginning to hit me. The gulf between self-image and reality can be an ego-crushing chasm. I like to think I have a competent grasp of the basic concepts of globalisation, human rights and social movements, but realistically I know on a bad day I'm about as incisive and cutting as a Haribo.

Like most big-heads I believe my abilities to be greater than they are, but even I have moments of clarity. This morning I visited the Coke museum, which is a testimony to the Company's history and its advertising blitzkriegs, and as I look around I realise I am witnessing a skirmish in one of those battles right now. In the immediate vicinity of my seat in the the airport lounge is a man-sized Coca-Cola fridge packed with Company products, an authentic Mexican diner serving drinks in Coke glasses, a massive Coca-Cola vending machine, a bottle of Coke sticking out of a seven-year-old's rucksack, a 30-something in a Coca-Cola T-shirt and numerous bottles of Dasani, Coca-Cola's brand of bottled water, being slurped by a school sports team that have arrived in tracksuits. Leaning back on the seat I can capture this entire scene within my field of vision. I am the odd one out, the exception to the Coke-drinking norm.

Coca-Cola is the biggest brand in the world, they have a greater global reach than a flu virus, they have lawyers who excrete spare IQ points and I am a dad sitting in an airport holding a teddy bear and an asthma inhaler muttering, 'Oh God, what have I done...'

1
THE HAPPINESS FACTORY

Atlanta, USA

'Coke is like a little bottle of sparkle-dust.'

Inside the Happiness Factory, The Coca-Cola Company 'documentary'

Everyone tells stories and a good story is a sleight of hand, distracting where needs be and discerning in its revelations. But the craftiest storytellers can tell you a tale without you realising it's being told. They are called advertisers – though some prefer the word 'twat'. Every product they sell has a tale to tell and an audience in mind to tell it to. They can tell a story with a phrase, a picture and sometimes with a single pencil line. Without them transnationals would become extinct because in order to sell they have to tell stories. They have to tell them to survive. Without adverts, brands do not exist and without brands modern corporations crumble.

No company spends money unless they feel it is for their financial benefit, so consider the estimated total global advertising budget for 2008: it is US$665 billion', or to use its technical term a 'gazillion'. With that amount of money you could run the UN and its entire operations for 33 years[2]. Or you could finance a totally new 'War on Terror'[3]: the US could invade North Korea and Cuba and still have change for a fair crack at France. For lovers of traditional forms of statistical comparison, the global advertising budget is Liberia's GDP for 600 years[4].

In the battle of the brands Coca-Cola are king. In 2007 news spread across the globe's financial networks that for the sixth year in a row Coca-Cola had been ranked as the world's top brand, beating well-known competition from Microsoft, McDonald's, Disney, IBM and Nokia to the title[5]. *Business Week*/Interbrand annual ratings and its evaluations are based on a distinct criterion: the belief that brands can be intangible assets, ie, something that doesn't physically exist yet can nonetheless have a financial worth. The value of a brand is calculated through surveys, which essentially measure the goodwill felt towards a company. Now I'm not an expert on high finance but the day that the trader or banker came up with the idea that you could put a price on...er...nothing tangible – well, that day must have ended very late at night with a taxi driver helping them to the front door.

Interbrand valued the Coca-Cola brand at $65.324 billion, which is a lot of goodwill. And the company must fight for every penny of it. For take away the brand, the image, the red and white colours and iconic script, take away the shape of the bottle, the advertising, the polar bears, the lights in Times Square, the Santa ads at Christmas, the Superbowl commercials, the sponsorship of the Olympics and football leagues, take all that away and you are left with the product: brown fizzy sugar water. And brown fizzy sugar water with no packaging, no logo and no built-in aspirations concocted in advertising land is not something any of us really need. Asa Chandler, Coke's first proprietor, knew this and set to conquering the world with a simple philosophy: advertise everywhere and make sure the drink is always available.

But there is one crucial thing about storytelling, as any narrator knows: the details that are left out of a story are as important as those that are left in. I am about to be reminded of this as I head for the World of Coca-Cola, a smooth silver building, with metal curves and a gleaming tower, half-corporate HQ, half-Bond-villain lair. It is essentially the Coke museum, the repository of the official Coke story, but this corporate autobiography leaves out some of the more uncomfortable truths.

* * *

The morning is cheerfully cold, a lovely Southern winter's day in Atlanta; the sun makes not one bit of difference to the temperature but it shines bright across the clear blue sky. A few police officers stand around Pemberton Park in the city centre, coats zipped up and wearing hats with earmuffs that dangle down each side of their heads, gently reducing them from figures of authority to parodies of Elmer Fudd. They drink coffee, smile and nod as I wander past. This is the entrance to The World of Coca-Cola and somewhere discreet loudspeakers are playing Coke's most memorable advertising jingle, 'I'd like to buy the world a Coke'.[6] Which may explain the earmuffs.

I like to think the company plays this song as a hymn of thanks to the Atlanta Development Authority who gave them $5.4 million to help pay for the park landscaping and the entrance plaza,[7] or the City Council who scrapped $1.5 million worth of sales tax for the company,[8] or indeed the property tax worth $2 million that the Atlanta city fathers decided they didn't want Coca-Cola to pay.[9] Coke might be worth billions but they are not averse to sticking out their hand for loose change, especially when the loose change has six noughts at the end of it.

In pride of place in the state-subsidised Pemberton Park stands a six-foot-four-inch bronze statue of the area's namesake, the founding father of Coca-Cola, pharmacist John Pemberton. Officially he created the drink in 1886 and sold it from Jacob's pharmacy[10]; now, over 120 years later, his noble image stands facing the park, one hand on a small Victorian table at his side. In his other hand he holds up a glass of Coca-Cola, partly in celebration, partly inspecting it, his impassive face considering his drink and offering it out to the world. It is the image of a pioneer, a scientist hero and benefactor to humanity. Sir Alexander Fleming wouldn't have minded having a statue like this and he discovered penicillin. The statue portrays Pemberton as thinner than the photos I have seen of him, where he looks a tad chubby. This apparently is not the only factual discrepancy. According to Mark Pendergrast, one of the most respected authors on the company, John Pemberton returned from the American civil war addicted to morphine.[11] So Coca-Cola's founder was a chunkie junkie, though in fairness, who would erect a statue of a fat druggie outside a family tourist attraction – with the exception of the Elvis Presley estate?

So for the greater good of the corporate image ol' morphine Pemberton loses a few pounds and gets clean. And inside the historical revisionism continues; bizarrely there is no mention of one of the drink's original ingredients, cocaine, which with hindsight is hardly the greatest sin, as there were other beverages of the late nineteenth century that contained varying quantities of Colombia's most famous export. Admittedly it's a slightly messy fact: one minute you want to teach the world to sing, the next you want to teach the world to talk really quickly and rub its gums with an index finger.

It is these 'messy facts' that the Company seem to have an almost pathological desire to try and hide. They are deviations in the Company narrative, grit in the PR grease. And Coca-Cola do not like grit in the grease.

The World of Coca-Cola's image control even extends to their choice of neighbours. Right next to it sits the Georgia Aquarium; in 2002 Coke gave nine acres for the aquarium. In 2006 Coke set aside two and a half acres for a civil rights museum – for an attraction that would celebrate Atlanta as the cradle of the movement, with plans to house some 7,000-odd pages of Dr Martin Luther King Jr's writings. Thus corporate and civic history entwine together in one single downtown location, so we can remember the fight for human dignity and visit the fish.

Coke's new neighbours may or may not choose to display details of Dr King's last-ever speech, made the day before he was killed. In it he called for African Americans to withdraw their economic support of companies if they 'haven't been fair in their hiring policies', that is, favouring white workers over black workers. One of three companies that was targeted for boycotting that night was Coca-Cola. Dr King's exact words were, 'we are asking you tonight, to go out and tell your neighbours not to buy Coca-Cola in Memphis'.[12]

Likewise there may or may not be mention of the lawsuit brought against the company by hundreds of Coke employees, accusing them of discriminating against black workers in pay and promotion. The Company made no admission to these charges, but in November 2000 announced they were paying $192.5 million to settle the case.[13] If you're measuring racism by the buck, that's a fuck of a lot of racism.

Another little story the Company are not fond of is linked to the Olympics. Coca-Cola's relationship with the Olympic Games began in 1928. But Coke downplays its sponsorship of the 1936 Games, the Berlin Olympics, where a certain psychopathic painter and decorator launched a PR drive to promote his Nazi state. The Coca-Cola Company are happy to mention that one of the US 1936 Olympic rowing team went on to become their chairman. They are also proud to point out that sprinter Jesse Owens advertised Coke – though this was years after he won four gold medals in Berlin, somewhat spiking the Aryan master-race theories of his host. The Company are keener to place themselves alongside those who are seen as 'fighting' the Nazis or promoting the 'Olympic ideal', rather than display themselves as a backers of the Olympic platform given to Hitler. And frankly, who wouldn't be?

But the Company have a few other Nazi items in the attic. Consider Max Keith, the managing director of Coca-Cola GmbH, Coke's bottler in Germany, during World War Two. As the war progressed the supply of ingredients to make Coca-Cola dried up, so Max invented a new drink to quench the German thirst. He named it Fanta. Now there's a strap line for an ad. Fanta: The Reich Stuff!

Company historians note that Max Keith never joined the Nazi Party but he did exhibit Coca-Cola GmbH at a trade fair organised to embrace the concept of the German worker under the Fuhrer. In another instance Max Keith decorated his Coca-

Cola stand with Nazi flags. This has been confirmed by The Coca-Cola Company which said: '[Max] Keith at a bottler convention displayed swastikas and ended with a salute to Hitler. [This] would not have been out of place in the US if it were reversed and the podium had an American Flag and the proceedings began or ended with the Pledge of Allegiance.'[14] I'll leave you to be the judge of that.

What I do know is that The Coca-Cola Company archives have pictures of the stand at the trade fair 'that depict swastikas used as decor'[15] under the Coca-Cola banner. It is merely a guess on my part that the archivist would rather burn in hell than release those photos for public viewing

It's fairly safe to say that these stories are not going to generate greater sales for Coca-Cola, with the exception of the odd Klan customer. None of these facts, whether it is Pemberton's naughty needle, Fanta's dodgy parentage or King's condemnation, tell the story Coca-Cola want us to hear and it is the story *they* want to tell that sells their drink.

* * *

To hear the Coca-Cola story, it is a $15 admission charge for adults, $9 for kids aged between three and twelve. But before you are tempted to visit the World of Coca-Cola ask yourself one question: what is on show here? They make fizzy drinks and advertise all over the world in order to sell them; all they have are bottles and adverts – they can't make a museum out of that, can they? Yes, they can. That is exactly what the World of Coca-Cola is: Coca-Cola, Coca-Cola adverts and a giftshop selling Coca-Cola merchandise.

The first gallery you come to is the misnamed 'Loft', situated on the ground floor. Essentially this is an open area in front of two display cases, with the capacity for about two hundred people standing. The room is wall-to-wall banners, bottles and posters, pictures of American footballers urging them – and therefore us – to 'Play Refreshed'. Another has a boy holding up a six-pack of Coke in the old-fashioned design: 'All Set at Our Home' it reads. Coke clocks, bold and bright shine from high up on the loft rafters, next to art deco leaded-glass lampshades, with stained-glass pictures of the company script. A huge banner reads 'Live on the Coke Side of Life', though it is not as if there is any other option around here. Even the lighting has a red hue, and my retinas are beginning to ache slightly from over-exposure to the Coke colours: everywhere is red and white.

The glass cabinets hold Coke memorabilia as if it were treasure from the time of the pharaohs: toy delivery trucks, Christmas decorations, a pair of promotional hip huggers from the Seventies and the jewellery Raquel Welch wore on a Coke modelling shoot.

In front of the cabinets, a young woman dressed like a zookeeper in boots, long trousers and a red collared T-shirt, is addressing the crowd with a hand-held cordless mic. She's probably a perfectly nice girl, but she has all the emotional intonation of a flight stewardess. She must have repeated this spiel countless times leaving her over-familiar with the lines and distant from any meaning they might have. But she musters all the gusto she can and launches into the company schtick one more time.

Running through the lines like a chore best done quickly, she says, 'You'll be in this room for just a few minutes then the doors either side of me will open and you will be allowed into the,' she pauses for theatrical effect before proclaiming,

'Happiness Factory.' The trouble is she loses interest before she finishes the phrase, so it sounds like 'HAPPINESS Factory.' She gulps down some more air before charging on in near-monotone 'In the Happiness Factory is an approximately six-minute-long animated documentary based on our 2006 Superbowl commercial and it gives you a little glimpse of all the magic that goes into each and every,' she pauses, 'Coca-Cola.'

I manage to hang on to a couple of facts that she reels out: there are four hundred brands and the logo of the white swoosh on the red background is called the Dynamic Ribbon. Then I hear that our time in the Loft is 'just a prequel to the rest of your day here'. Frankly, I don't know which is more alarming: the prospect of staying here for a whole day or the use of the word 'prequel' to describe waiting in a room. Next time you're on hold at the end of a phone waiting for an operator to become available, just remind yourself you are not in a queue but experiencing a prequel.

Carla, the woman with the mic, continues by drawing our attention to the fact that the lights have just dimmed, which is the signal that 'our audio artefacts have cued up, which are basically eighty years' worth of Coca-Cola jingles. Feel free to sing along to them if you know the words.' I raise an eyebrow in concern as snippets of ads get blasted at us. The second eyebrow goes up as a mum in tracksuit bottoms starts mouthing 'Can't beat the feeling', while she wanders past the Rachel Welch jewellery. People are joining in, a group of thirty-something men who told me they're from Florida start on 'Always Coca-Cola'. I just know that if they play 'I'd like to teach the world to sing...' the whole room will burst forth in harmony. Oh fuck, I'm in a cult – this is what the Hari Krishnas would be like if they took sugar in their chai.

The doors to the cinema open and I move rather too quickly through them and into a large auditorium with raked seating. There about twenty-five of us dotted around the empty space facing a big cinema screen, in front of which a tour guide called John stands grasping a microphone. 'I'm here to welcome you to Happiness Factory and living on the Coke side of life, and having fun is what it's all about,' he says, adding 'Now I understand we have a birthday in the house', at which one of the Florida thirty-pluses delivers a half-hearted cheer. 'So let's all sing happy birthday after three. One. Two. Three . Happy Birthday to you...'

The audience, such as we are, mumble through Happy Birthday, while John throws himself into his mirthless task. If by bizarre chance anyone were ever to ask me, 'What do you think it would be like to be taken hostage by Ronald McDonald?'

I can reply, 'I have a vague idea.'

'OK,' shouts John, 'How many of you have seen the commercial "Inside the Happiness Factory"? A show of hands? A couple of you. It was actually shown last year during the Superbowl and it was the second-highest rated commercial and because of that we turned it into a documentary. So, how many of you have wondered what happens every time you put a coin into a Coca-Cola vending machine, anyone wondered that?'

A lone and slightly strangled voice yelps, 'Yes.'

'Let me tell you what happens,' says John. 'Everyone say a little bit of love, let me hear you say 'Love'. '

'Love' croak six or seven of us.

'Magic' he gleefully urges.

'Magic', reply even less than the first time.

'Magic *and* Happiness!'

'Happiness' I find myself saying almost alone.

'And that is what goes on inside the vending machine.
Enjoy the show.'

The lights go down and the advert begins. If you have a TV
you'd recognise it. A young man puts a coin in a Coke vending
machine, but as the money rolls down the chute the advert
becomes an animation with a sub-Tim Burton soundtrack.
A small swarm of huge insects, overweight maggots with
helicopter blades strapped to their backs, fly in an empty Coke
bottle, which a mechanised decanter promptly fills. A track-
suited figure with a gold tooth and a plume on his helmet,
half-knight half-pimp, is catapulted – holding a bottle cap –
on to the top of the bottle. A gang of fluff ball lips are released
from a cage, ambush the bottle and frantically kiss it. Then
penguins in goggles throw a snowman into a large fan that
blows the flakes from the now decapitated snowman on to the
bottle. Finally the drink is led down a parade ground by a
band, with cheerleaders and a fireworks display, before being
dropped into the trough at the bottom of the vending machine
for the young man to collect.

As ads go it is actually a very good one, but it is odd that the
company guides keep referring to it as a documentary, which
it isn't. It is no more a documentary than Snow White is an
academic study of interpersonal relationships within
polygamous communities. But as the ad finishes the
'documentary' element begins. Various Coca-Cola employees
were interviewed, their words re-voiced by actors and assigned
to different cartoon characters from the commercial. So the
majorette, all blue hair, lips and eyelashes has a voice of an
All American Mall Girl, whose words at least are a real
worker's testimony.

'Are we rolling?' she asks in true behind-the-scenes

documentary style. 'Hi I'm Wendy, I'm single...and it's my job to keep everybody happy,' the coy cartoon trills. How would she describe Coca-Cola? 'Coke is like a little bottle of sparkle dust.'

Later the maggot with the helicopter blades (who upon closer examination looks like he has nipple rings or piercings of some kind) says in a deep husky voice, 'It's a relaxed atmosphere, it is not like some jobs that are tense when you get [t]here, it is a good working environment.'

These, remember, are the words of Coca-Cola employees, recorded and revoiced. According to these real employees, Coke is a great place to work, so it must be true. It is such a good environment that all sorts of creatures line up to testify, including a blue, long-necked chimera, a weasel salamander in a hard hat with a monkey wrench held over his shoulder. He speaks in a gruff ol' southern voice 'I smile ten minutes before I go to bed and ten minutes before I wake up every morning...It is people like me an' Eddie who make this company, the fact that we have been here and stayed here, to me that is the heart and soul of Coca-Cola.'

And as if that wasn't enough a shy Hispanic woman tuba player, demurely whispers, 'What have I given to Coca-Cola? My loyalty and my love. I give that.' She pauses before adding, 'Don't make me cry.'

Is she glad to work for the company? 'We are lucky to be one little piece of this wonderful company.'

The room momentarily goes dark as the feature finishes, people begin to shift in their seats, when the music suddenly swells louder. I turn to the noise just as the auditorium lights come on and catch the cinema screen swiftly gliding upwards, to reveal a secret corridor behind it. Guides are now on their feet, arms outstretched, beckoning us to leave our seats, descend the stairs and enter the tunnel, leading us to the next part of our tour, while a voice booms 'Welcome to the Happiness Factory.'

* * *

There are seven more rooms in the Happiness Factory and with the exception of the miniature bottling plant they all contain yet more adverts, Olympic ads, sports ads, ads in Arabic, German, French...on rolls the Happiness Factory with its TV screens blasting even more ads...onwards to the Perfect Pauses Theater, a small movie screen where you can watch Coke ads on an endless loop – and people do! Couples sit arm-in-arm watching adverts together. If by some perverted act of sabotage a film started to play in the middle of the ads the audience would get up and walk out, bored and confused. The final chamber, The World of Coca-Cola's colon if you will, is the tasting room, where dispensers pour Coca-Cola products from around the world for all to sample. It is packed with kids on a school trip, shouting over the music and tearing from tap to tap with plastic cups, while the teachers look on powerless to stop the sugar-rush tsunami that is heading towards them.

Naturally the exit is via the gift shop. And equally naturally every item on sale is covered in Coca-Cola logos, thus turning customers into walking adverts. The school kids from the tasting room will pass through here soon and at that thought I silently offer up a prayer to the god of small shoplifters.

* * *

'What did you expect Mark?'

Well, that is a good question and I am glad you asked it. It is hardly surprising that the company self-promotes to the point of nausea. It is the company's showcase attraction – a fizzy-drink version of Disneyland. Actually it is more Chessington World of Adventure, but you get the point. The attraction is unlikely to be a thorough critical examination of the Company's business practices. By now you might be thinking: 'Lighten up Mark, it is a Coke fun house, there is free fizzy drink, a working bottling plant which is vaguely educational and kids can get their picture taken with a polar bear! What more do you want?' Or you may think, 'It employs thousands of people around the world, it sponsors some worthy projects, surely that is a good thing?'

It'll come as no surprise that PR is designed to show companies in the best possible light and this will always be different from cold reality. But consider this: the animated majorette from the Happiness Factory commercial just called Coke 'a little bottle of sparkle dust'. Consider the disparity between eight teaspoons of sugar in each can of Coke and 'sparkle dust'. Frankly, it would be nearer the truth if the huge maggot with the strapped on helicopter blades were to appear crying, 'I'm so fat because I drink this sugary shit everyday! Now I need to get my stomach stapled!' There can be a wind-blown plain of tumbleweed between the image a transnational promotes and the reality of working for them or having them as a neighbour.

This is a globalised economy, where goods and money move with ease to the cheapest work force and some of the cheapest labour is found in some of dodgiest countries with poor human rights records and few or no environmental standards. And just as transnationals move in and out of tax havens, labour markets and emerging economies, so their critics have found an emerging world of dissent. If the familiar jingle of the Coca-Cola crates bouncing on a delivery truck can be heard in the furthest reaches of a mountain track, then a phone can get there too, or an internet connection and a camcorder, even an old camera will do. If your company gets caught dumping toxic materials in a village stream then it only takes one photo and a send button for your logo to be wired up to a world of trouble.

Coca-Cola say they strive 'to enrich the workplace, preserve and protect our environment and make a positive difference and effective contribution to our shared world.'[16] They say that they have 'long been committed to using our resources and capabilities to help improve the quality of life in the communities where we operate.'[17] But it is not the company tale I am concerned with. I'm interested in hearing from those who deal with the Company every day – the villagers, farmers, workers and shopkeepers. These are the people I want to find, these are the people I want to talk to, these are the stories I want to tell.

In the World of Coca-Cola, not only have folk paid $15 to watch, celebrate and have a chance to purchase the company's adverts, Coke have even found a way for their visitors to contribute to the company's PR machine. Up on level two the Pop Culture Gallery houses some kitsch retro-style furniture, a few Andy Warhols and a large Perspex display filled with handwritten letters. The identical writing paper and legibility of the script suggests that these are not the originals, but the content at least is written by Coke's customers. A sign reads 'Whether it's a childhood memory, a moment of refreshment far from home, or a recollection of good times with friends, Coca-Cola touches the lives of millions of people. Do you have a favourite Coca-Cola story? Share your story with us...' Which is exactly what I am doing. Going around the world, hearing stories from people whose lives have been touched by Coca-Cola and its bottlers.

For there is one missing detail from the tale of Coca-Cola's brand value. It is true that company profits have risen, they have bought other brands and sold more Coca-Cola and it is also true that the Company was rated the world's top brand for the seventh year in a row. Yes, the brand value is estimated at $65.324 billion.[18] Yes, that is a huge sum of money. But the missing detail is that this figure of $65.324 billion is actually a drop in value. In 2006 the figure was $67 billion,[19] in 2005 it was $67.525 billion.[20] Which means the company has lost $2.2 billion in brand value, that's $2.2 billion of goodwill the company has lost in the past couple of years. Something is beginning to make people like Coca-Cola less.

It is a small irony, given Coke's original ingredients, that the company's current PR problems started in Colombia. The murder of a trade unionist working for Coca-Cola's bottler and the subsequent campaign has inspired students, campaigners and activists around the world to challenge the company and has brought the mighty drinks giant up against a stark fact: if you are a transnational at the forefront of globalisation, then opposition to your practices can be globalised right back at you. So that's why I'm sitting in an airport waiting lounge bound for Colombia. I am going to hear just how some of those billions of dollars worth of 'sparkle dust' started to turn to dust.

2
GIVE 'EM ENOUGH COKE!

Bogota, Colombia

> *'Everyone has the right to peaceful assembly and association.'*
>
> **UN Declaration of Human Rights Article 20, 1**

The lighting in the hotel lobby is dim and so is the porter. The lift is tiny, room enough to fit one person and a bag. I go to get the lift. But I don't. The porter takes the lift. I take the stairs. He leaves the bag. I take the bag. He takes the tip. Hmmm. They must have a different definition of dim around here...

The city of Bogota is situated on a plateau approximately 8660 feet above sea level, thus making its altitude the second-most likely thing to give you a nosebleed in Colombia. It is not uncommon for travellers to suffer from altitude sickness, which for me takes the form of being tired and clumsy, not to mention tipping dim people who turn out to be clever.

The room is two floors up on the corner of the building overlooking the police station. Its stone frontage is picked out of the night by lamps around the arched doorway, under which a young man in uniform stands, stamping his feet wearily against the chill. Drawing the curtains forces my attention back to my immediate surroundings, a cold, small room with dark wood panelling and a reinforced doorframe. The reinforcement is only vaguely reassuring as it looks as though someone has tried to prise open the door with a large screwdriver, so I am glad to have company. Watching me slowly unpack are Emilio and Jess. Emilio is a Spaniard by birth and a Colombian by marriage; this will be the second trip to Colombia where he has translated for me. Jess, a London photographer doing a feature on firefighters, has stayed on past her assignment to photograph some of the people I hope to meet. The altitude sickness has given me the mental agility of an ex-boxer who has turned his talents to sports commentating. So I am currently holding my toothpaste in my hand while looking frantically round the room for it.

Emilio notices the teddy bear in a US Marines outfit propped up on the bedside table.

'Wha' the fuck is that?'

'That is a kitsch *memento mori*.'

'A wha?'

'A reminder of death. *Memento mori*, it's Latin, for reminder of death,' I say, cheerfully spotting the toothpaste in my hand.

Emilio furrows his brow and says, 'I don' think you need that here in Colombia, no?'

Which is true. More than forty years of conflict between governments, paramilitaries, drug cartels and left-wing guerillas has left the country with a well-deserved reputation for violence. It is the most dangerous place on earth for trade unionists caught between employers eager to be rid of them and barbaric paramilitaries who are quite capable of doing just that.

Across the world trade unions have traditionally been at the forefront of the great battles for democracy, education and decent working conditions and as trade union membership has gone down since the start of the Nineties, it is worth remembering that the right to belong to a trade union is a fundamental human right, enshrined in the UN Declaration of Human Rights.

In Colombia, the attacks on human rights are not limited to labour rights violations. 2004 saw 1440 people kidnapped in Colombia:[1] one person every six hours. That was the year I first visited Bogota with Emilio, accompanied by another friend called Sam, who was a good two stone heavier than me. And this weight difference is significant because before arriving in Bogota I took the precaution of learning key Spanish phrases from Emilio, the most important of which was *Dispara el gordo primero*: shoot the fat one first. Fortunately I only needed to use it once. This is what happened.

The dub sound-system night took place in a club that inhabited the top two rooms of a building accessed by knocking on the door nicely and ascending some long and narrow stairs. What the place lacked in fire exits it made up for in atmosphere and the friendly squatter-chic decor, though without the chic. The club was full of swaying bodies and a small serving hatch produced cans of beer from a mountain of trays visible over the shoulder of the barman.

Leaning against a wall wet with condensation was a tall chap wearing a brown leather coat and, with what I now know to be a chemically assisted smile. Turning to face me he said, 'Your first time in Colombia?' in impeccable English.

'Yes.'

'How do you like it?'

'Great, people are very friendly here,' I shouted over the bass lines rattling from the speaker.

'Very friendly...' the decibels increased. 'Yes, friendly!' he yelled, then he nodded to his hand, which had not left his side, 'Would you like?' He was holding a glass bullet-sized chamber with a plastic nozzle, full of cocaine.

'No thanks,' I said.

'No?' He seemed flabbergasted.

Perhaps it was his reaction which prompted me to forcefully add: 'I have just spent the day listening to trade union leaders talking about the hundreds of their members that get killed by paramilitaries – who are funded by cocaine. I don't buy Nestlé products because of their baby milk, so I'm certainly not going for that.' I shouted over the music jerking my thumb at his container.

'No, no, no, this is okay,' he said, genuinely upset, 'This Is FARC cocaine – left-wing cocaine. Not paramilitary. This is fine.' A smile crept up one side of his face, and his eyes glinted.

Sneeringly I declared, 'Sure it's fine, it's probably Fairtrade, right.'

And as quick as it came the smile left his face, in fact he looked quite cross and started to lean towards me. At that point it dawned on me that it may be unwise to pick an argument in a Bogota nightclub with a drug dealer. With hindsight I think a polite 'no' would have sufficed.

'Your first visit,' he shouted over the music, with a blank menace. 'First time, right?'

Sam suddenly loomed from the dance floor, sweaty and clutching a can of beer. He slouched on to the wall with a bump and a smile, 'All right?'

And for some reason the next words I said were, *'Dispara el gordo primero.'*

There was a pause, the man looked at Sam, Sam looked at me, I looked at the man, the man stared back, Sam looked at the man, the man turned to Sam, Sam turned to me, then turned to the man and with an innocent grin yelled, 'All right?'

The man in the jacket shook his head and walked away.

* * *

Nearly four years and one good night's sleep later Emilio guides Jess and me on our walk through the rundown side streets. Downtown Bogota may proclaim itself a modern city with skyscrapers and a financial centre, but the world of international commerce seems far away as we pass old men selling cigarettes from trays. There are no smart suits and briefcases as we wander by the small and cramped shops, where stock spills out of the doorways and hangs into the street. Half in and half out, overflowing packs of chewing gum on cardboard strips, sweet tubes of mints, boxes of matches, plastic toys and plasters. Here glass cabinets perch on stands, full of brown glazed buns, small dumplings, primped and crusty, cornbreads, *arepas* with melted cheese fillings that sit drying on the heated racks. The coffee shacks have radios that tinnily grate out songs while groups of men smoke in doorways and sip coffee from little white plastic cups that bulge out of shape with the heat of the drink. Carefully we pick a thread through the potholes that litter the roads like concrete acne and dodge the rasping roar of trail bikes and the nasal splutter of mopeds that scythe the thoroughfare.

In minutes we have moved from the morning havoc of the back streets into Teusaquillo, an area where the roads are slightly wider and the craters fewer. Trees periodically dot the pavement and white walls and grilles harbour little gardens of yuccas and palms. The terracotta roof tiles give each home an air of stability, while the buildings themselves are set back a little from the road. The well-to-do used to live here but they moved on long ago, leaving it inhabited by human rights lawyers, civic groups and non-government organisations.

We stop at a house with a low brick wall. The front garden consists of one patch of grass, one patch of concrete and two oil stains. It is the kind of place that back home in England would have a disused caravan parked in one corner. Here the front doors of the building are large, wooden and nondescript, and give little clue as to the identity of the occupants. Especially since the old graffiti that used to read 'Death to trade unionists!' has been painted over. Now there is nothing to announce that this ordinary house is home to Sinaltrainal (*Sindicato Nacional de Trabajadores de la Industria de Alimentos* – The National Union of Food Workers). They are the biggest trade union in the 'Coca-Cola system' in Colombia, representing over half the organised Coke workers, though after over a decade of attacks and intimidations the membership isn't as big as it was. In fact, with a current membership in the Coca Cola plants of only 350 it is fair to say they have been decimated, but (and the but in this case is enormous) this is the group that started Coca-Cola's current woes. This is the union that has seen its members and leaders murdered. This is also the union that took on one of the biggest companies in the world. These two things are not coincidental.

This building is where we meet two men, Giraldo and Manco. They arrive on different days and subsequently give their testimonies separately but they tell the same story and they both tell it from an old table in the middle of a union office covered in campaign posters. The propaganda slogans demand boycotts and justice. The images are of handguns painted in the company colours of red and white. The names and pictures of dead trade unionists are everywhere. Giraldo and Manco knew these men, they were friends and relatives, and now they sit under the watch of the dead as they speak of how they died.

* * *

On a Saturday morning Oscar Alberto Giraldo Arango (Giraldo) walks into this office. He is forty-two but he carries a few more years on his shoulders. His shirt is as thin as his face, worn and frayed too, his cheeks look like they are down to the last layer of skin. Hunched and with an old black cap on his head ready to be pulled down, he sits looking out of big dark eyes, void but for an impassive watery stare.

The first time I met the men at Sinaltrainal they told me, 'To be a trade unionist in Colombia is to walk with a gravestone on your back.' I initially took this as a reference to the fact that Colombia is the most dangerous place in the world for trade unionists: since 1986 2,500 trade unionists have been killed, that averages two a week. But the men I met looked weary – as if they had physically borne their stone.

Giraldo sits down, looks up, takes off his cap, stiffly rubs the top of his head with his hand and begins. He was born and bread in Carepa, Urabá, in the north-west of the Colombian countryside near the Panama boarder. He started work for Coca-Cola in 1984 at the Bebidas y Alimentos de Urabá bottling plant – which translates as Drinks and Foods of Urabá. When he told his friends of his new employers they congratulated him, 'Well done, that's great! You got such a good job!' And it was too. The union had done well for the men, securing bonuses, overtime and health benefits. But this was not to last. Graffiti announced the paramilitaries' arrival in Carepa in 1994. 'We are here!' it declared. Shortly after the graffiti arrived so did the bodies. The first Coca-Cola worker and trade unionist in Carepa to be assassinated was José Eleazar Manco in April 1994. The second was killed days later on the 20 April. He was Giraldo's brother, Enrique.

In the mornings Enrique travelled to work on the back of a friend's motorbike. There is only one road to the bottling plant and that morning three men emerge from the side of it. They stand in the middle of the road and aim guns at the bike forcing it to stop. Enrique is dragged from the publicly exposed lane, into the trees and bushes with the armed men. As the paras disappear they shout to the driver -'Go!'

News travels fast and when Giraldo gets to work everyone is talking about what has just happened. The shock of Enrique's kidnap circles the plant, disbelief and confusion growing with the telling. The deliverymen, production-line workers – all of them try and grasp the facts and speculate on why Enrique was picked up in this way. But the gossip quickly turns to mourning. Another man arriving for work has seen Enrique's body dumped at the side of the road.

THE PARAS

'We are the defenders of business freedom and of the national and international industrial sectors.'
Carlos Castano, leader of the AUC paramilitaries[2]

The Colombian paramilitary groups were spawned in the conflict between the state and revolutionary guerillas. In 1982 officers under General Landazabal, the Defence Minister of

Colombia, worked with multinationals and cattle ranchers to organise and fund 'defence groups'. Ostensibly they were to fight left-wing insurgent groups but increasingly the paras, as they are known, became entwined with the drug cartels and the army, often leaving it difficult to see where one group finishes and another starts.

Spreading out countrywide, the paras grew steadily into the AUC (in Spanish this stands for the *Autodefensas Unidas de Colombia*, its English translation is the United Self-Defence Forces of Colombia). They quickly became known as death squads, attacking and killing anyone considered to support the left-wing guerillas – basically anyone working in human rights or trade unions. It is a common refrain amongst the establishment and security forces that the guerillas and trade unionists are one and the same. As if to illustrate this point Colombia's President Uribe as late as 2007 said 'Either carry out union organising or carry out guerrilla warfare, but this wicked mixture does much damage to Colombia.'[3]

The paras have a bloody history of working with the security forces. Human Rights Watch published a report in 2001 called 'The Sixth Division'. The title comes from the fact that there are five army divisions in Colombia but so great is the level of collusion between the army and the paras (sharing equipment, information and personnel) that the paramilitaries are often called the Sixth Division.[4]

Carlos Castano, the charismatic leader of the paras, claimed that 70 per cent of his organisation's funding came from the cocaine industry. However, he was also an ardent supporter of neo-liberal economic policies and of multinational investment in Colombia. Castano said of their relationship with the AUC, 'Why shouldn't national and international companies support us when they see their investments limited...We have always proclaimed that we are the defenders of business freedom and of the national and international industrial sectors.'[5] Perhaps not surprisingly for a group so committed to multinationals, the paras developed their own logos, branding almost, and one of their logos was crossed chainsaws – the preferred tool of choice when carrying out massacres.

In a newspaper interview Carlos Castano was quoted as responding to the accusation that the paras attacked indiscriminately by saying, 'Blind attacks? Us? Never! There is always a reason. Trade unionists for example. They stop the people from working. That's why we kill them.'[6] Given that statement it's perhaps not surprising that Colombia is the most dangerous place in the world to be a trade unionist. The International Trade Union Confederation (ITUC) puts the conviction rate of trade union murderers at 1 per cent,[7] although even that figure is considered a little on the high side by those on the ground. Certainly President Uribe has shown little inclination to rectify this situation. His public statements on the matter include, 'There are no assassinations of workers in Colombia'[8] but there are 'rotten apples' in the trade union movement.[9]

Perhaps the most startling statistic with regard to violations of international humanitarian law is the dramatic escalation in the direct role played by the Colombian State. When President Uribe assumed office in 2002, the State was responsible for 17 per cent of all human rights violations. Four years later – at the end of Uribe's first term – the State was responsible for 56 per cent of human rights abuses; with the paramilitaries and FARC accounting for 29 per cent and 10 per cent respectively.[10]

Giraldo has lived with the story of his brother's murder for twelve years and betrays little emotion when he says, 'they contacted the body collectors in the area who went in search of the body.' No one was charged with Enrique's murder. He was dragged from the motorbike and executed, his body left at the side of the road, and as far as the authorities were concerned that was that; it was an unpleasant incident that generated a little paperwork. 'There wasn't very much of an investigation,' says Giraldo. But a definite pattern emerged when almost a year to the day another Sinaltrainal leader working at the Coca-Cola plant in Carepa was killed. His name was Enrique Gómez Granado and on the 23 April 1995 he was shot on his doorstep in front of his wife and children. It seems almost indecent to mention the end of this man's life and the searing horror endured by his family in so brief a sentence. But it is with brutal ease a man's life becomes a statistic. So Enrique Gomez became the third Sinaltrainal leader murdered in just over a year, leaving the unavoidable link between union organising at the Coke plant and being killed.

When the surviving union leaders were threatened and intimidated it became blindingly obvious that there was a campaign against the union at the Coca-Cola plant. These men were followed as they left work, cards and letters delivered to their homes that read 'Go now or face death!' The entire union leadership opted for the first option and fled to Bogota en masse, which left the workers with no effective union in the Carepa plant, a situation that appeared to suit the management just fine. Giraldo claims that, 'some of us had been working for the company for nine or ten years but the company would call us in one by one and say to us, "Come on, look, the union has fallen...the union doesn't exist any more so you need to do what the company tells you to do".' As the union was attacked and its leaders murdered, managers at the plant were making it crystal clear that they intended to take full advantage of this situation.

So the workers remaining in Carepa meet in secret. 'We agreed to set up a new underground union,' says Giraldo. The president was Luis Hernán Manco Monroy (Manco). A few days after talking to Giraldo at the old table in the Sinaltrainal office in Bogota, I speak to him. At 1.9 metres he is a tall man with receding black hair and a maroon coat that looks like a battered driving jacket. But the thing that catches your attention when you meet Manco is the way he holds himself. He has a cautious swagger, his whole frame seems to bob slightly, like a boxer. He is sixty years old but has the awkward twitch of a man who expects to be hit.

As president of the newly formed union leadership he helped draw up a collective agreement, the terms and conditions they wanted the company to negotiate over. Then the union came out into the open. 'We informed Coca-Cola that we had new leadership and so we started having meetings with the management at the Coca-Cola plant.' The manager at the time was a man called Ariosto, who, they allege, not only knew but socialised with the paramilitaries. On one occasion, Manco said Ariosto sat drinking with the local paramilitary commanders outside the plant. 'There was a meeting with Cepillo and Caliche [the commanders] at the kiosk, they were drinking with Ariosto and he said that if he wanted to end the union, it would be very easy.'

Giraldo recalls another instance when Ariosto said, '"The union exists because I let it exist, if I don't want it here, that will be the case", but we didn't think about this because we didn't know how bad it would get...'

They didn't have to wait long to find out. On 6 December 1996 Carepa's darkest day began.

* * *

The body of Isidro Gil lay inside the plant. The first bullet had hit him between the eyes. The remaining five shots were fired out of spite or anger or bravado – who knows, perhaps it was just a way of saying 'We are here!' But he died where he fell in the courtyard. No one touched him until his brother Martin arrived. Crying, he held Isidro in the courtyard as the Coke workers looked on until the police came to take them away. It was just after 9am, and he was the fourth Coca-Cola union leader to be killed in Carepa.

The two paras who killed him had arrived on a motorbike and gone to the security hut by the main gates, where Isidro was working. As he opened the large iron gates to allow a delivery lorry to leave the paras saw their chance, slipped past the office, through the gates and shot him. Giraldo 'was 10 metres away from him when they shot him, and then I ran inside because I didn't know what...' His voice trails off. 'When I heard the first shot, I was walking nearby the entrance. Those of us who were nearby ran off.'

Manco looked up when he heard the first shot. 'The machine that I was working on was quite near the door...When I heard the shots, I looked behind me because the door was behind me, and Isidro had already fallen to the ground.'

Ariosto the manager had disappeared and was nowhere to be found. So without knowing what to do or directions from the company the men hung around the plant. 'We didn't know where to go and we were waiting for [the police] to come and take the body and tell us that we could leave,' said Giraldo.

Even when the men were finally told to go home they didn't.
'The production line stopped,' said Manco, 'but we stayed
there in the afternoon because we were too scared to
leave...not working, just waiting there.'

Eight hours after Isidro had been killed the men finally left the
plant to go home. They were right to be fearful. One of the
worried men was a trade union organiser called Adolfo Luis
Cardona, nicknamed El Diablo. El Diablo was a local footballer
of some renown, a former champion in fact. He too had seen
Isidro killed and that afternoon, while his friends and
workmates waited in the plant, he went to Carepa. The paras
spotted him and called out that the local para commander
Cepillo wanted to see him, 'Come with us, Cepillo wants
you...Come, nothing will happen. Get in the lorry we will drive
you there.' But this lorry was of some local infamy. It was said
people got into it but did not return alive. 'Come and get in we
will take you to meet the Cepillo,' the paras insisted.

There and then El Diablo made the most important decision of
his life. He ran. He took off running down the village street
screaming *'Van a matar a mí!'* They are going to kill me! He ran
and ran and ran towards the police station four blocks away.
There were few cars but the road was full of people, fetching,
carrying, hustling, bustling, shopping, walking, working
people. Into the oncoming crowd he ran, dodging anything
that came towards him, twisting his body to avoid a collision,
his legs churning and scuttling to keep upright. On he ran
through the narrow streets crying, panic filling every part of
him as he screamed to onlookers, 'They are going to kill me!
They are going to kill me!' Behind him the paras gave chase,
one on motorbike the rest on foot charging after him, all
pretence of normality thrown away. They were hunting him
down in broad daylight. The bike weaved its way through the

traffic of people as the foot soldiers bumped and jostled those in their path. No one said anything. No one did anything. What could they do? How could they stop the paras stalking a man in broad daylight? But the assassins lacked the adrenalin of a condemned man and the instincts of a footballer. El Diablo burst frantically into the police station begging for protection and sanctuary.

The police all but shrugged: 'What can we do?'

This is what they managed to do: they escorted El Diablo home, waited while his family packed and then drove them to the airport. There they went first to Bogota and then on to the USA, where El Diablo lives today. In this case Colombian justice was no more than a taxi service into exile.

The morning had seen the murder of Isidro Gil, the afternoon the attempted abduction of El Diablo and that night saw the final event. Sinaltrainal's offices in Carepa were firebombed. Metal bars had smashed the doors apart, files and papers were scattered around the building, joining the litter of the broken tables and chairs. And then the entire building was burned to the ground. A blazing beacon shone out in the night as the union office crackled and smoked in the flames, a warning beacon, to which the message was clear: your union is finished, go or die!

Manco had gone into hiding but the following day the para leader, Cepillo, sent out messages that he wanted to talk to the union men, to hold a meeting with them. Manco's world had been destroyed, his certainties had vanished, the only coping mechanism he had left was fear. In order to survive in abnormal situations we need to make abnormal reactions and fear helps us make them. Manco certainly reacted abnormally... he agreed to see the paras, persuaded by another union man that he should go.

The meeting was to be held at the paras' local hang out, an ice-cream shop in Carepa, called La Cieba. Two other union men arrived with Manco to find Cepillo at a table with a group of paras. The killers' commander was a chubby man, aged about 25, wearing jeans and a short-sleeve shirt. The shutters were rolled down, the shop was closed. Manco sat opposite the chubby leader. There were no pleasantries, no one drank, no one smoked, there was none of the usual Hollywood paraphernalia you might expect with such a scene, just an ice-cream shop with armed killers at a table.

'Cepillo said that they had killed Isidro, and they said it was them who burned down the headquarters. And they said that the union was over, that the union was the guerrillas,' said Manco. As they sat in the shuttered shop the paras calmly issued their orders for what was to follow. 'We could have killed you all today,' said Cepillo, 'but we can be reasonable.'

The following morning the killers' version of being reasonable was unveiled for all to see, at 9am they assembled all the Sinaltrainal members at the Coca-Cola bottling plant. There the paras made them sign letters resigning from the union. The letters were prepared by 'Rigoberto Marín, who worked for the company...He gave them out one after the other, like "here's yours, here's yours",' said Manco.

The union in Carepa was smashed. The leadership was in hiding and exiled – they had fled or were dead. The members, cowed by guns, threats and intimidation, had signed away their rights. Meanwhile the managers of the Coca-Cola bottling plant surveyed the wreckage of the union and promptly introduced a pay cut to the workers. According to Sinaltrainal the wages dropped from between $380 – $450 a month for experienced workers, to $130 a month: Colombia's minimum wage. When asked about this drop, Coke failed to respond. Given that they would have met resistance to this if Sinaltrainal was still there, it is fair to say that, from the point of view of company profits, murder and arson did have an upside.

* * *

Back in the union office sitting at a table littered with empty coffee cups and grains of sugar, Manco and Giraldo finish their tales as all exiles do, by talking of the life they fled to. They lived for six months in the building they now tell their stories from – the union office – there was nowhere else for them to go. Both men were in the office when the paramilitaries' package arrived containing the letters of resignation they had made the union members in Carepa sign. The paras even included blank copies for Manco and Giraldo to sign. Eventually Giraldo's family left Carepa to come and join him in Bogota and he moved out of the union office. He has not had a full-time job since. 'I haven't been able to earn much. I have just been doing odd jobs with three- or four-month contracts...sometimes days go by here where we have no food, because sometimes there's work and sometimes there's not, it's not like it was.'

I asked Manco if he has stayed in Bogota since leaving Carepa.

'Yes, of course, but it's horrible. I don't always get food here, I lost my house, my family, and everything.'

'Your family?'

'They didn't want to come so they stayed there, the mother took the children there. And of course I can't go there, I haven't been there.'

I watch Giraldo leave. Instinctively and without display he stands by the front door of the building with his coat zipper pulled up tight, tugs his collar around his neck, opens the door, looks across the street and then along it. He steps out through it glancing both ways and then slips away, a hunched silhouette heading to a home in exile, to wake to a dawn of few certainties. Where work may or not be found, where bellies may or may not be empty; where dead friends' faces haunt posters and memories of home are full of longing. And if you ask 'Why did he fight so hard and take so many risks to be in a trade union?' The answer is this: so he would not have to live the life he does now.

COCA-COLA TRADE UNIONISTS KILLED IN COLOMBIA

AVELINO ACHICANOY ERAZO
Worked at Embotelladora Nariñense SA – COCA-COLA (Nariño Bottlers Ltd) in Pasto. Killed on 30 July 1990. Sintradingascol leader (Colombian National Union of Fizzy Drinks Workers).

JOSÉ ELEASAR MANCO DAVID
Worked at Bebidas y Alimentos de Urabá SA – COCA-COLA (Drinks and Foods of Urabá) Carepa. Killed 8 April 1994. Sinaltrainal member.

LUIS ENRIQUE GIRALDO ARANGO
Worked at Bebidas y Alimentos de Urabá SA – COCA-COLA, Carepa. Killed 20 April 1994. Sinaltrainal organiser.

LUIS ENRIQUE GÓMEZ GRANADO
Worked at Bebidas y Alimentos de Urabá SA – COCA-COLA, Carepa. Killed 23 April 1995. Sinaltrainal regional union leader.

ISIDRO SEGUNDO GIL
Worked at Bebidas y Alimentos de Urabá SA – COCA-COLA in
Carepa. Killed on 6 December 1996. Sinaltrainal leader and
negotiator. ALCIRA DEL CARMEN HERRERA PEREZ, Isidro's
wife, was murdered on 18 November 2000 in Apartado.

JOSÉ LIBARDO HERRERA OSORIO
Head of Technical Maintenance at Bebidas y Alimentos de
Urabá SA – COCA-COLA in Carepa. Killed 26 December 1996.
As a manager he had been very supportive of Sinaltrainal.

ADOLFO DE JESÚS MÚNERA LÓPEZ
Worked at Coca-Cola plant in Barranquilla, Atlántico
department. Killed 31 August 2002. At the time of the killing
he had been sacked but had been reinstated after legal
process. Sinaltrainal union leader.

ÓSCAR DARÍO SOTO POLO
Worked at Embotelladoras Román SA – COCA-COLA (Román
Bottlers) Montería plant. Killed on 21 June 2001. Union leader
of Sindicato Nacional de Trabajadores de la Industria de las
Bebidas en Colombia (Colombian National Union of Drinks
Industry Workers) 'Sinaltrainbec'.

Source: Andy Higginbottom at the Colombia Solidarity Campaign

3

SERIOUS CHARGES

New York, USA

*'Serious charges demand a
serious response...we take
accusations regarding labour
rights violations seriously...'*

Neville Isdell, CEO The Coca-Cola Company'

'Serious charges demand a serious response,' said the
company CEO Neville Isdell, referring to allegations of
abuse by Coke's Colombian bottlers, in what seems a
reasonably appropriate statement; though in all honesty he
was hardly likely to say, 'We lost a couple of Latinos, who
gives a fuck.' However, serious statements deserve serious
evaluation. According to Sinaltrainal, the murders at the
Carepa plant were part of a countrywide campaign against the
union. These are the serious charges they make:

- A worker is killed inside the bottling plant, six other union
  leaders are killed by paramilitaries, many are killed during,
  or approaching, negotiations with the bottlers and during

industrial action. The bottlers are alleged to have contracted with or directed the paramilitaries.

- Bottlers are accused of union busting, intimidation and harassment of workers.
- The security manager at the bottler company's Bucaramanga plant falsely accused union leaders of terrorism, resulting in the workers being imprisoned for six months for a crime they did not commit; one was tortured.
- Paramilitaries operated from within the Barrancabermeja plant at a time when attempts were made on the life of the union leader. It is alleged that this was with the knowledge of a plant manager.

These would, by most people's standards, qualify as serious charges. So what was The Coca-Cola Company's serious response? Did the Company itself investigate the allegations of collusion between plant managers and the paramilitaries? The answers are: not much and no.

The Company website proudly displays the first and only public audit by The Coca-Cola Company into their bottlers in Colombia.[2] This was conducted in spring 2005, over eight years after Isidro Gil was shot dead. Intriguingly, the audit conducted by the Cal Safety and Compliance Corporation does not examine or investigate any charges of collusion or paramilitary activity in the plants. Focusing on the plants' compliance issues, the report does however note several health and safety breaches, including:

- the absence of a protective guard on a syrup container at one plant
- the incorrect number of fire extinguishers at two plants
- incorrect documentation for an employee at one plant[3]

Fortunately there is no need to get up a petition or start a letter-writing campaign, as I am happy to report that the appropriate remedial action has been taken so as to comply with health and safety regulations. However, reassuring as it is to know that a protective guard now covers the syrup container in the Bogota plant, there still remains the outstanding 'serious charges' to be addressed by the company. To this day The Coca-Cola Company has not investigated the alleged links of Colombian bottling plant managers with the paramilitaries, despite a man being shot dead under their logo.

From the outset the first line of defence coming out of Atlanta was the denial of 'any connection to any human-rights violation of this type' and to distance themselves from the bottlers saying, 'The Coca-Cola Company does not own or operate any bottling plants in Colombia'.[4] This is the standard use of the 'Coca-Cola system' operating as an entity but claiming no legal lines of accountability to The Coca-Cola Company. TCCC does not own the bottling plants, the bottlers operate under a franchise. But the case here is similar to that of Gap and Nike in the 1990s. In these particular instances the clothes giants had outsourced their production to factories in the developing world that operated sweatshop conditions. It was not Nike or Gap who forced the workers to do long hours for poor pay, it was the contractors. However, campaigners insisted the companies should have enforceable human rights standards applied throughout the supply chain, compelling the companies to take action. The argument was then, and is now, that no matter where the human rights abuse occurred, if it's your name on the label then you're responsible for sorting it out. In The Coca-Cola Company's case the argument is made more compelling by the fact that, although they franchised Coke production to Bibedas y Aliementos and Panamco, they held 24 per cent of

Panamco's shares[5] – a controlling interest. Which gives them considerable clout in how the business is run.

This view of the Company's responsibilities is shared, in particular, by Councilman Hiram Monserrate from New York City. He represents a large Latino community and through some of his constituents became aware of the situation. Appalled, he took up the matter and has investigated Coca-Cola's response to the events. And so I visit New York for the first time, to talk to him.

* * *

I love New York. I nearly bought the I ? NY T-shirt but for adhering to the only rule of fashion that I know: namely don't buy things worn by people you don't like. Walking around the place I keep pointing and shouting, 'That's where *King of Comedy* was filmed...see, that's the bridge in that scene from *Saturday Night Fever*...if that's Ben Stiller let's heckle him...'. The city is a vast historic map of films and music. I get a coffee on the Bowery hoping that the Ramones once sat here before appearing at CBGBs. Lexington gets me singing the Velvet Underground and Central Park has me quoting Woody Allen.

Tall apartment blocks are dotted with white air-conditioning units sticking out of the windows, as if a swarm of flying fridges have just crashed straight into the side of the building. And the sight of them is suddenly wonderful. The plethora of pointy water towers stuck on rooftops like fat fireworks on stilts is amazing. I'm happy enough to gaze idly at hanging traffic lights suspended over the streets or fire escapes and ladders that criss-cross entire blocks. I am a fan. So much so that when I wander past a blue wooden police barrier outside a mosque, presumably ready to corral anti-Islamic demonstrators, I instinctively squeal, 'Oh look bigotry...they have that here too.'

My visit coincides with Super Tuesday, the big day in the US Primaries when Democrats and Republicans vote to decide who will be their presidential candidate. It is the Democratic race between Hillary Clinton and Barack Obama that focuses New York. Stickers on cars proclaim 'I'm backing Billary!' and Obama's face decorates Brooklyn windows.

I'd gone into a deli to eat and the primaries were the talk of the lunch queue. Now, being English, I'm a little baffled by the number of decisions required to get a sandwich: you have to choose your bread, spread, filling, dressing, condiments, extras and opt out of getting a pickle. Essentially you have to tell them how to make the bloody thing, leaving me momentarily resentful and wanting to shout, 'I'm not Jamie Oliver, all I want is a sandwich!'

As I ponder on rye or sourdough a man behind me strikes up a conversation. He's on a wheelie Zimmer frame, has a face like a tomato with stubble and is dressed in a green jacket. He looks like he should smell of alcohol, though he actually doesn't.

'Yew voted today?' He says as I catch his eye.

'No, I'm not eligible to vote, I'm English.'

'Yew want me t'vote for yew?' he says in a kindly manner, 'I'll vote for yew. Who yew want me t'vote for?'

'No, I'm all right, thank you.'

'I voted twice already today, I did it for my friend here,' he says, gesturing to a man beside him in a black pleated leather jacket and a bobble hat. 'They didn't recognise me,' he continues.

'They didn't?'

'Nah, one time I went in backwards.'

New York City Councilman Hiram Monserrate represents District 21 in Queens. Queens is across the East river from Manhattan Island, but on his side of the river the houses and salaries are much, much smaller. Queens is dirty and quirky. It is essentially a working-class area, you can tell this by the significant increase in 'Beware of the Dog' signs. Households tend to sit on the side streets off the main road, expressways tend to sit over the main roads and the traffic from LaGuardia airport sits on top of it all.

Just off East Elmhurst, on one of those side streets, sits Councilman Monserrate's office, opposite a parking bay for school buses. It has a sign in the glass front window, *'Por favor registrese para votar hoy'*, a polite reminder to his Latino electorate: don't forget to vote, folks. Inside, some plastic chairs and a sofa provide a waiting area for his constituents. The rest of the office is small and open plan by necessity. Six staff members sit at desks, handling casework, phoning housing departments, debt agencies or whoever needs to be called off or brought in. Councilman Monserrate's office is tucked away at the back.

The councilman does not appear to be a typical corporate critic, if indeed such a thing exists. Monserrate served in the US Marine Corps for four years, spent twelve years in the NYPD and to be honest he looks like his CV. He is stocky and strong-jawed, with a neck you could moor tugboats to; and I'd bet if you were able to snap him in half you'd find the word COP running all the way through his body, like a stick of Brighton rock. His politics is that of a Queens Democrat, a combination of liberalism on issues like immigration mixed with a strong populist streak. He appeared on breakfast TV pitching a notion that New York should be nicknamed Gotham City, as he was inspired to fight crime by his boyhood hero Batman. The idea has all the political rigour of renaming London Beanotown, but in terms of political PR it underlines his police credentials and 'record of public service'. So in the context of American politics he is not yet part of the establishment but boy, does he want to be.

Despite this, the councilman has been a persistent critic of The Coca-Cola Company since 2004. He worked with New York City's pension fund about how they might use their stockholding in Coke to influence the company, tabling critical resolutions at shareholders' meetings. He has spoken out against the company on US campuses, with students subsequently boycotting Coke.

'So you want to talk about Coca-Cola...' he says as he drops his black overcoat across one chair, scrapes another across the floor and leans back in it.

The councilman was introduced to Sinaltrainal's officials in New York in 2003 and found their tale compelling enough to help organise a delegation to Colombia in 2004. 'My initial impulse: I wanted to know more. At the very least it seemed to me there had to be some truth in what the workers were telling me. That labour reps and workers were being killed.'

While planning for the delegation, Councilman Monserrate decided he ought to invite The Coca-Cola Company along too. 'We have to have some fairness,' he explains, 'they were invited to participate. They were invited to visit the plants with us. They were invited to join the meetings and join in the discussions. They could have been a partner in this delegation: they refused.'

Whether he asked them out of a political desire to be seen to be fair or a genuine sense of fair play, I don't know, but nevertheless the Company declined the offer. 'I wasn't trying to malign Coca-Cola or FEMSA[6]...I'm not a socialist revolutionary.

I am an elected official from New York City.' He says this as if one might harbour a notion the breeding grounds of Trotskyism are to be found in the US Marines and New York Police Department, two bodies not noted for their adherence to dialectical materialism. In truth it is precisely because of his relative orthodoxy that I want to talk to him about what the delegation found out and why he seems to be picking a fight with the company that is so symbolic of America.

Councilman Monserrate's 2004 report on the Colombian allegations found not only a distinct lack of action by The Coca-Cola Company and the bottlers but an alarming laissez-faire attitude to the charges levelled against them. Although the delegation was denied access to Coke's bottling plants, Coca-Cola/FEMSA representatives Juan Manuel Alvarez and Juan Carlos Dominguez did meet with them. The delegation asked outright what they had done to investigate the allegations of ties between plant managers and paramilitaries. At first 'these allegations were vigorously denied,' the report states, but it continues, 'Alvarez and Dominguez acknowledged that Coke officials had never undertaken any internal or external investigations into these assertions, nor into any of the hundreds of human rights violations suffered by the company's workers.'[7] That is, the Colombian bottlers themselves admit that these serious allegations were not taken seriously at all.

In his office Councilman Monserrate leans forward, puts one hand in between his legs, grasps the seat of the chair and hauls it closer to the table. 'Isidro Gil was killed inside the bottling plant. That alone, to me, puts the onus on The Coca-Cola Company to say, "Hey, we have a problem here and we have to deal with this problem one way or another".' He nods his head and stares at me, like he's Robert De Niro. 'There's a causal relationship between the trade unionists' deaths and working at Coca-Cola. So at the very least the company in Atlanta has an obligation to try and get to the bottom of it... Coca-Cola, just like any other major corporation, has a responsibility to be responsive corporate neighbours. You can't just chalk it up to the politics of the country. You're Coca-Cola and your logo is worldwide and it started here in America.' His forefinger taps the table pointedly, as if the company is in the room and he is telling it off. 'I mean we wouldn't accept it in America. Could you imagine it if in a Coca-Cola plant in the USA, a worker was killed because he was part of the union – what kind of outrage there would be!' His mobile phone rings, he looks at the caller's number before pushing it to one side.

And as he sits with his back to the office wall which is covered in honorary degrees, citations, community awards and other such chaff of public office, it dawns on me that it's the councilman's patriotism that has put him in the fight with Coca-Cola. American patriotism often entwines love-of-country with love-of-country's-economic-system. The councilman seems to fall into this category. 'They do represent American Capitalism,' he says in such a way as to put capital letters on both words. 'And American Capitalism should never be about allowing your workers to be subject to violence or death because they are organising to defend their rights. What does it say about America?'

The Carepa murders were the starting point of a new saga of violence and intimidation for the union and though these were the worst cases they were a long way from being the only human rights violations. Sinaltrainal alleged a campaign of murders, intimidation and harassment against trade unionists working at Coke bottling plants across Colombia. But so far The Coca-Cola Company had shown little, if any, interest. So the union responded by doing three things:

- They brought a lawsuit against The Coca-Cola Company and its Colombian bottlers in July 2001 in the USA
- They initiated a call for an international boycott of Coca-Cola products in 2003
- They went around the world telling as many people as they could about the first two things

This got the Company's and the bottlers' attention. So what did the company do? Was there finally a moment of corporate self-reflection and realisation? No, the bottlers took the union to court claiming that in bringing the US lawsuit the union had libelled and defamed them. I'll repeat it for those of you who might be distracted picking your jaw from off the ground: the bottlers said the union had libelled them by taking them to court in the US. The bottlers even went after 500 million pesos in damages, until the case was dismissed as being without merit in 2004.[8]

Councilman Monserrate discussed the case with Coca-Cola FEMSA representatives in Colombia and he reports that one of the men 'characterised these criminal charges as a "consequence" of the ACTA case [ie, the US lawsuit], which the delegation interpreted to mean that the company intended the charges as a direct reprisal.'[9]

So according to the bottlers, when the victims of violence and intimidation seek legal remedy they become criminals. Which I would suggest is akin to Union Carbide suing the inhabitants of Bhopal for inhaling their property without permission.

In his office in Queens the councilman is flabbergasted. 'They were facing criminal charges because they filed a lawsuit in the US...this is outrageous! This is ridiculous, this is worse than ridiculous!'

He leans forward in his chair, furrows his brow and purses his lips. With the phone ringing and meetings stacking up around him the councilman has little time, so he seems to be gathering his thoughts and momentum for a final verbal assault. And it comes.

'My question to The Coca-Cola Company,' he pauses, 'is: are you saying this is just the cost of doing business or is this the business that you are in? Which one is it, because either one is not a good choice. Right? Are you saying this is what Coca-Cola does by design or is it just complacent and allowing these things to happen? Either option is bad.'

THE ALIEN TORT CLAIMS ACT AND SINALTRAINAL'S CASE

The legislative spectrum in the USA varies from the progressive – their Freedom of Information Act, for example, is light years ahead of the UK – to the bizarre: in Alabama it is illegal to play dominoes on a Sunday. However, the Alien Tort Claims Act is one of those laws that actually elicits a genuine expression of 'God Bless America'. This bit of legislation also deserves a further cheer, as President George W Bush tried to 'reform' it and failed. Which is always worthy of a quick hurrah!

The Act allows for companies and individuals to be taken to court in the USA for complicity in the crimes of kidnap, torture and murder committed outside of the USA. The Alien Tort Claims Act of 1789 was not widely known, or used for that matter, until the 1980s when the Filartiga family used the act to sue an Inspector General of Police from Paraguay, who was visiting the USA. They claimed he tortured and killed their seventeen-year-old son Joelito in Paraguay in retaliation for his father's political activities. The courts found in favour of the Filartiga family and awarded them over $10 million and although the family never received any money they did finally get some form of justice. Their case had been denied in Paraguay and when national legal systems fail to deliver justice then one of the only avenues left is ATCA.

Increasingly, human rights' advocates are using the Act to bring multinationals to the courts. In 1997 suit was filed against the oil company UNOCAL for alleged human rights abuses in the construction of its oil pipeline in Burma. In 2004 the company went for an out-of-court settlement, paying an undisclosed sum in damages.[10]

Another case relates to Chinese dissident Wang Xiaoning, who used a Yahoo! email account to post pro-democracy articles anonymously. Yahoo! complied with a request by the Chinese authorities for information on the account which led to the arrest, detention and torture of Wang, the lawsuit filed against the company claimed. Yahoo! also settled for an undisclosed sum out of court.[11] Wang Xiaoning remains in custody serving a ten-year sentence.

Currently Firestone, Exxon, Shell and Wal-Mart have suits filed against them under the Alien Tort Claims Act.[12]

Pro-corporate lobby groups have sought to limit the scope of the law. Senator Dianne Feinstein introduced a bill to do just that. She said her bill was 'designed to balance the interests of US companies and human rights groups.' She also received $10,000 that same year for her re-election fund from Chevron[13] – another company with a pending case against them. She shortly after had a change of heart, and withdrew her bill, 'in light of concerns raised by human rights activists'.[14]

Given that the law can be applied to acts of kidnap, torture and murder, attempts to limit it or reduce the law's effectiveness in order to balance US interests seems to imply that US multinationals can't compete in the global marketplace without the odd incident of complicity in murder, kidnap and torture.

SINALTRAINAL

July 2001, the United Steelworkers of America union and the International Labor Rights Fund filed an Alien Tort Claims Act (ATCA) suit on behalf of Sinaltrainal in the US Federal Court in Miami. The suit, claiming $500 million compensation for the plantiffs, alleges that the bottlers Panamerican Beverages (Panamco) and Bebidas y Alimento 'contracted with or otherwise directed paramilitary security forces that utilised extreme violence and murdered, tortured, unlawfully detained or otherwise silenced trade union leaders,' and that The Coca-Cola Company as the parent company bore indirect responsibility. The Colombian bottlers deny the charges.

The Coca-Cola Company argued the Colombian bottlers were separate companies and The Coca-Cola Company had no case to answer, stating 'We deny any wrongdoing regarding human rights or any other unlawful activities in Colombia or anywhere else in the world' adding that, 'The Coca-Cola company do not own or operate any bottling plants in Colombia'.[15]

The union's legal team argued The Coca-Cola Company exerted control over its bottlers by way of a legal agreement, called, unimaginatively, 'the bottlers' agreement'. The argument went thus: The Coca-Cola Company licences the production of their drinks, they provide the syrup with which to make them and dictate the types of bottles, cans, industrial processes, adverts and promotions that the bottlers are to use. Thus they exert a degree of legal and economic control.

Furthermore, The Coca-Cola Company not only possessed 'a controlling 24 per cent interest' in Panamco's stock, but had two seats on Panamco's Board.[16] And whilst Bebidas y Alimentos was owned by US citizen Richard Kirby, the union's lawyer claimed that The Coca-Cola Company had such an influence on the company that it refused to agree to their request to sell the business in 1997.[17]

The case is being brought by the International Labor Rights Fund, supported by the United Steelworkers of America on a no-win no-fee basis (though this does not apply to any money settled on for the victims of violence).

March 2003 In an landmark ruling, District Court Judge Martinez ruled that the case against the bottlers Panamco and Bebidas y Alimentos can go ahead – the first time a US judge has allowed a case against a company for alleged human rights violations committed overseas to be heard under the ATCA.[18]

But the judge dismissed the case against The Coca-Cola Company on the grounds that the 'bottlers' agreement' did not give the Company explicit control of labour issues over the bottler.

2006 District Court Judge Martinez reversed his previous decision and dismissed the case against the bottlers, now arguing that the case can't be brought in the US because of 'lack of...jurisdiction'.[19]

2008 Sinaltrainal lawyers submitted an appeal on both rulings on 31 March 2008[20] and a result is expected by the lawyers in 2009. If successful it means the case can be heard and Sinaltrainal will have their day in court in the USA with The Coca-Cola Company and their bottlers.

3.5

THE HUSH MONEY THAT DIDN'T STAY QUIET

'We envisage a world in which ...we improve lives in every community [we] touch.'

TCCC Strategic Vision[1]

Neville Isdell, the Chief Executive Officer (CEO) of The Coca-Cola Company from 2004–2008 and current chairman of the Board of Directors, is a tall balding man whose hair leans to ginger and is cropped short in the way soldiers and men of a certain age prefer. His body is trim but his face is baggy and craggy; its shape is that of Charlie Brown, the Peanuts cartoon character, but with the muscle tone of Keith Richards. In short, he looks like a typical upper management man – and I mean that in a pejorative sense. At the 2005 Annual Meeting of shareholders, Isdell stated, 'there are no threats or attempts by management to attack or intimidate workers for being affiliated with a union or for being a union organiser or for being a union official.' He went on to say that, 'the people employed by our Colombian bottling partners work in facilities where their labor and human rights are respected and protected.' It was a noteworthy event, as the CEO of the world's most popular brand felt compelled to defend the company but the true significance of his robust public pronouncements can only be measured by what the company was doing in private.

In Colombia the pressure on Sinaltrainal was immense: the intimidation of workers by the paras was relentless, and the company's drive to casualise the workforce was driving down union membership. 'Every time we recruit new workers and members they get sacked,' said Carlos Olaya, the union's researcher. Indeed Councilman Monserrate's delegation claimed that Coca-Cola FEMSA, 'continually pressured workers to resign their union membership and their contractual guarantees. Since September 2003, they have pressured over 500 workers to give up their union contracts in exchange for a lump-sum payment.'[2]

Across the world the boycott met with mixed results. In Ireland Trinity College and the University of Dublin voted to 'Kick Coke off Campus' and refused to stock their products in student-run facilities. They were joined in the UK by Sussex, Manchester, Middlesex and the School of Oriental and African Studies, and in the USA by New York University and Michigan University. Even though the contracts with US universities are usually worth millions, kicking Coca-Cola off campuses is unlikely to dent the balance sheet of a company that made $5.98 billion profit last year.[3] But the accompanying media attention and headlines like 'Is Coke the new McDonald's'[4] in the *Guardian*, and *The Nation* calling Coke 'the new Nike'[5] must surely be part of the reason Coca-Cola has lost billions from their 'brand value'. Something had to be done.

Publicly the company's attitude to the Colombian issue was not hostile nor was it dismissive, it was both. Coke increasingly described the lawsuit brought by Sinaltrainal as an 'out of date' allegation[6] or 'an old story'.[7] But this is not the full picture and behind the scenes the Company was involved in negotiations with the union to settle the case.

Timing is everything – from boiling an egg to having sex to deciding it is time to talk with the trade union taking your company to court. The US lawsuit was going nowhere fast but that all changed when District Court Judge Martinez dismissed the case against Coke's bottlers on 4 October 2006. It might have looked as if the Coca-Cola system had been exonerated in court but the judge had opened up a world of potential pain for the Company. Crucially the court decision was *not* the hearing of the case itself, instead it was to decide if the US courts were the correct venue for the trial. And once District Court Judge Martinez decreed the US courts did not have jurisdiction this left the union lawyers free to launch their appeal, bringing The Coca-Cola Company back into the dock to face the whole thing one more time.

If the union lawyers were successful in their appeal then the case would go to full trial and The Coca-Cola Company would face the legal procedure of disclosure, forcing them to hand over internal documents detailing their relationship with the bottlers. I can't speak for the company but I would imagine this prospect was about as appealing as syphilis. Timing is everything – and six weeks before Judge Martinez cleared the way for the union to get the Company back into court The Coca-Cola Company began to negotiate with Sinaltrainal on 19 August 2006.

When I asked The Coca-Cola Company about these talks they portrayed them as 'fruitful and informative'[8] as if remembering the biscuits served. They went on to describe the negotiations as 'warm and buttery', 'sweet and moist' and 'chocolaty on the top'.

The purpose of the talks the Company said was 'to assess whether a mediated resolution of the parties' differences could be achieved.'[9] In short they were looking to settle out of court and with a settlement like this comes money...a lot of money. How much money? A barrow full. Although I can not disclose the exact sum offered to Sinaltrainal and the plaintiffs in the lawsuit it is my understanding that it had six noughts at the end of a dollar sign and a couple of digits in between. For those working in the British coin of the realm it would the same number of noughts but a single digit in front of the pound sign. For those working in the Zimbabwean Dollars, I am afraid the world has run out of noughts.

If the Company was offering money what were the conditions attached to it? I spoke to Ed Potter, The Coca-Cola Company's Global Workplace Rights Director, a man with intimate knowledge of these negotiations. I said to him that the company had history in this department, 'financial settlements are reached, but part of that financial settlement is that you don't criticise us again, you shut up, you go away.'

Ed Potter replied, 'All I will say as a general matter is we've had several different resolutions...you've described one of them.'[10]

Whereas Coke describe the talks as 'fruitful and informative', Sinaltrainal use an altogether different set of words. 'We were in a process that lasted almost a year and a half where we talk and talk and talk with them in order to find a solution to the conflict...and it didn't give us any result at all,' said Edgar Paez, the union's International Officer. He is sitting in his office, by the same table Giraldo and Manco gave their testimonies from. Edgar is a man prone to smiling, with a touch of a South American George Michael to his unshaven appearance, but throughout our conversation he remains grim-faced. The only reason Coca-Cola negotiated according to him was, 'because they don't want us to keep reporting them [campaigning]...What the Company wanted was to buy the silence of the people involved. They give some money to the victims in order not to denounce the problem.'

The negotiations broke down in early 2008. Coke said 'no final resolution was possible. An impasse was reached and no further discussions are anticipated at this time.'[11] Arguably, the impasse was the conditions of the settlement – Coke would pay millions of dollars but anyone working for Coca-Cola FEMSA and involved in the lawsuit had to leave their jobs, they could no longer work at Coke. But more than this they would be legally bound never to criticise Coca-Cola ever again. According to Edgar Paez this would apply 'not only in Colombia but everywhere in the whole world. They wanted us to sign an agreement that no one would denounce Coca-Cola any more, for the rest of their lives.' In effect, the agreement, if signed, would prevent them from campaigning against any multinational that Coca-Cola had business with. From the moment they signed until they day they died.

The end result of key members of the union leaving Coke and being unable to criticise or organise against the company from the outside would effectively mean the union would be finished. Sinaltrainal would cease to exist in the Coca-Cola plants. That is, after all, what is meant by my phrase 'you shut up, you go away'.

The money was on the table and all Sinaltrainal had to do was agree and take it. So the men and women who had fought for the right to be in a trade union would become silent. Their right to free speech and freedom of association would be gone for ever. All they had to do was take the money and sign the paper. For men like Giraldo and Manco the prospect of compensation was money they literally could only dream of.

The union refused to sign. They refused to be silent. Leaving The Coca-Cola Company with an 'old story' that would not go away.

4

'CHILE'

Bucaramanga, Colombia

'There are no threats or attempts by management to attack or intimidate workers for being affiliated with a union or for being a union organiser or for being a union official.'

Neville Isdell, CEO, TCCC Annual Meeting 19 April 2005

This is the story of the first time I stayed with a man called Chile, a Sinaltrainal member who lives in Bucaramanga, to the north of Bogota. The city sits in the basin of a plateau ringed by hills, a packed urban island sprawling over its convex foundations and is surrounded by terracotta soil and the ripe light green of the trees. It's the seventh biggest city in Colombia – the English equivalent would be Leicester or Coventry.

Given that most Catholic countries draw the line at evoking cooking spices at christenings it should come as no surprise that Chile is a nickname. Though the name derives from the spice, here folk spell it after the country. His real name is Luis Eduardo García, and he earned his moniker after a particularly heated argument with a manager at the local Coca-Cola bottling plant. I met Chile in 2004 on a fact-finding mission, which is how I came to be on a bus travelling through Bucaramanga with a crowd of trade unionists, leftists, Christians and human rights' campaigners. Each day we would set off to visit displaced people, families of murder victims, NGOs and lawyers, listen to their stories and then head off to our next destination – a sort of human rights coach trip.

The bus is knackered. Very knackered. You may be familiar with the type of American bus that Evel Knievel used to jump over on his motorbike. Well, our bus looks like the one that he accidentally landed on. Inside it is incredibly hot: were we to be parked in England, someone would be checking the back seat to see if the dog was still alive. There is little respite from the heat. The windows come down only a few centimetres at the top of the frames. In the absence of a breeze to force the air around a little I am trying not to come into contact with the seat's back, lest I stick there – though given the lack of suspension on this vehicle it is unlikely that any of us are going to sit anywhere for long.

On board we divide up into our various gangs. Near the front are Pax Christi, a Christian peace outfit, made up of elderly Germans who have traipsed around the fact-finding trip with grim faces and even grimmer clothes. They have an air of concerted concentration and gloom, giving them the appearance of someone trying to digest an espadrille. Everywhere we go they appear with notebooks and pencils ready to catch every misfortune. They are the stenographers of the apocalypse.

Just a few seats back are the two male Swiss trade unionists, who never sweat and have duty-free breath mints in their rucksacks. They gently nudge, natter, whisper and giggle together: I wouldn't be surprised if they had a password and a tree-house in their garden back home. Around them are the Americans, who subdivide into those from Brooklyn and those not. Those 'from' are loud, brash and, despite the fact that they have never been to Bucaramanga in their life, are prone to shouting directions at the bus driver. He in turn ignores this advice.

Chile has a square build. His black hair is receding, his T-shirt bulges around his gut and no one save a Krankie could call him a tall man. But he has a confident and determined presence and must have been quite a catch 25 years ago. He stands by the driver, hanging on to the rail up by the front door, and gives a running commentary as we drive past sites of local oppression. It is essentially a historical battlefield tour, except the history is recent and the tour guide personally knows the dead.

As we pass a large prison, one of the Colombians shouts out. 'Here!' he points at the building we can see through the window. 'Here! This is where they put Chile!'

The passengers crick their necks in unison to see the jail, the prison cell bars visible from the street. Others join the loud chorus, shouting, 'There is the prison where Chile was jailed!'

The man in front of me has both of his arms in the air, almost appealing for sanity. 'That is where Coca-Cola sent him!'

   'They locked him up because of Coca-Cola's lies!' shouts another.

'It is true,' says Chile to the German heads that are now bent over their notebooks, scribbling frantically. His admission serves only to unlock further floodgates of communal anger and it seems everyone has to shout

'There is where they tortured him!'

'There is where they abused him!'

'There!' screams the loudest voice of all, bellowed from one of Chile's closest friends, 'There!' he shouts along the suddenly silent bus, declaring to the fixed faces turned to him. 'There ...is where Chile lost his virginity!'

And he promptly erupts into raucous laughter, undercutting the sombre and angry mood in a deft moment. The whole bus laughs. Chile laughs hardest of all. He is bent double, slapping his thigh and looking like he might choke.

By the time we finish the day's journey and return to Chile's home it is late, everyone is tired and no one has thought about supper. So Esmeralda, Chile's partner, gets a Chinese takeaway and for a few moments there is only the sound of cutlery on tin trays and the background hum of the family fish tank. Away from the bravado of the bus Chile drops his nickname and returns to being Luis Eduardo. Assisted by Esmeralda, their daughters Mayela and Laura, and their son Alexander, he tells a less rumbustious tale of how he become a plaintiff in the USA courts accusing the Coca-Cola bottlers of engineering his wrongful imprisonment.

Luis Eduardo started work for the Coca-Cola bottling plant in Bucaramanga in 1988, working his way up from a cleaner to the position he currently holds, assistant to José Domingo Florez, his best friend who drives a huge red Coke truck. Luis Eduardo is the crate shifter and stacker for the truck. This tale has a familiar start. Initially there was respect for the union but that changed in the mid-1990s when the manager of the plant accused the trade unionists of being 'guerillas' and employees' medical insurance was suddenly cancelled. This provoked a strike, led in part by Luis Eduardo. Then events took an altogether more conspiratorial turn. After the strike the head of security at the Coke plant, José Alejo Aponte, contacted the police accusing Luis Eduardo, Domingo Flores and Álvaro González Pérez, another trade union organiser, of planting a bomb in the bottling plant. The three men went to prison in March 1996 to await trial and spent the next six months there.'

'Coca-Cola employees publicly accused us, before the authorities, that we were terrorists,' says Luis Eduardo illuminated by the glow of the fish tank. As proof of the terrorist plot, 'The boss of security in the firm, he took a packet, a metal box, put it beneath his arm and he ran around the plant saying that it was a bomb, it was a bomb!' Luis Eduardo shakes his head in wonderment that any sane individual might walk around holding a real bomb under their arm. And, more than this, that the authorities might credulously believe the word of a man who claims he has a bomb tucked under his armpit. Not content with finding a fictitious bomb, the company then said it had actually gone off. Where was the damage then? Ah, those cunning terrorists had cleaned it up afterwards. Obviously following a new insurrectionary trend: tidy terrorists, terrorists your mother could like – they may blow up buildings but they always leave some potpourri in a bowl by the smouldering rubble.

'The company [security manager] says that the bomb exploded but there was never any damage inside the company,' says an incredulous Luis Eduardo.

Indeed the Regional Prosecutor shared his view, finding that not only were the men innocent of plotting to plant a bomb but that no such bomb existed in the first place.[2]

'We managed to prove our innocence and Coca-Cola had to return us to our jobs,' says Luis Eduardo

But by then the damage had been done, as they had spent six months in prison awaiting trial. Domingo Flores, Luis Eduardo's best friend arrested alongside him, claims he was tortured by the police. And if it was tough for the men it was even worse for the families.

'For the kids it was really hard,' says Esmeralda, her arm draped casually around Mayela as they sit on the sofa.

Luis Eduardo nods in the direction of Laura, 'My youngest daughter – I had to remove her from the school because her friends said to her that her father was a delinquent and a terrorist.'

'Because it was all on the TV news and in the newspapers,' adds Esmeralda. So the nine-year-old Laura would demonstrate outside the prison gates, banner in hand, demanding the release of her father. 'The girls would visit their dad once a month,' she continues, but the official visits were not enough. 'They wanted to see him, they'd wait outside the prison and he would see us through the window and throw us a note.'

'In prison in order to communicate with your family, you have to write a note,' Luis Eduardo explains, so he would wrap the note around a sweet or something he could hurl through the bars of the open cell window, over the wall. Nothing too personal was ever put in it in case it fell into unintended hands. The contents would read, 'I am OK. Don't worry, the lawyer came and it's going OK.'

Except it was far from OK. With no wages for six months Esmeralda battled to keep the bank from taking their home and had to resort to begging to get by.

It was far from OK for Luis Eduardo too. He and Domingo Flores were placed in the highest security wing of the prison alongside the paramilitaries, the people who were trying, and often succeeding, in killing trade unionists. Both men avoided showers and toilets for fear of being attacked, and Luis Eduardo's face displays his revulsion as he revisits the stench of the cell, the humiliation of being forced to piss in bottles and shit in bags. And so they lived in the stench and the fear for six months, throwing notes wrapped around sweets to his children in the street.

'Coca-Cola bottlers were involved in this conspiracy because the ones who denounced us were administrators within the company, managers of the company,' he says. So alongside the family of Isidro Gil the names of Luis Eduardo García, José Domingo Flores and Álvaro González Pérez were added to the suit filed in the USA, under the Alien Tort Claims Act. The court documents allege the Coca-Cola bottler, Panamco Colombia,[3] 'brought charges against the aforesaid Plaintiffs in retaliation for their trade union activities. Their resulting prolonged unlawful detention and accompanying torture was therefore the result of Panamco Colombia's malicious prosecution.'[4]

The Coca-Cola Company have never apologised for the bottlers' actions or sought to investigate them, preferring to stick to their original defence, namely that The Coca-Cola Company does not own the bottlers in the 'Coca-Cola system'. When questioned on this the company replied, 'TCCC have *discussed* [my italics] the matter with the bottler and understands that the bottler's employees gave truthful statements to the Colombian government investigators...Messrs García and Flores were compensated for their time away from work [back pay], provided additional security and protection and have remained employed by the bottler.'[5]

And that just goes to show how caring the bottler is: having made accusations that the men were terrorists the bottlers kindly gave the men their jobs back when the claims turned out to be bollocks. Though the men were not actually paid any compensation for being falsely imprisoned by the security manager's 'truthful statements', they were 'compensated for their time away from work' and I imagine the men felt that they were compensated merely to be back in the caring bosom of their employer. Though they have not expressed that.

With unintended irony TCCC have described the lawsuit brought by Sinaltrainal against them as 'aggressive'.

Over the past couple of years The Coca-Cola Company have taken great pains to promote themselves as a union-friendly company, which 'respects our employees' right to join, form or not to join a labor union without fear of reprisal, intimidation or harassment.'[6] In fact they say 'the Company have shared the Policy [for respecting trade union rights] with our independent bottling partners and is committed to working with and encouraging them to uphold the principles in the Policy.'[7] You don't need a degree in semantics to see that a dead worm could wriggle through the gaps in this. Seldom has the word 'encouraging' been used in such an unencouraging manner – this state of affairs also applies to the words 'committed and 'principles'. It is a mini masterpiece in stating the bloody obvious, as they have 'shared the Policy with our independent bottling partners'. They are 'committed to working with and encouraging' the bottlers to respect workplace rights. Frankly I know nursery school teachers with better discipline policies than that. So what form will Coca-Cola's encouragement take? Praising the good and ignoring the bad? So if no paramilitaries shoot Coke workers, do the bottlers get a sticker? Essentially we can paraphrase the statement as: We'll ask them to be nice but don't blame us if it goes tits up.

* * *

It was time to visit Luis Eduardo aka Chile one more time. It has been seven years since he and the union launched the court case in the USA in 2001, five years have passed since the call for an international boycott and four years since I last visited him. I wanted to find out how his family and the union had faired under Coca-Cola's new-found respect for employees' rights, what had changed for them?

'We'll find some examples of how they [the bottlers: Coca-Cola FEMSA] respect our rights.' Chile told me, so once again he is taking me on a tour of Bucaramanaga, though this time on foot. As the morning sun has yet to rise to the humid midday prime and the traffic pollution hasn't had time to build up a head of fug, it is the perfect time to bustle through the city. We pass the market carts piled high with star fruit, pineapples and grapes, dusty from the orchards and the city dirt. The juice sellers lounge by their stands, pausing after the rush-hour surge, chatting and cleaning the fresh pulp and pips from the blades of their blenders. Occasionally people call out his nickname, 'Chile!' and wave as we march through. The market bingo hall is just getting started, and those who can't play watch from the street as the numbers are called in a rapid-fire monotone by a man who mistook hair oil for charisma. On the pavement a patchwork of vendors sit on their haunches beside rolled out mats decorated with random wares, from small packs of screwdrivers to hair dye, pens to lighters, duct tape to yo-yos and nail clippers to radio batteries. They are laid out in a deliberately random fashion, like objects in a memory test. Unified by nothing but cheapness, I marvel at the world of possibilities this incongruous mix of goods represents. A world where someone might stop to pick up some industrial gloves and while they are at it impulse-buy some joss sticks.

Onwards we stride, searching for a specific man. The trouble is that we don't have the man's name, we don't know where he lives and he doesn't know we are coming to see him. All of which sounds rather unprepared; after all, the key to any quest is to know what you are going in search of before you start. I doubt Jason would have found the Golden Fleece were he to have set out with a vague idea of getting some duty-free knitwear. Nevertheless, there are two facts that will help us in our endeavour: one, Chile's certain that he knows the district the man lives in and two, the man we are after was recently knocked over by an out-of-control police car. Of all the things that might mark a man out in his community, being run over by the cops is definitely a distinguishing feature: misfortune is the satnav of a community. So we have only to end up in the right district, approach a local and say, 'We are looking for the guy who was waiting at the bus stop for work when for no reason whatsoever a cop car ploughed into him' and in theory they should know where to find him...and they do.

In a back street where old men sun themselves in fold-out chairs and unemployed dads gather round the underside of a broken-down van while their children help them work, Chile approaches a guy in an oil-covered vest holding a hammer. He says words to the effect of, 'I'm looking for the guy the cops fucked up...' and the oily dad lifts his arm, hammer still in hand, and points out directions.

The road bends where it starts to run up the hill. This is where Carlos Maldonado Anaya rents a room in a bungalow. Behind it palm trees grow and their wilting leaves hang over the roof, under the shade of which sits Carlos in a wheelchair. He shoots a brief smile when he sees Chile, recognising him from other days, and leads us cautiously inside. The cool small front room is the lounge, the dining area and the parlour. The room is three steps long, with a kitchen to the rear and two bedrooms to the side. What it lacks in size it fails to make up for in decor: the doors are plain unpainted plyboard affairs, with bolts rather than handles to keep them shut. Old faded photos of children long grown and gone decorate the wall, a solitary china cat sits on a shelf. Positioning himself opposite a cheap print of the Last Supper, Carlos tells us he is fifty, but in poverty years this translates as about seventy-five, he's skinny enough to evoke the word 'wretch' and sits in a raggedy pair of shorts and a shirt. The most eye-catching thing about him though are his legs, thin and brown with silver metal tubes and pipes sticking out from the flesh. The pins holding his bones together emerge from his skin and run at angles down his leg, like a homage to the Pompidou Centre.

Before the police ran him over Carlos was a *fletero* – literally translated the word means transporter or porter. He worked in the dense streets of Bucaramanga where the lanes are sometimes inaccessible to a truck, where the crowds flow down the narrow capillaries of the city, so crates of Coca-Cola have to be delivered by hand. Weaving amongst them shouting warnings of his presence Carlos hauled crates of Coca-Cola to the shops and cafés for twenty-five years.

The system worked liked this: the company supplied the stock, Carlos provided the manpower, 'they give me the product so that I can distribute it,' he says. Using a sack barrow that can balance fifteen crates on its iron frames he would deliver during the day and return to do the paperwork at night. Carlos said, 'I have had to work almost eighteen hours, in previous seasons. I used to work from 6am and sometimes until 11pm or 12pm' his fingers arc through the air to show the passage of time. As you might expect his earnings were far from great. 'The last year I worked I earned the minimum wage. The minimum. I was earning around 360,000 pesos a month.' That's about £100.

Carlos explains the set up, 'The company gives us the job, but from that job we had to to pay the warehouse.' This is often just a small lock-up with a roll-down shutter where you can stack crates of pop. The Coca-Cola trucks come round and deliver the crates of soda to the warehouse. They tell you how many crates you have to deliver. They tell you what drinks each order needs, where you have to deliver them to, the routes. They make you wear a Coca-Cola uniform. They tell you who you can hire as an assistant and they sometimes say, 'Sack so-and-so, they're no good.' Effectively the Coca-Cola bottlers control their working lives, which sounds remarkably like the role of an employer, but the job of a *fletero* is a sub-contracted one, hired by contractors, not directly by the company, so they do not appear on Coca-Cola's books. 'No, I don't have any contract, nothing signed at all, never, I have never signed any document with the company.' This means that he can be fired any time.

Given this precarious state it is perhaps not surprising when Carlos spoke of the wish to unionise and spoke about this with his fellow workers, 'but the problem is that we cannot join our union because of the fear that when the company realise that you belong to the union they will sack you. They will say that you know that the company does not allow you to join a union. Then they say "no, you have become a trade unionist there is nothing else for you to do here".'

So to sum up the relationship: Coca-Cola bottlers don't employ Carlos, but they do tell him when to collect the stock, where to go, what to deliver, who to deliver it to and when to do it, what to wear, who to hire and who to fire and threaten him with the sack should he join a union. None of which sounds like the declarations The Coca-Cola Company have made to respect workplace rights.

Carlos has kindly given us the name of another person who used to work delivering Coke so we set out to search for him, though having the name of the person we are looking for feels slightly like cheating. Leaving the bungalow we cut back through the side streets to the centre, squeeze past the cattle trucks parked up on the kerb side, dodge buses as they lurch out of the station and wander against the lunchtime market crowd of shoppers, where shoulders hunch with the weight of bags, jaws chomp on snacks held in napkins and feet tango through the surge of fellow humans. There are wide-eyed chickens stacked high in wire boxes with guinea pigs and geese as neighbours. We pass stalls selling cutlery, crockery, lace and knives as we head out of the market, along the main roads and on to the quieter roads. Here Ivan works in a kiosk, a small café selling sweets, beer, hot food and cigarettes, with a few tables and chairs outside. The boundaries of this establishment are an ambiguous affair, as the pavement runs into the dining area and vice versa. This is the epitome of Colombian café culture: a café, a street and a complete absence of culture.

Ivan only has two customers – a young man in denim with a proprietary arm draped around an even younger woman whose crop shirt allows her puppy fat to gently lollop over her tracksuit bottoms. Ivan leaves the counter when he sees Chile, and nods a friendly smile. He is twenty-nine years old, with a baseball hat pulled back on his head and a grin that collapses to hide an overreaching top set of teeth. He's as eager to talk as Carlos was cautious, but constantly checks the couple drinking beers lest they want another round.

Ivan was a delivery assistant. 'I had to go with the lorry and deliver the bottles.' These were long days, 'to be honest we started at quarter to six in the morning and we finished around 7, 8, 9pm.'

Like Carlos he too talked to Sinaltrainal about joining the union, but Coke said 'that if we join a trade union we would have been sacked'.

In one single motion Ivan lets out a little 'hmmph' through his nose, his head twitches to one side, eyebrows raised and he pulls his lips tight together in an expression of disgust.

Just to be absolutely clear I ask again, 'So they would sack you if you joined the union?'
　'Yes.'
　'Is that a common occurrence?'
　'Nowadays it is happening...The project, the plan the company has, is to end the union.' He explains, slightly perplexed that the question was even asked.

Under the bottlers' system of subcontracting, which is referred to simply as contracting in Colombia, Ivan was employed by four different subcontractors. In this kind of environment the possibility that workers might have some kind of job security is non-existent.

'There was an indefinite contract,' Says Ivan

'Could they sack you at any point?'

'They sacked us because the company gave them the order to do it...' he shrugs matter-of-factly. 'There was a verbal agreement contract, there wasn't any signed contract. It was kind of indefinite.' According to Ivan it was the bottlers who decided who was hired and fired; if the bottlers didn't like you 'then they called one of the men and they said 'we don't want to see this man any more. He cannot work for you any more.' Ivan hmmphs with increased vigour and as if to prove his point adds that in 2006 he became ill with tuberculosis. 'They sacked me, I never had any help from them...they turned their back and they didn't help me, not even five pesos.' Hmmph.

His head twitches with a sideways tilt as he adds, 'Lastly I want to clarify that I want the trade union to carry on its duties. And to carry on fighting as they always have done.'

With that, right on cue, a denim-clad arm appears in the air behind him to order another beer, Ivan turns instinctively, says 'Thank you' and politely returns to serving beer.

So far our morning tour of the city has found two men who claim to have had their right to join a union denied them; Chile thinks there is another nearby and it turns out there is. His name is Jorge Santana Acostaho. The metal doors open inwards from the bright light of the sun into the shadow-dim world of the lock-up. A step down leads to the bottle bunker. It is a maze of narrow walkways created by stacks of crates with room enough to fit a small sack barrow. God knows how far back the place goes, there are endless crates, red ones, yellow, brown ones too. Stacks of Aguila beer, Coca-Cola, Pepsi, Gatorade, 7Up and Crystal. A small workbench is to one side by the wall with a desk lamp on it and above it, on the brick, a calendar features the obligatory woman in a swimsuit. This is very much a man's world. The place has the faint whiff of fresh sweat and pride. Jorge Sanatana leans with one hand on his desk, the collar on his shirt open, revealing a red V where the sun has caught him over the years. His face is hard and his hair is short and greying. Now maybe I am just a soft hand-wringing middle-class Englishman abroad and maybe all the men are like this around here, but I swear to whatever God you want that I don't think this man is capable of standing up without looking defiant.

Jorge worked for three years on the delivery lorries and for nine years in the warehouse. Back then the bottlers were more reliant on the *fleteros* not just delivering the drinks but for drumming up the orders too. 'Coca-Cola gave me an area and said I had to find the customers, so I got two or three people to go and find them. They told me to sell 200 crates a day. They used to call saying you have to sell more…So Coca-Cola pressured me and I had to pressure the employees.' According to Jorge Santana the pressure to sell that number of crates was so intense that, 'sometimes I would cheat and buy the crates myself just to make up the numbers.'

As with the other testimonies 'They used to tell me "this guy is no good, sack him". And I have to sack them.' Coca-Cola ended up sacking him for arguing, and Jorge Santana set up as an independent *fletero*. He is happier now, but 'Coca-Cola won't sell to me directly. I have to buy Coca-Cola on the black market as they refuse to sell to me.'

So far none of this paints a picture of 'respecting workers' but at this juncture I should mention my relationship with The Coca-Cola Company, which is this: I ask them questions about their practices, a PR person prevaricates on answering, waits until after my deadlines expire, then sends over a wodge of PR guff last thing Friday and buggers off on holiday for two weeks so I can't ask a follow-up question. It would be sad but for the fact that the company accidentally sent over their lawyer's notes on how to answer my questions [see Appendix B].

Trying to get TCCC to answer a question directly is like trying to run a quiz night in an Alzheimer's care home. So I have taken the liberty of imagining what they might say were they to imbibe the original recipe and get a little talkative. The Coca-Cola Company could say that I had merely spoken to disgruntled former employees, people with a grudge against the company. To which I would reply, 'That is most surely true, they do indeed have a grudge.'

The Coca-Cola Company could also say that I have spoken only to people known to Chile, a Sinaltrainal member who is in dispute with the company and that the views expressed are not representative of the workforce. Which makes the next person I talk to all the more significant.

We leave Jorge and walk through the alleyways in the hot afternoon, skipping across to the shady side of the street to avoid the sun. I become aware that we are walking, purely by chance, behind a Coca-Cola deliveryman – a *fletero*. The red shirt with the Coca-Cola logo on it is the first clue. The enormous metal frame on wheels that he is pushing, the second. The large crates of Coca-Cola merely confirms my suspicions. So ambling at his side I whisper to Chile,'Do you know him?'

'No.'

'Can we talk to him?'

'We can ask.' And with that Chile strikes up a conversation, the result of which gains me a five-minute audience in the *fletero's* warehouse – on the condition he remains anonymous. Hiding your identity for fear of reprisal is one thing but denying yourself a name seems a bit too impersonal, so I have taken the liberty of giving this *fletero* a false name: Pemberton, after Coca-Cola's founding father.

No doubt the daily delivery of 300 boxes containing 9,000 bottles of drinks has helped keep Pemberton trim, unlike his historically lard-arsed namesake. He stands legs akimbo with one hand on his hip, like an action hero, and with his other hand holds a clipboard at his side. Just like the other *fleteros* Pemberton says he is told what to deliver, to who, in what amounts and at what time, as well as what to wear by the bottlers, 'You have to buy this uniform from Coca-Cola,' his hands now motion to his clothes, a red T-shirt, with a green collar to match the green company approved trousers. The T-shirt bears the words COCA-COLA FEMSA on the breast.

Pemberton is matter-of-fact and businesslike even when he tells of the precarious nature of his employment. 'They can get rid of me whenever they want. I have no job security at all. I have been working [here] for ten years and I have no security for those [years]...So I have to do whatever they ask and agree to everything.' He looks to his assistant and whistles out a call, pointing at some crates stacked tightly together at the side of the lock-up, which the assistant starts to load on a barrow. Pemberton turns unsmiling and continues, 'Coca-Cola say I can only employ one other person to help me.' But he explains there is too much work for the two of them so he has to break the rules and employ two assistants. Running with the theme I ask, 'Has the bottler ever mentioned who you should or should not employ?'

'Yes, two years ago they told me to sack someone.'

'Who told you?'

'The Coke Supervisor.' Mimicking the supervisor, Pemberton says, '"This guy is useless, get rid".' Shrugging he adds, 'What can I do? If they ask me to do it I have no choice.'

'What about joining a union?'

He laughs and shakes his head with a mild contempt. Joining a union is simply not an option.

It was not always like this, Chile says. The Coca-Cola deliverymen (like the *fleteros*) used to be unionised: 'In 1992 80 per cent of the distribution workers were fixed contract workers and unionised. Today in Bucaramanga there are only two workers in distribution who are on fixed contracts,' himself and his driver Domingo Flores. For Chile, sub-contracting is one of the main causes for the decrease in Sinaltrainal membership, 'In 1992 there were 282 Bucaramanga workers in Sinaltrainal, and in Bucaramanga today you will only find sixteen.'

Meanwhile The Coca-Cola Company proudly boast of their good employee relations, 'In Colombia, a country where 4 per cent of workers are unionised, 31 per cent of the employees of Coca-Cola Colombian bottling partners belong to unions.'[8] So why are the *fleteros* telling such a different story? The answer lies in the statistic...oh yes, my friends, statistics: the thinking man's lie. Calculating a statistic is similar to normal counting but with different rules and when dealing with an entity like a transnational corporation it is important to remember that statistics are facts that have been shaped to fit the story. So, is the Coca-Cola statistic accurate? Let us suppose for a moment it is and consider the implications. The rest of Colombia has only 4 per cent union membership, yet the Coca-Cola bottlers have created such an employee positive environment that union membership is up nearly 800 per cent on the national average. If true the appropriate response has to be *Viva Coca-Cola! La Lucha Continua Hasta La Victoria Siempre con Coca-Cola!*

Meanwhile, back on my planet, logic dictates that this surely cannot be the case, how can Coke bottlers be so pro-union in such an anti-union environment? The answer is they are not. Coke's calculations are based on the number of *permanent* employees they have working for them, and as for the casual labour, or the sub-contracted workers – they are simply not included in the figures. Neither Carlos, Ivan, nor any of the other *fleteros* I spoke to are counted as employees.

A few days earlier in Bogota I had spoken with Sinaltrainal's researcher Carlos Olaya, who told me that since the Nineties Coke bottlers have taken full advantage of a change in the law,[9] which enabled them to remove swathes of workers from their books as direct employees and push them into casual contracts. Huge sections of the bottlers' operations were sub-contracted out – hirings, delivery, maintenance services (like canteens), security, accountancy; all of it was outsourced. 'Now the Coca–Cola bottlers have about 9,000 workers but only about 1,850 are directly or permanently employed, of that figure about 600 are in a union – about 32 per cent.' Which is close enough to the company figures of 31 per cent. 'However, when you include the other 7,150 workers, the true figure is about 6.5 per cent of the workforce are unionised, higher than the national average, true, but still ridiculously low.'

So Coke can say, 31 per cent belong to a union , because the rules they use only count every fifth worker employed under the Coca-Cola logo. Now I am not saying that this special counting method is necessarily bad; there are times when it would be nice to count five as only one, *Die Hard* movies for example.

The *fletero* testimonies raise some serious issues. If the

Coca-Cola bottlers do not employ these workers, why do they keep insisting that these workers cannot join a trade union? Answering this question TCCC's global workplace rights director responded by saying, 'Colombia has unique labour laws in that contract workers are not allowed under Colombian law to belong to industrial unions...it's a unique law in the world...'[10] Implying quite clearly that the 'Coca-Cola system' was just obeying the law on the issue. This is somewhat disingenuous.

Colombian law, according to the Colombian Trade Union Federation 'recognises the right of association only to the workers who have a labour contract [permanent employment]'.[11] This means temporary or casual workers are being denied one of their basic human rights – the right to freedom of association.

So is Coke merely an innocent party here? Is the Pope a lesbian? According to Sinaltrainal, in 1990 75 per cent of workers under the Coca-Cola system in Colombia had permanent employment and 25 per cent casual employment. Today that figure is basically reversed, 80 per cent of workers in the 'Coca-Cola system' in Colombia are casual labour. The 'Coca-Cola system' has subcontracted its workforce at an incredible rate thus denying them the right to join a union and keeping wages low and work hours high.[12]

* * *

I wake up the next morning at Chile's house to find that the family rush hour has just kicked in. Amidst the washing and dressing, shouting and shushing, beating and stirring, sweeping and feeding, homework and cleaning, Esmeralda is showing me how to make *arepas*, a flat round griddled cornmeal patty stuffed with cheese. Frankly, this is the last thing she needs and after tasting my efforts it is the last thing the family need too. Laura is finishing her homework while glancing urgently for her breakfast. Mayela feeds the baby while trying to ignore the smoke from the griddle tray. The baby's attention is caught by the smoke and so hangs open-mouthed over the bottle. Esmeralda is making dough balls, coaching me, doing up a child's shirt while serving as a human clock by periodically shouting out someone's name and the time. Jess leans over the table to snap the scene with an enormous camera, Laura's college friend is eating eggs and ducking to miss Jess's lens. Someone is in the shower upstairs shouting 'What's burning!' Emilio stands blankly in his underwear and Luis Eduardo frantically searches for the latest batch of death threats he has received.

'Luis Eduardo aka Chile' is what the paramilitaries call him in their death threats, that and 'you trade unionist son of a bitch.' Luis Eduardo collects death threats like my mum collects parking tickets.

It's a trivial point, but considering the nature of death squads and their primary purpose, namely killing people, they rarely come up with catchy names for themselves. The old Colombian paramilitaries were called the Autodefensas Unidas de Colombia (AUC) which translates as The United Self-Defence Forces of Colombia. The new paras, both nationally and in Bucaramanaga, have opted for the Águilas Negras – The Black Eagles, which doesn't sound that threatening, evoking as it does, the name of a Goth Folk band.

What isn't so trivial is that they regularly send death threats to prominent Sinaltrainal members. This one was sent to Chile in February 2007: 'The Paramilitiaries of Magdalena Medio, The Black Eagles, call on the terrorist Coca-Cola trade unionists to stop bad mouthing the Coca-Cola Corporation given that they have caused enough damage already. If there is no response we declare them military targets of the Black Eagles, and they will be dealt with as they prefer: death, torture, cut into pieces, coup de grâce. No more protests!'

There are a number of significant points about this threat: 1) The Black Eagles target Luis Eduardo because of his work as a Coca-Cola trade unionist and clearly object to the campaign against Coke. 2) They insist that trade unionists are terrorists. 3) They bizarrely offer a menu of physical assault, as if murder à la carte is somehow classy.

This particular threat came shortly after the vice-president of Colombia, Francisco Santos, made some particularly unhelpful remarks. In a thinly veiled reference to Sinaltrainal, Vice-President Santos called on those agitating against 'Coca-Cola, Nestlé, and other private companies' to stop their campaign, adding that this was fuelled by interference from 'sectors of the extreme left, radicals infiltrated into trade union sectors that are generating absolutely absurd campaigns against the corporations.'[13]

'It was after the State's version of the events that the threats started coming through to the trade union leaders...the security situation became much worse in 2007,' says Chile.

'How many death threats have you received in a year?' I ask, expecting a rough estimate.

'Eight threats,' he says precisely, as it dawns on me that death threats by their very nature are not likely to be forgotten. Death threats rarely illicit the response of, 'Oh Lord, I've been that busy I've lost count of them.'

Alongside the eight threats came a visit to the family home. Two men got past the security hut, crossed the wide courtyard in the middle of the blocks, passed the grocery shop with a tray of eggs on the counter, then turned left through an archway that goes under an apartment, emerging quickly into the cool shaded walkway that nips and tucks between the homes. Small iron fences balance on top of low brick walls where little front patios are littered with clutter – kids' plastic toys, spades, garden chairs and lots of pots sprouting firs, ferns, palms and red-leaved lilies. At the end of this is a home with bigger railings, with proper locks on them. Laura, the youngest daughter says, 'I was inside, on my own...I came down when they knocked on the gate.' She curls up on the chair. 'They said they wanted my father.'

'It's really bad and we're really scared,' says Esmeralda.

While Coca-Cola might call this an 'old story' it is a crucially current one for the family and the familiar chaos of breakfast belies the strain. A couple of years ago their eldest child Alexander had to jump from a moving bus to escape two men who clearly knew who he was and seriously threatened him. Alexander has moved well away with his wife and child and now manages a restaurant. Esmeralda spends most of her week working for him there and returns home when she can. Laura is receiving counselling as the recent visit by the paras has triggered memories of her childhood exclusion from school while her father was in jail.

The Coca-Cola Company says that the bottler, Coca-Cola FEMSA, has given assistance to workers threatened by the Black Eagles, including:

- 'Paid leaves of absence from work.'
- 'Loans to install security cameras at the homes of affected workers.'
- 'Set flexible working schedules for those workers upon their return to work.'

- 'Provided individual transportation for those workers to and from work.'[14]

Which sounds reasonable, but let us balance the books – what is in the credit column and what is in the debit column? In the debit column we have The Coca-Cola Company whose bottlers have been accused of collaborating with paramilitaries and they themselves have been accused of making little or no effort to redress the situation despite an employee being killed in the bottlers' own plant. In the debit column the bottlers' security manager falsely accused union members of terrorism, for which they are wrongfully imprisoned for six months, while their families have to beg to survive. Those bottlers have made no effort to redress that wrong. In the debit column Coke wanted rid of the union, which was the logical outcome should a settlement have been reached. In the debit column the bottlers have subcontracted workers so they do not have to give them permanent employment and refused to let them join a union. The bottlers are accused of undermining Sinaltrainal while The Coca-Cola Company claims to respect their rights.

And so on to the credit column. This entry in the balance books is not quite as long as the previous column. In the credit column is: when workers receive death threats the company lends them some money for a camera, gives them some time off and provides them with a lift to work. It is a list you could sum up as: a day off, a taxi and a loan...

Luis Eduardo has by most standards led an eventful life. There was an attempt on his life, when a para appeared with a gun while he was delivering Coca-Cola. He was saved by a shopkeeper pulling him into the store. On top of the false imprisonment on trumped-up terror charges, he has been on hunger strike for better conditions at work. Paramilitaries visit his house and his children have been threatened. His friends are either dead or carry pistols, tucked inside their shirts. Yet paradoxically I feel totally safe in his home. Perhaps my sense of security is the result of rationalisation, namely: the paramilitaries are more likely to kill Luis Eduardo than they are to do anything to me and it is a reasonably good bet that they are not going to kill Luis in front of a foreigner with a press card. Ergo, as long as I stay with Luis Eduardo, everything will be fine...it is when I leave that the problems will start. I reckon Jackie Kennedy had similar feelings, figuring that 'no one is going to bother shooting at me when they can shoot at John.'

* * *

Leaving, under the cloud of this calculation, is an unsettling affair.

'This is a little thank you.' I say handing Luis Eduardo a bottle of single malt whisky.

'This is for you' says Esmeralda, handing me a rolling pin and an *arepa* mould, 'But you must promise to make them when you get home.'

'Thanks, that is really kind of you and thank you for putting up with me,' I say.

'These are for you,' says Luis Eduardo, handing over a bundle of photocopied death threats. Not a traditional parting by any means, but I don't think he had time to get me a presentation tin of regional quality biscuits.

5

THE DAYS OF THE GREAT COKE PLEDGE

© Jess Hurd/reportdigital.co.uk

Istanbul, Turkey

'Coca-Cola acknowledges that Coca-Cola workers are allowed to exercise rights to union membership and collective bargaining without pressure of interference. Such rights are exercised without fear of retaliation, repression or any other form of discrimination.'

Joint Statement issued by The Coca-Cola Company and the International Union of Foodworkers on 15 March 2005[1]

Everyone is a mere six phone calls away, so says the theory of six degrees of separation. It works like this: you can contact anyone in the world merely by phoning someone you think might be able to help track down your target and creating a chain of contacts until you reach your goal. Admittedly, anyone who has used NHS Direct at a weekend would beg to differ. But, for example, if I wanted to reach Vladimir Putin I would try and find someone who in turn knew someone else in the Russian Embassy and go from there. Admittedly, in Putin's case you would only have to make a couple of calls before he came looking for you, probably with a plate of sushi with a half-life of a few million years, but you get the point.

In practice though, this is far from foolproof. One unforeseen consequence of attempting to utilise the 'six degrees' theory is that once you start the ball rolling, people come back with all sorts of unrequested information. You might start out looking to track down Eddie Murphy and end up getting through to Aleister Crowley's cousin.

And so it was that I had set out for Istanbul with the intention of talking with ex-Coca-Cola workers sacked for joining a trade union, and ended up nattering to a host of other, unexpected folk, including the man who wrote a history of Coca-Cola in Turkey. Someone I knew knew someone, who knew someone, who thought it might be interesting for me to meet with a Coca-Cola obsessive. Partly out of curiosity but mainly out of a desire not to appear rude I said, 'Sounds great.'

Which is why I am sitting in a patisserie just off Taksim Square fighting to keep a polite smile from turning into jowl cramp. The writer opposite me is slouching across the table. In fact everything about him slouches, his sixteen-stone frame

slouches in the chair, his black driving jacket slouch
shoulders slouch, even his thick-rimmed glasses slo...
nose. He doesn't so much sit at the table as nearly melt over
it. If I were him I would be worried in case the Buddhists are
right and in the next life he comes back as an ice-cream.

He's a knackered guy in his mid-forties but has the glint of a
young believer in his eyes. The front half of his head is bald
and the back full of black curls, flecked with the odd grey.
These same colours are sported by his stubble, making his
chin look like a badger recovering from chemo.

Our man here has written a history of Coca-Cola in Turkey.
Naturally he orders a bottle of the stuff, while I opt for the
traditional Turkish apple tea. He slugs, I sip and I feel the
better man for it. His book has not been officially 'authorised'
but is currently 'with Atlanta' awaiting a decision. There have
been a few hoops to jump through too as, according to our
fellow, the company doesn't like any mention of their cocaine
history – of all the C words to take offence at, it seems that
'Cocaine' tops the Company's list. I imagine it must be quite a
task, writing a history of a product with Coca in its name and
not actually mentioning cocaine. But our slumped fellow
avoided this pitfall by reference to alkaloid compounds
throughout the book to avoid the dreaded 'cocaine' word and
is hopeful that he will get it published.

On mentioning that I am researching communities and
groups who have found themselves in conflict with the
company, his reaction is livelier than his posture belies.

'There is no story here,' he says in good English, 'there is no
story about Coca-Cola in Turkey.' Pausing to look at me
directly 'The only story here...' he spreads his hands out across
the table top, palms up, Jesus-style '...is of a miracle drink...'

his eyes widen in wonder '...the miracle of Coca-Cola. The drink that unites people across the world.'

I don't mention the Istanbul Coke deliverymen I've just met who would probably interpret 'uniting people across the world' in a slightly different fashion, seeing as they were sacked for joining a union. For the time being I'm not uttering a single word, as I have an unnerving feeling that if he's interrupted he'll go back to the beginning and start all over again. Blinking, I focus on what he has to say. 'I was involved in one of the bridge projects, it was partnered by a Japanese firm and at the end of it there was a party to celebrate.' He leans forward in the way that racists do when they are about to say something they know they shouldn't. 'The Japanese...' he says on cue, 'served up this food...' his face is full of disgust, '...that soup with seaweed, really disgusting, you can't drink it,' he informs me as if this is scientific fact. 'Then these vegetables and rice, it smells disgusting, like vomit, you know what I mean.' He looks around and finding no disagreement, sneeringly spits out the word again, 'Vomit. No one could eat this shit. But all of us...' his faces smiles at his conclusion '....we could all drink Coca-Cola.' And he toasts the sky with his bottle.

This fellow is a zealot, Coca-Cola to the core, you could cut him and he would spill fizzy brown blood, possibly with a slice of lemon. His feelings towards Coca-Cola are intense enough to border on love, although this kind of love is the type one normally associates with restraining orders. I find his obsession fascinating, indeed it is almost an asset as it gives him a certain gauche charm. I do not, however, have much like for him.

It's not his physical appearance at fault, because to be honest I am at best only five years behind him. Nor do I dislike him because he idolises Coke so much; life is too short to hate someone over a fucking fizzy drink. Believing Coca-Cola to be the greatest thing in the world is neither a crime nor an affliction. I actually don't even mind pushing cake around a plate, while he tells me all about his collection of Coca-Cola memorabilia – a topic that is as endless as it is dull. Nor do I dislike him because his obsession has led to the suspension of any critical faculties he must have had. No, all of these things are kinks and quirks, the odd strand of DNA that defines who we are as people. No, I dislike him for the simple fact that he is a bigot.

'Coca-Cola has brought only good to this country.' He explains that he and his wife visited the east. As the south-east is the Kurdish region I wince in anticipation. 'We went into a shop and the grocer used disposable gloves to cut the cheese.' He holds his hands up in wonder and mimes putting on the gloves. 'Those people have never been able to understand basic personal hygiene...' In this particular instance the subtext is more 'text' than 'sub' and the message is quite clear: 'Kurds are filthy'. 'And do you know who taught them about hygiene? Coca-Cola. I talked to the shopkeeper and he told me how Coca-Cola had taught him about hygiene in classes...Their hygiene was terrible, no one could do anything about it, not even the government could teach them. But do you know who taught these people? Coca-Cola taught those people.'

If I have interpreted this correctly Coca-Cola are great because they and only they have managed to teach the Kurds to wash their hands. It is fair to say that logic plays no great part in our man's analysis. He sees a world where Coca-Cola brings western values and civilisation to the heathen hordes, where the company are missionaries travelling the globe for converts. It is a cap-doffing vision of 'our betters' doing their bit to improve us, one drink at a time.

I finish the Turkish apple tea, and as I get up to say good bye it dawns on me that our man here is one of those rare people whose Ralph Steadman portrait would actually look prettier than the subject.

Yet while sitting in judgement, like some south-London Solomon, I have been equally delusional. I have gently sipped the sweetness of my tea and appreciated its fine apple aroma. I have dangled my tea glass by its rim between my finger and thumb, gesticulating with it like a contemplative sophisticate. Yet it turns out this traditional Turkish apple tea is neither, tea, apple, nor indeed traditional; it is made of a bright pink powdered concoction, that was invented by a pharmaceutical company and marketed to tourists. Indeed, it is Turkish only in the sense that powdered milk is traditionally English. More than that, the tea has enough sugar in it to make my man boobs go up a cup size at the mere thought of it. In short this Turkish apple tea is about as natural as ketamine, as healthy as a sherbet dab and I would be shocked if real fruit has been anywhere near the production process.

And to cap it all, do you know how I found this out? The drummer from Turkey's entry in the 2008 Eurovision Song Contest told me! I have been tutored in cultural authenticity by a man who aspires to be liked by Terry Wogan. Oh the post-modernism of it all...

* * *

It came about because Jess the photographer was to ply her trade, photographing an interview with a Turkish rock band called Mor Ve Otesi. Unfortunately the journalist who was to do the interview dropped out at the last minute.

'You should do it,' she said.

'I don't know who they are.'

'So? They'll tell you who they are.'

'Why interview a band I know nothing about?'

'Because they were going to perform at RocknCoke....'?

'What?'

'Big festival. The biggest in Istanbul, sponsored by Coca-Cola and they pulled out of it.'

'Oh great. I can see the headline, "Obscure Rock Band Snub Sponsor Shock!"'

'No the point is that...'

'Or maybe "Coca-Cola hardly notice as Turkish band don't take their money sensation!"'

'No, there is more to it than that.'

And then she told me that the group who turned down Coca-Cola's gig were none other than Turkey's entry for the 2008 Eurovision Song Contest. The Cliff Richard of Istanbul, the Turkish Brotherhood of Man, the Katrina and the Waves of the Orient turned down Coca-Cola's moolah...And that extra sequin, well that puts a whole different set of goggles on the story for me.

* * *

On arriving at their office the band are far more hospitable than a bumbling ignoramus deserves.

Lead Singer, a balding, skinny thirty-something in a white jumper asks, 'Do you know who we are?'

'No.'

'Have you heard our music before?'

'No.'

'Do you know anything about us?'

'No.'

'Would you like a drink?'

'Yes, that would be lovely.'

Drummer, who has cropped short hair and a goatee that can only be described as jazz-wizard style, says 'I'll get some albums for you to have.'

He disappears for a moment then re-emerges with Bass Player, who is suitably adorned with floppy hair, and is clutching a fistful of CDs for me.

We drink and chat, and I learn that Mor Ve Otesi have been around for a few years, are a respected rock band, with a string of albums and whose members work on the Turkish anti-war organising committee. Not your normal Eurovision fare but as Lead Singer points out, 'Turks take Eurovision very seriously.'

'Which is not something I understand coming from Britain,' I say, 'we just put anything up for it.'

'We noticed,' he replies.

I also learnt that the first RocknCoke festival in Istanbul was held in 2003 and the line-up included the Pet Shop Boys, Simple Minds, Suede and the Dead Kennedys.

'And just a few Turkish acts...' said Drummer.

'...Four Turkish acts, and we were asked to be one of them. We said "why not?"' adds Lead Singer.

The band were touring at the time and on returning to the capital, 'We heard that there was a global campaign that started with what happened in Colombia,' says Lead Singer, 'we decided not take part in this festival and we decided to take part in Rock for Peace.'

'That was seen as a big success for the alternative festival,' says Drummer, 'as we were perceived as a band coming from the other side.'

So I promise to listen to the music, thank them for having me and put my notebooks in the rucksack. Drummer kindly waits to see me out and while we head to the office door I mention that it seems fitting that Coca-Cola, the outriders of globalisation, should reap global disapprobation. If the image of a brand can travel from Atlanta to Istanbul, then criticisms of it can likewise arrive from Bogota. As the brand travels the world, negative stories can stick to the logo. So, I conclude, when people ask how can I challenge a brand as big as Coke, we can reply that it starts by individuals learning to look past the PR image.

Drummer nods, standing at the open door and as we exchange pleasantries he politely enquires, 'What else have you got planned for your trip?'

'Well, the one thing I do need to do is to find some traditional Turkish Apple Tea to take home.'

'Erm...You do know...' he begins.

* * *

The Coca-Cola Company are but one of a multitude of companies that shape the image of their brands to suit their marketing needs and in the case of apple tea I am but one of a multitude of consumers prepared to suspend reality. But the statement from our man in the patisserie that 'there is no Coca-Cola story in Turkey,' is a suspension of reality too far. I tracked down the ex-Coke workers I had originally come here to see and I set out for the offices of the Transport Union of Istanbul, to hear their allegations of how Coca-Cola bottlers drove down their wages with sub-contractors, sacked them for unionising and then colluded with the police who attacked them and their families. The union's name is Nakliyat-Is, pronounced knack lee yat – eesh.

Alpkan, the man who is going to act as my interpreter, is a lecturer. As a native of Istanbul, he told me that 'The union is easy to find from where you are staying, just head across the bridge and up the hill...' Directing someone to walk up the hill in Istanbul is a little like saying, 'Oh, just follow the canal' in Venice. In Istanbul it is impossible not to walk up a hill. Here the streets are narrow and steep, and halfway up every single hill seems to be an old man pushing a cart with an unfeasibly enormous load. I'm beginning to suspect that it is a legal requirement for steep inclines to have an old man on them.

Fortunately the union offices are on a main road that runs under the slightly more eye-catching landmark of a huge and ancient aqueduct. Some 500 yards away uphill (naturally) is a five- maybe six-storey structure which seems to make up the entire block. Every apartment, office, warehouse, shop and storeroom exists in one extremely large building. It has the look of a Soviet construction from the 1960s, though the sight of shops stocked with actual goods for sale spoils that particular illusion. At pavement level the block's entrance is tall wooden doors, a garland of nameplates and buzzers at their side.

On the other side of one of these doors lies a circular stairwell encased in frosted glass, tinted a light brown with nicotine and age. The echoes of our footsteps rush up the stairs before us to the second-floor landing. Here, through what looks to be an apartment door, lie the offices of Nakliyat-Is. The meeting room is a small place with a low ceiling but about sixty seats have been packed tightly together, forming five rows of chairs which all face a desk at the front of the room. Behind the desk, hanging from the wall is a red banner with yellow letters declaring, 'Organised labour will defeat the forces of capital!' It is as if someone had set up a union hall in a council flat living room. I wouldn't be surprised if halfway through lively meetings there was the sound of banging from the other side of the wall and a shout of 'Keep it down in there! I can't hear the bloody telly!'

The union came into conflict with Coke in May 2005, just two months after the company in Atlanta had issued a suitably foot-shooting statement. On 15 March 2005 The Coca-Cola Company made the Great Coke Pledge and said, 'Coca-Cola acknowledges that Coca-Cola workers are allowed to exercise rights to union membership and collective bargaining without pressure of interference. Such rights are exercised without fear of retaliation, repression or any other form of discrimination.'[2] Exactly sixty-six days after the Great Coke Pledge Turkish deliverymen were sacked for organising a union. The four men sitting in front of the red banner are going to tell me the story.

Let me introduce you to them. Behind the desk sits President Küçükosmanoōlu. My translator explains that even Turks have problems pronouncing his name and so he is more often than not just called President K. He looks constantly determined and has a glare that could make a statue blink. Such is the force of his stare that I would not be surprised if there is a scientific gauge for measuring its magnitude. Today it is turned on a low setting – which would be about 2.5 on the Ayatollah Khomeini Scale. President K is a smart man, who sports a side parting and a moustache that is a classic of the region. His suit informs the room what his words confirm, that he has been in negotiations all morning. Sitting next to him is Fahrettin Takici, a lean and trim forty-nine-year-old with hair cropped close to his scalp; hunched over his chair, legs apart with his forearms leaning on his thighs. He is dressed all in black: black roll-neck sweater, black leather jacket, black trousers, all of which combine to give him the air of a loyal lieutenant. Next to him but sitting to the side of the desk is the oldest-looking man in the room, Ahmet Gakmak, whose suit is as grey as his hair. Under his jacket is a V-neck jumper with a brown and purple diamond pattern, but this description gives this garment more colour than it deserves, as it blends into the suit with an effortless ease borne of penury. Ahmet has poverty teeth, where the gaps between them tell of a life of thin wage packets. In complete contrast in front of him sits the last and youngest member of the quartet, Erol Turedi. His hair is pure Tony Curtis, his shirt crisp, his tiepin tidy, his enamel badge of the Turkish flag perfectly positioned on his lapel and his black zip-up boots are straight out of Austin Powers. And when he flashes you a cheeky smile it is the kind of grin that deserves its own theme music.

Erol, Ahmet and Fahrettin worked for Coca-Cola Icecek, the Turkish bottling company jointly set up by the Anadolu Group in Turkey and The Coca-Cola Company in Atlanta. Coke now owns 20 per cent of CCI shares.[3]

Their story starts in a manner similar to the *fleteros* in Colombia. Originally the deliverymen worked directly for Coca-Cola Icecek and considered it a good job – then they were subcontracted, they ceased to work for Coca-Cola directly, and everything changed.

Their new employer, the sub-contractor, was called Trakya Nakliyat Ve Ticaret Ltd STI (Trakya). The wages went down, overtime money went down and they were forced to resign from their old union, Oz-Gida Is in 2000 on the insistence of the management. The one thing that did not change was the job itself, as Erol points out, 'We were driving the same trucks, wearing the same Coca-Cola shirts, we changed our clothes in the same place.' In fact, according to Erol, the managers they were working under remained the same too, so not even the personnel changed. 'They were absolutely the same people.'

President K reiterates this point in his deep voice, 'The relationship between [the sub-contractors] and Coca-Cola Icecek is only a bureaucratic relationship, the whole management is led by Coke managers, [the decisions of] who to hire and who to fire were all taken by Coke managers. Coke choose the route, what brands, how much, when it was to be delivered. Everything went from Coke, even the receipts, even the paperwork was on Coke papers. The only issue that Trakya appears on is on the workers security payments [that is, the national insurance].'

The four men telling this tale have a curious unity. They're all distinct personalities yet they speak as one. An odd ensemble – I was going to call them a Greek Chorus but this being Turkey it's probably best to leave the Greeks out of it. However, there is something beyond the normal workplace camaraderie here, as they finish each other's sentences and join in together on certain refrains and sayings. It is the nearest I have seen to barbershop storytelling.

You can see this in action when the men discuss one aspect of the story, which is that The Coca-Cola Company says that 'the labour dispute does not directly involve the [Turkish bottlers] CCI.'[4] President K starts to explain why he thinks the sub-contractors are used. 'Consider the law in Turkey,' he says. 'Coca-Cola can divorce itself from any problems with the subcontractor...'

Ahmet chips in, 'Trakya was set up to decrease wages and stop any attempt at unionising.'

Erol fills in some detail, 'when we were working under Coca-Cola the wages were four times more than when we worked for the subcontractor...' he throws his hand away in unconcealed scorn '...and the working conditions used to be better.'

Ahmet starts to say, 'When we went to the management for a wage increase the management said...'

But Fahrettin jumps into the tale and along with Ahmet, they chant in unison the words of the manager told them, 'Get off the job, many people would work here in these conditions.'

Erol says nothing but his head bobs sagely and he stares at me as if to affirm the truth. President K adds a comment too, he lights a cigarette and his stony impassive face raises an eyebrow in a rare emotional outburst.

So with pay down and overtime squeezed they quietly began to unionise the deliverymen at two of Coke's plants in Istanbul, Dudullu and Yenibosna. Ahmet had the first clandestine meetings with President K, preparing the legal work they would need to comply with. When these meetings began 'a maximum of five people in each plant initially knew of the plans...' confides Erol '...we were very careful and very secret.'

Their caution was borne out of concern of how the management would react. They were right to be worried. On 19 May 2005, sixty-six days after the Great Coke Pledge was made public – six days after announcing their intention to form a union, they were sacked. Without any indication or warning the five union organisers were laid off. Erol and Fahrettin arrived for work at the Dudullu plant and were informed along with the three other men that they were being sacked for poor performance.[5] Considering Fahrettin and Erol had recently been rewarded by the company for their good work this seems an odd reason. 'I have many awards for being a good worker,' Erol insists, 'Awards the firm gave me, presents and certificates, for Best Driver.'

Which just goes to show how complex business really is these days. Those of us not involved in the corporate world would think that the best driver would be the last driver to be sacked for poor performance. How wrong we would be. Indeed a quick study of the bonus and share options for the world's top business executives illustrates how the system works: the more the Chief Executive Officer runs a company into the ground the more they are rewarded.

To the untrained eye it might appear suspicious that the five men sacked for poor performance just happen to be the five main union organisers. Indeed, Erol alleges that on the day they were sacked, 'Coke management agrees to have a meeting.' He sits bolt upright as he continues, 'And I stress this is the Coke management not Trakya...They meet the five of us and they say, "Why are you doing this? You have brought this action upon yourselves but still let's talk".'

'We have unionised.' says a friend.

A manager replied, the delivery men could '[go] on working by resigning from the union.'

According to court documents submitted in the US the union also alleges that one of the managers went on to say, 'We, as The Coca-Cola Company, shall let no members of the union work for us.'[6]

The next day, 20 May, another fifty deliverymen are sacked at Dudullu; all but a couple were members of the new union, though these non-members joined swiftly afterwards.

Five days later on 25 May the unionised deliverymen at the Yenibosna plant were sacked too – another fifty men. Within sixty-eight days of signing up to protect and respect trade union rights Coke had overseen the sacking of over one hundred workers for joining a union. At this point I fear the gap between pronouncement and reality is so great that only the likes of Heather Mills dare brook the chasm.

Every country in the world has its own customs, some old, some new, some cultural, some religious and some just for the tourists, but perhaps Turkey's most enduring tradition has been the random use of excessive force at public gatherings. Though this societal norm is not exclusive to them the Turkish authorities do excel at it, thanks to the notorious police rapid deployment force called the Çevik Kuvvet. It is at this point in the union's saga that these same police enter the story. Now, according to human rights groups the Çevik Kuvvet is responsible for about 80 per cent of the accusations and reports of torture and abuse committed by the Turkish security forces.[7] According to Nakliyat-Is 'Coke arranged for the Turkish Çevik Kuvvet to attack, gas, beat and arrest the union members and their families' so as to terrorise them into accepting 'mass terminations without further protest'.

The events took place 97 days after Coke signed its pledge to respect union rights. Up until then the deliverymen had been busy campaigning for their reinstatement. From May to July they had marched, rallied, petitioned, lobbied and protested, becoming quite a cause célèbre on the way. But after two months there was still no prospect of Coke giving them back their jobs. So the union planned a demonstration for 20 July at the Dudullu plant – the operational headquarters of Coca-Cola Icecek.

* * *

This plant at Dudullu is ringed with black ornate iron railings. Inside, there are trimmed hedges and lampposts placed just so to mark out the pathways and borders, while a concrete walkway sweeps to the administrative office. This is a long building, wider than it is high, with a domed tower in the middle of it, like a town hall clock. Except this building has no features to speak of and appears to be made entirely of dark reflective glass. If Lego made their blocks out of Ray-Bans and Nihilists designed shopping centres, this would be the result. Or if you fancy, imagine Corbusier had rebuilt Trumpton.

Beyond the iron railings on the street lies a less precocious construction, the union's protest shelter, erected by the men to keep the heat of the sun at bay while they continue their vigil. The shelter resembles the summer self-assembly shades that crop up in south-London back gardens, long-poled affairs with all the stability of Amy Winehouse, under which entire families sit clutching paper plates while fathers in shorts ritually turn meat into charcoal.

The morning of the demonstration finds the men from Dudullu under this same protest shelter, though half of the gathering consists of their wives and children who are with them for the day. The plan is to start the demonstration just as soon as their friends and colleagues arrive from the other Coke plant at Yenibosna. They do not have long to wait. At about 10am a coach draws up alongside the shelter, screeching to a halt with its air brakes hissing. The Dudullu families are instantly up and out of their chairs to welcome the newcomers. Women in headscarves and coats, kids in T-shirts and jeans are climbing off the coach with their fathers in their white Coca-Cola delivery shirts, now adorned with slogans scrawled in marker pen. No sooner have the first protestors got their feet on the ground than a shout goes out, then another, an arm is raised and motions the protestors forward. Suddenly and with no further ado a group of men cross the few metres to the perimeter of the plant's iron railings and start to scramble over them. Hands go up to steady the climbers before they launch themselves from the top. Hollers and whistles rise as they jump off into the plant. Quickly both groups, those inside the railings and out, start towards the main gates and in an instance they are prised open. Then with a slight look of disbelief at their own audacity 200 people stroll into Coke's plant. Older children hold the hands of the younger ones, women hold bags and banners, men wave flags as they wander past the trimmed hedges. Just for a moment they pause under the Coca-Cola logo that sits above the main entrance of the black-mirrored building. A few kids glance around with a look of 'Oh blimey, what have we done', then turn back to the entrance and everyone simply walks on in.

A handful of police in white T-shirts appear at the door. They were supposed to keep an eye on the demonstration but have been taken completely unawares; frankly, in this situation, a lollipop man would have more authority. Powerless to stop the crowd from walking in, one policeman tries to halt the crowd's progress before a protestor pins the officer's arms to his side and moves him out of the way, lest he hurt himself. As they stride past the stunned constabulary the workers urge, 'Keep out of this.' And on they go, into the corporate reception area of the main atrium. This is an open-plan and air-conditioned large glass box, placed squarely in the middle of the building – a box within a box. Around its glass walls run corridors and offices. An escalator whirrs to the other floors, while a balcony overlooks the vista of a reception desk and a floor dotted with pot plants – the corporate equivalent of flowers bought from a petrol station. Ceramic and metal basins stuffed with an unimaginative selection of greenery mix with genteelly roped-off sculptures of Coke bottles. This place is bland, grand, almost featureless and easy to wipe clean. It is what I imagine a waiting room looks like in a Swiss euthanasia clinic.

And into this antiseptic lounge surge the protestors, twisting and turning to take in their surroundings, craning their necks, holding hands, shouting 'Our goal is bread!' and 'Reinstate the dismissed workers!' clapping, cheering and embracing each other.

In their midst President K motions them to sit down on the floor. They have made it into Coca-Cola's Turkish operational headquarters, they want to speak to the Coke managers about getting their jobs back and they are not going to leave until President K negotiates with Coke.

Coca-Cola say that the protestors 'illegally broke into the facility'.[8] Which is true. Though there is a certain innocence to their intentions. 'This was not an occupation, it was simple: we wanted our jobs back and we wanted to talk to the managers or whoever is responsible,' the President tells me.

Erol flicks his hair and elaborates, 'We never declared this an occupation or anything like that, we said – you did an illegal act, we came here to talk about this issue and find agreement.'

As the general manager for the entire Coke operation in the region had his office in the Dudullu plant it made complete sense for the families to walk into the place. In their eyes they were simply knocking on the door asking for justice.

Most of the white-collar workers had been sent home leaving only key management in the building. Messages were sent up to them and for a while the atmosphere stayed relatively calm. There are a few arrests, but the presence of the children and women (one woman pregnant and some elderly) keeps everyone on good behaviour. The cops even bring in some food and water for the families. 'At first we didn't eat it,' I am told later by one of the protestors who was there on the day, 'as this was from Coke and the police...but then we got hungry.'

Both the union and Coke describe a relatively peaceful interim period. Coca-Cola say that 'No action was taken to remove the protestors for ten hours...and several meetings were held between CCI management and the protestors to try and resolve the situation peacefully.'[9]

That charity was over by 3pm. TV cameras set up at the gates on the street. Police buses park outside the main entrance. Istanbul's second most senior policeman appears at the plant to oversee operations. But the biggest development was the arrival of 1,000 police drafted in to cope with the 200 protestors. The Çevik Kuvvet – 'robo cops' in full body armour – mass outside and are deployed into the building in groups. They fill the corridors. They occupy the balcony. They take the floor above the workers. Hundreds of police appear in the atrium, with riot shields and batons at the ready. The police charge nets six arrests and forces the protestors into a corner, the women and children huddled at the back by the walls. The men stand in front of them. They have linked arms together in an effort to protect themselves and their families, but when the assault finally comes their efforts are proved to be instinctive rather than practical. In front of them are 1,000 police and behind them the children have started to cry.

Finally Coca-Cola's managers agree to talk to the union. So while the police corner the families downstairs President K and the union lawyer go upstairs for talks. It is late afternoon when they gather in a meeting room, which is small. Around a table, which is large. Alongside the managers, which is essential. And next to the police...which is baffling. Why were the police sitting in on reinstatement negotiations? Riot police are rarely, if ever, known for their roles as conflict resolution facilitators. I tend to think the words, 'Perhaps you could express your thoughts and feelings,' would ring hollow when uttered from behind a reinforced Perspex visor. It just wouldn't foster confidence in the non-violent aspect of mediation.

The union had no say as to whether the police were present or not. 'We obviously didn't want the police there,' says the President, as the cops 'said that they would attack the workers at any moment. So the meeting was very tense...On one hand we're talking to the managers and we are near an agreement but the cops are intimidating and abusing the workers.'

Despite this the talks seemed to be more fruitful than might be imagined. According to Coca-Cola, the bottlers CCI tried to 'resolve the situation peacefully, asking the police to delay action'.[10] Indeed the union thought they were going to reach a positive outcome. 'The meeting with Coke gave me the impression that we were close to agreeing to the demands,' President K recalls. 'In the meantime the police are constantly pressuring us in the meeting, "Time is late. You must stop." We said to the police "You can see we are close to an agreement, please wait a little more".'

In fact it is curious that Coca-Cola's managers did not address this anomaly. 'They could have said, "please leave now because we are close to an agreement or do not increase tensions".' The fact that the company did not do this 'implies that Coke are happy with the police behaviour,' says President K. Perhaps the Coke managers in Turkey were just too busy subcontracting workers into lower wages to read that The Coca-Cola Company (owners of 20 per cent of their shares) respected the rights of trade unions to 'collective bargaining without pressure of interference'.

If events were going badly upstairs, events downstairs took an expected turn for the worse. On the frontline Erol looked out at the police – 'they just pulled down the gas masks and that was when we knew.'

Two years later, listening to the men describe these events it is obvious that neither the outrage nor indignity has left them. Erol is on the edge of his seat, Fahrettin and Ahmet are out of theirs as they describe the whirling chaos as the canisters spun furiously, spurting out chemical clouds. Their arms shoot into the air in improbable directions to show how it engulfed them. Their eyes widen as they tell of stumbling into each other in panic and blindness, gasping for breath. They curse the police as children were separated from their parents and the men beaten with riot sticks. And they hold out their hands when they talk of being bundled into the police wagons outside, of reaching up to the small windows to gasp for fresh air – only to be sprayed in the face by the police.

After finishing their story the men relax, stirring sugar into their glasses of black tea and lighting cigarettes. Alpkan the translator has not seen these folks for a while so he catches up with the gossip about their families, lives and work. Union staff who up until now have stayed out and left us alone now feel able to wander into the room. A few papers for the President to sign are informally dropped on the desk. Fahrettin has to be dragged away from his mobile phone as we just have time to pose for photos. Erol and I grin madly with our arms around each other's shoulders, and the whole place feels like a post-show dressing room. Though in truth the story is not quite finished...

In the aftermath of the attack the union continued its campaigning. 'Originally it was about getting jobs back,' continues President K after the break is over. 'When we said this to Coke, they said "we have changed the transportation system and can't give you back your jobs". After that point we talked about money.'

So they started working on compensation and five months after it all started Trakya settled with the union in October 2005, paying out for the dismissals. Shortly after settling Trakya suddenly and strangely ceased to exist. Though the agreement once again forbids disclosure of its contents, it is understood the payment was approximately £500,000. This was divided amongst the 105 sacked men giving an average of £4,760 per person – about a year's pay on the minimum wage. However, this settlement was for the dismissals, not the attack by the police at Coke's HQ, for which Coke has always denied any responsibility.

Turkey is not a country noted for its access to justice or respect for human rights. For example, under Penal Code 301 it is an offence to even mention the Armenian genocide, hampering any inquiry into such a matter, as it is illegal to describe what happened. So as a trade union, especially one banned by the Generals after the military coup in the 1980s, Nakliyat-Is believed they stood a better chance of pursuing their claims through the USA. So they followed the Colombian route, bringing a case against The Coca-Cola Company and Coca-Cola Icecek in the States under the Alien Tort Claims Act. Nakliyat-Is claims in court documents that the Çevik Kuvvet 'attacked them with a particularly lethal form of tear gas that under international standards is not permitted to be used indoors, and then brutally beat the workers and their family members with clubs. Most people were paralysed from the gas, and when they were felled by the clubbing, they were kicked repeatedly.'[11] The writ alleges that the police were acting with the 'agreement' of the local Coke managers.[12]

The Company has a different interpretation of events saying, 'the Public Prosecutor made the decision that the situation could not be allowed to continue. The Coca-Cola system respects the rights of people to hold peaceful protests and regrets that a peaceful resolution to the illegal occupation of the CCI building could not be achieved.'[13]

They have also described the situation as a 'local issue' that has been 'resolved'. But once again, while they are publicly dismissive they are privately concerned. In a parallel manner to the way in which Coke handled the Colombian trade unionists, the Atlanta company has been involved in talks to reach a settlement out of court with Nakliyat-Is. As both cases were being brought by the same lawyers, it is my understanding that The Coca-Cola Company decided to tie the labour issues – both Colombian and Turkish – into the same negotiations, enabling them (were an agreement to be reached) to staunch their PR misery regarding trade unions. It is also understood that a figure close to $1 million to settle with Nakliyat-Is was being discussed when Sinaltrainal pulled out of the talks and the Company ended any further discussion on the case. The failure to resolve the issue has left the court case ongoing.

* * *

The following morning sees me hunched on a wooden seat at the side of a ferry, clutching a coffee in one hand and in the other a bread ring covered in sesame seeds. The ship's engine makes a low thrumming sound, harbour air smells of diesel and I'm off to Asia in a minute. The Bosphorus Strait divides the city of Istanbul, leaving part of the city in Europe and the other part of it in Asia.

With a slow blast of the horn the ferry leaves Europe and heads for the declared cultural centre of the Asian shore, the district of Kadikoy, from where the next income bracket down is but a bus ride away and is followed by a car ride literally to the edge of a residential development area. Here fresh builders' rubble splashes across the grass expanses between the housing blocks, casual litter in the shape of paint pots, timber, copper wire and sacking. The windowpanes in the new builds still have X-shape tape stuck on them and unconnected wires hang from lamp fittings. Beside one such unoccupied set of apartments, opposite a lone cherry blossom, is a modest three-storey affair where Mr Pomba, an ex Coca-Cola deliveryman, lives with his family. He is going to tell me about his experiences inside the plant on the day the police attacked.

He is a quiet and gentle man, wearing what looks to be his 'for best' V-neck navy blue jumper, with a Windsor knot tie under it. He is older than the other workers and silver hair sits happily on top of his head. Bowing slightly he holds out his arms beckoning me to sit on the sofa. Opposite is his chair, part of a suite, and between us snugly fits a coffee table, with a glass top and a scented bowl of plastic flowers placed precisely in the middle. Two framed texts from the Koran hang opposite a wooden cabinet that is a shrine to his daughter's passion for Besiktas football club. Anything in the team colours of black and white is placed here: scarves, shirts, rosettes, teddy bears and even photos of her in black and white face paint, with the club initials drawn on her cheeks.

Mrs Pomba and her daughter Ebru quietly enter the room, their heads shyly bent and covered with headscarves, carrying a large shiny metal samovar on a tray. This is for the Rize tea, Turkish black tea –cay – it heats the water and brews the cay which comes out of a small tap at the base.

'Please make yourself at home,' Mr Pomba says with a slight clearing of his throat.

The plastic flowers are removed and the samovar is carefully laid on the coffee table. Saucers soundlessly appear with their white rims dotted in red paint like petals and small thin glasses stand in the saucers like daffodil flutes.

'I wonder if we could start with talking about working at Coke?' I say.

Mr Pomba's reply leaves me uncertain as to whether he said 'yes' or 'let us wait until after tea', he says, 'Please.'

Not knowing what to do...I begin. 'Others have said it was a prestigious job to be working at Coke...'

'Yes it was. It was job number one.' He says smiling slightly, 'I really loved my job.'

Ebru produces photos of her father receiving a gift from one of the managers. 'The present they are giving him is this clock,' and from the other side of the coffee table she produces a metal encased carriage clock. Smack bang in the middle of the face is the famous script of the Coca-Cola logo. The arms are frozen still as the clock no longer works, but Ebru still carefully places it in a box to return it to safe keeping.

Mrs Pomba in her big dark housecoat puts a plate on the table. It's the best china. A perfect ring of royal blue on each plate's border is overlaid with golden threads of vines and leaves.

'After you were dismissed did you go to the protests outside the plant?'

'Every day. I was going on a daily basis. As if I was going to work.' He clears his throat softly, 'I was going there at 8am and was leaving at 6pm' He motions to his daughter Ebru and she comes and sits on the chair next to him. Her face flushes as she looks up and places her folded hands on her lap. She was on the demonstration with her father and two younger sisters. 'I wanted to get my father's job back,' she says tucking her chin into her chest.

'We had a lot of hope, expectation of getting our jobs back,' Mr Pomba explains, 'we were very joyful when we went there.'

Silently, neatly folded triangular serviettes and tiny dessert forks are put on each plate, just as Mr Pomba reflects on how close they were to getting reinstated when the police attacked. 'The head of the union was just about to get a deal with the company. We probably needed another ten minutes and we would have got a resolution.'

He smiles and offers his hand to table indicating I should take some food. There are plain puff pastries on the serving plate. I have been given the best food in the house. I unfold my serviette and slowly pick apart the layers with the dessert fork.

Hot black tea is poured into my glass and two cut-glass sugar bowls added to the table, the sugar in each one piled into a perfect mound. Opposite me Mr Pomba continues. 'Then they start spraying gas at us and attacked us...they were beating us and putting whoever they caught inside the police vehicles. My youngest child's eyes have been affected by the gas....she had to have an operation.'

Ebru was there when this happened, she too was gassed and so I say, 'How did you feel when all of this happened?'

'Don't even remind her,' says Mr Pomba, shaking his head.

Ebru cannot look up, 'I am upset even now, with my father just talking about it...'

She stops and silence takes over and I notice the steam rising gently from our glasses. Alpkan stirs some sugar making a small sound with his spoon. Ebru's head stays firmly down. Her father looks to her. Then her mother, the nigh invisible tea lady suddenly screams across the living room, 'I would kill those police!' She explodes with unrestrained rage. 'I'd shoot them now if they were here!' We're staring as her fists beat the sky, declaiming to the heavens. 'The dogs sprayed gas in my people's eyes! Like you see on TV – the Israeli police and the way they treat people! They are like them!'

And then she catches herself and with a flutter of her hands to fidget herself calm, she is quiet. Her voice is gone as quickly as it came. She shakes her head, collects herself, Mr Pomba clears his throat and his wife pours another glass of black tea.

For this family there is no doubt, 'Coke is responsible. They are responsible for the whole thing. They made the police attack us.'

I genuinely don't know if they did or did not, but I ask 'Do you really think Coca-Cola could have stopped the police attacking you?'

'Yes, they could have if they had wanted to,' he sighs and forces a smile on to his reddened face.

Some things did change after the great Coke Resistance, here is a list of them:

1) Mr Pomba and Fahrettin Taciki both got new jobs as drivers with different companies, though on lower wages.

2) Erol Turedi is now a salesman for Nestlé.

3) Ahmet Gakmak has not worked since being dismissed for unionising, he insists this is because he has been blacklisted.

4.) Mor Ve Otesi came seventh in the final of the Eurovision Song Contest with the song 'Deli'. They scored 138 points, receiving one maximum 12 points from Azerbaijan.

Legendary broadcasting phenomenon Sir Terry Wogan was very encouraging of them. The UK song came last in 25th place, receiving only 14 points.

5) To the best of my knowledge no book has come out on Coca-Cola in Turkey.

6) President K recently won the world glowering competition.

7) After the mass sackings, the campaigns, the protest shelter, the gassings and the settlement, the Turkish government, sensing the need for reform and change, grasped the nettle and acted decisively. The erection of protest shelters without permission is now illegal.

8) Coke has allowed the trade union Oz-Gira-Is back into the plant. Eagle-eyed readers will remember this is the union that workers were forced to resign from in 2000. So it is nice of Coke to let them back...

9) The Nakliyat-Is court case brought in the USA against The Coca-Cola Company and Coca-Cola Icecek is ongoing. The case is currently pending in the 11th Circuit USA.

6
MAY CONTAIN TRACES OF CHILD LABOUR

El Salvador

> ## 'Any child labour allegation is a very serious issue that we fully investigate.'
>
> **The Coca-Cola Company'**

It's early morning and it's hot. Long palm leaves lollop over the country lane, dark and shiny in the warm coastal mist. Few appear to be about at this hour, save the odd delivery van for the hotels or night watchman finishing a shift. But along one otherwise deserted stretch of road, a small gaggle of elderly Miami joggers wearily pounds its way up the incline. They comprise mainly of women, with one gasping male in their company. Their lungs are greedy for air, their heartbeat races, though they do not. You can practically see Death on their shoulder, taunting cynically, 'Whoa there, this one's a quick one!' You may well ask how I know they are from Miami? Well, it's a series of deductions. Firstly when Salvadorean women get old, they don't jog, they sit. They sit on benches, on rugs in the streets, in doorways, by churches and always in the shade. But jogging, no. Clue number two is the brightly coloured wrist and headbands, which just seem to scream the words 'Florida Retirement Community'. However, the final give away is their security guard. Striding lightly behind them is a Salvadorean man in his mid thirties, wearing a brown company shirt and matching baseball hat. He has a massive pump action shotgun, hanging from a strap around his neck while one hand holds the handle and his forefinger rests over the trigger guard. There can't be many people in this area other than Miami tourists who'd have armed security accompany them for a jog. Though in all honesty I'm not sure if he was there to protect them or to step in at the first sign of a coronary and administer the mercy shot.

I pass them in a van driving from a place called La Libertad on the El Salvador coast. It's a popular holiday haunt where the waves pull in large groups of surfers and the beaches are big enough for everyone else to avoid them. My destination is north to the Department of Sonsonate and its eponymous main city. This city is essentially one long high street packed with car-repair workshops, fast-food bars and strip joints. However, it is the journey to the city that takes us through sugar cane country. The place is packed with plantations. The sugar is why I am here – sugar and children.

Sugar comes second to water as the main ingredient in a can of Coca-Cola, and with nearly eight teaspoons in each 330ml can,[2] the sugar gives the water a good run for its money. It is sugar that has left a bitter aftertaste for the company in El Salvador, as the sugar Coke uses is tainted with child labour.

In 2004 Human Rights Watch (HRW), an NGO with considerable experience documenting and campaigning in the area of child soldiers and child labour, produced a report criticising Coca-Cola for not doing enough to prevent child labour in its supply chain. The report, 'Turning a Blind Eye, Hazardous Child Labor in El Salvador's Sugarcane Cultivation' said:

- 'The Coca-Cola Company buys sugar refined at the Central Izalco mill.'
- 'At least nine of the twelve children Human Rights Watch interviewed in the Department of Sonsonate worked on four plantations that supply sugarcane to Central Izalco. These children ranged in age from 12 to 16. Their testimonies and the accounts of adult workers on those plantations confirmed that those plantations regularly use child labor.'
- 'Coca-Cola's guiding principles apply only to its direct suppliers, who must not 'employ' or 'use' child labor.... Coca-Cola can itself turn a blind eye to evidence of human rights abuses in its supply chain as long as its direct suppliers do not themselves use child labor.'
- 'In Coca-Cola's case, child labor helped produce a key ingredient in its beverages bottled in El Salvador. In that sense, Coca-Cola indirectly benefits from child labor.'[3]

Not surprisingly Coca-Cola was not pleased to have such practices associated with its products. They get in enough trouble over their drinks being too sugary for kids, without the public finding out that children are helping to supply the sugar in the first place.

Surely for Coke there are two essential questions: if there is child labour in the supply chain for our drinks, are we content for that to be the case or are we not? And if we are not, what are we going to do about it?

Coke says 'any child labour allegation is a very serious issue that we fully investigate'.[4] But they were less adamant when they said to the *Washington Post* that their ability 'to assist in addressing these fundamental issues of tradition and norm that surround rural poverty is limited.'[5] It is an interesting use of the word 'tradition' in relation to child labour. To my mind traditions should be warm and pleasant things – brass bands and summer fetes, rather than stuffing kids up chimneys. It is also historically and morally flimsy to defer to tradition, tradition is subject to change. After all, slavery was traditional, as was burning witches, indeed child labour in America was traditional; some even eulogised its beneficial nature, like Coca-Cola's first proprietor Asa Chandler who said, 'The most beautiful sight that we see is the child at labour. As early as he may get at labour, the more beautiful, the more useful does his life get to be.'[6]

'BEAUTIFUL' CHILD LABOUR IN EL SALVADOR

There are approximately 5,000 children harvesting and a further 25,000 children 'helping' their parents on the harvest in El Salvador.

Some children will get up at 4.30 in the morning in order to walk to the cane fields. Harvesting is hazardous and classified as one of the worst forms of child labour by the UN. Children are vulnerable to injuries from the machetes used for cutting, the cane sap can cause rashes and irritations, a significant proportion develop respiratory problems and a working day from 4.30am to 1pm leaves no time for school.[7]

On a more positive note The Coca-Cola Company inspected the sugar mill Central Izalco, stating that 'we again verified that it [the refinery] and its supplying mill had sound policies against employing underage youth.'[8] Laudable as this inspection is, there was never any allegation that the mill employed child labour, HRW doesn't say the problem lies in the sugar refinery, but rather it says child labour is rampant in the harvesting on the plantations. It often helps in an investigation to look in the right place and the right place in this instance is in the fields.

It can't be that difficult to check for child labour, all you have to do find the fields, turn up and look. And that is exactly what I am going to try and do: turn up and look for child labour. I'm making a programme for Channel 4 and I want to find out if, three years after the report, child labour is still in Coke's supply chain and if it is, how commonplace is it?

* * *

The crew is international, coming from the States, New Zealand and El Salvador and we have to gain entry to the plantations, film what is going on and hope the gang masters don't get too angry when we arrive unannounced. The challenge to find a way on to the fields proves to be more difficult than we thought as most of the plantations lie behind a curtain of trees and villages unseen from the road. Which is why Armando, our Salvadorean translator and driver, has taken to stopping at roadside stalls and quizzing locals as to where the crops are being harvested. The first attempt is unsuccessful, as is the second and the third too. Asking folk at random if they can help us in our search yields but one fact, which is this: the phrase, 'We're looking for working children' just sounds bad in any language.

David the American cameraman curtly says, 'Someone has got to know what the score is. Pull up and ask again.'

'I'll ask we need to be more direct.' I'm worried that Armando might just be a tad too polite to his fellow countrymen and women.

So I lean out of the front window at the next stall. Two old men in buttoned-up shirts and leather strap sandals stand staring at the empty road. They appear as if their whole purpose in life is just to stand there and collect furrows on their faces. And they are not doing too badly at it. I ask, in my admittedly imperfect Spanish and with help from the others, if the good gentlemen might know of any plantations cutting today that have a reputation for employing child labour?

They both shake their heads with one slow and barely discernible twist of the neck.

'*Gracias, señor,*' I say, turning back inside the van. 'Let's try again at the next stall, Armando.'

He swings the van off the dirt and back on to the tarmac, leaving the men to continue the wrinkle harvest. We drive in silence for a minute before Armando nonchalantly says, 'You are aware that you just told those people that we were 'hunting' children.'

'What?'

'You said to them 'we are hunting down children, can you help us?''

'Oh God...'

My head hits my hands. Here we are trying to investigate one of the blights of the developing world and I have made us look like the Child Catcher in *Chitty Chitty Bang Bang*.

Field one

There is one place we know for sure will be harvesting today, as we visited it last night to watch the foreman burn the crop ready for harvest. The sugar grows higher than a man and close together too, with big dry leaves and debris bunched in with the cane, making the job of harvesting all the more difficult. The simplest method of clearing this is set it alight.

The foreman is a young guy with not an ounce of fat on him and a metal plate over his front teeth. Last night he was happy for us to film the burning and even introduced his wife and child who have wandered over to watch the palaver of a film crew. He used a long dry leaf as a taper, lit it, inserted it deep into the detritus that litters the forest of tall cane, then stepped back. The flames jumped ten feet high with a low rushing rumble and a loud cackle that sounded as if the fire were chewing through the field. Left in its wake was black and dry earth and the prized cane, burnt on the edges, still hot to touch, scorched but standing in the drifting smoke ready for the next day.

The foreman had not expected to see us this morning and he does not smile this time. He just nods and snorts before turning his back and getting on with his work. Filming the burning is one thing but now there are children working in the fields and he is deeply suspicious of our presence.

'*Hola, buenas días,*' I call, cheerfully and ineptly.

But he just looks blankly and continues grabbing the long cane with one hand and swinging the machete with the other. In a single motion he chops the stalk at the base, twists it free, cuts off the shoot end, clipping the remaining leaves and throwing the cane at a pile, where it lands with a rustle.

Nearby is a ten-year-old boy with his father who's cutting the cane. The boy's name is Jonathan, this is his first year working on the sugar cane harvest, he tells me. His job is to collect and stack the cane.

'You've come to earn some money?' I ask Jonathan.

He laughs and so does his dad. This work is piecework so a family needs as many helping hands as possible to earn a wage. Jonathan is one of the 25,000 child 'helpers'.

The kids are uneasy with our presence, so after a quick chat there is little need for us to stay and even less of an invitation to do so. But our first search has found two children working on a small six-acre site. If we are to find if the practice is commonplace or not we will need to look in other locations.

Heading back to the main drag we pass the company transport parked at an angle on a bank of earth just by the field. It's an old American-style yellow school bus, with Transporte de Personal Agrícola Ingenio Central Izalco (transport for the agricultural staff working for Central Izalco) written on the destination plate above the driver. Central Izalco the sugar mill has driven the workers down here to the fields, as they often do. Given the reputation for child labour in the area I wonder if the use of a school bus is an act of corporate irony.

As we bump along the narrow mud track, dodging dogs and grunting pigs, at one point we slow right down and inch past a homestead on the roadside. It consists of a sloping shelter made of palm leaves. The roof nearly extends to the ground at the rear and the two side walls are almost triangular. In the shaded light we can make out a wooden framed couch. To say there is no door on this shelter would be to miss the point, as there is no wall on which to hang it. Standing in front of it is a young mother washing bowls and she smiles as we pass. Her kids have all got thick scruffy morning hair, they look up too, while a chicken scuttles round their legs. They were all standing in the kitchen. But the use of the word kitchen in this instance leaves the word straining and groaning at the seams of its own meaning. The kitchen is an area in the dirt that has been swept. One sheet of corrugated iron stands upright to support a board and a bowl. In the middle of the orderly dirt is a table, with a couple of chairs and a single piece of wire runs around the whole area at waist height – tied to a tree here and a stick in the ground there – it is a boundary, just so we all know where the 'kitchen' actually is. I have wandered into this world without walls carrying a simplistic set of values picked up off the Fairtrade shelf, where kids working = bad. And I curse myself. I have forgotten that there is another equation here in this place where a piece of wire marks out a room, and this is as true as the first one and it is this: kids not working= really bad.

HRW clearly identifies the kids working/not working equation as they recommend that the sugar mills 'should never take actions that would deprive child laborers of their livelihoods without ensuring that children and their families are receiving programs and services designed to provide them with alternatives to hazardous labor.' It is better that children do hazardous work than go hungry. But, in an environment where the only options open to these children are starvation or hazardous labour, then The Coca-Cola Company has only one option, which is to make sure it isn't responsible in any way for either.

Field two

Barely minutes later along the highway we happen upon another harvest. Slowing as we approach we peer out of the van window. David the American squints, 'I can't tell how old these people are, they must be 200 metres away...'

At that moment a young man pops up and looks at us from the field. He was bent over cutting thus making it impossible to see how old he is, but straightening reveals he must be all of 13 – though David is right, it is hard to get an accurate age. Regardless of his exact age this young man is definitely too young to be working here. We know this because as soon as he sees our van with the camera, he runs rushing into the uncut cane and disappears. We have had only seconds to catch the look of panic on his face before he is swallowed by the dense green and brown stalks and hidden from sight.

The original HRW report had said, 'Plantation foremen turn a blind eye to the fact that children as young as eight cut cane.'[9] Since its publication I had heard that the foremen were now concerned not so much with using child labour, but with being *seen* to use child labour. Perhaps that is what the boy was doing. Trying to make sure the plantation was not seen to be using child labour.

Field three

Another ten minutes down the way and my suspicions are aroused again. This time a young lad, machete in hand, trims cane. Having learnt our lesson from the first incident we don't slow down, we drive on. Once out of sight, we turn around, head back and stop. The child is out in the open field when the van brakes suddenly, men near to him shout and he breaks for the refuge of the sugar cane, his legs splaying awkwardly as he hops over the stumps and stalks protruding from the ground. He disappears momentarily but can only have gone a few feet into the dense wooded canes, as he pokes his head out to take a quick peek, catches sight of us, and then vanishes once more.

Barely moments later a white jeep arrives on dirt track by the side of the field, carrying three officials from the Ministry of Labor. This looks like a spot check of some kind and they dismount the vehicle with considerable officiousness. Civil servants they may be but their walk is pure Sweeney. Or at least a version of the Sweeney that works out. Wearing smart short-sleeve shirts and even shorter necks, the body-building bureaucrats start to go through paperwork with the plantation foreman. Coca-Cola say the Ministry of Labor 'has labor inspectors whose only task is to detect child labor.'[10] Could we be witnessing the authorities clamping down on child labour? How will they find the lad who has just hidden? What will happen to him and the foreman?

Actually, nothing happens. Their inspection seems to be just checking papers. It might appear brusque but it is short, sweet and painless. As they get back into the jeep I run over with Armando translating and say, 'I wonder can I grab a few quick questions? My name is Mark Thomas from the UK.'

Sitting in the front passenger seat an official turns to me. His expression is that of a man who can't quite be arsed to be menacing, like a bouncer with a minor case of ennui. He rolls his shoulders and blankly says 'Hello' – though I am sure his shoulders just told me to 'fuck off'.

'I'm making a programme for TV in Britain and it looked like you were making an inspection and I just wondered what you were doing?' I say, all breezy and blasé.

He replies with a mixture of boredom and aggression, 'What the ministry does is check for children working here and for illegal immigrants.'

At this stage I realise I might as well be standing before him in plus fours with a 12-bore under my arm, spouting like a toff, 'I'm on a child hunt don't you know...'

Nonetheless I plough on, asking, 'Oh...is there much child labour here?'

   'Here? No.'

'None at all?'

'Not here...' He says through rigid lips.

'None?'

'Not on this plantation.'

'You've checked for children working here illegally have you?'

'There is none here...at the moment...none.'

He rolls his shoulders at me. Twice.

* * *

Solving the problem of child labour involves a lot of different groups of people, including the Salvadorean Ministry of Labor. The HRW report highlights the complexity of the problems and is clear that it is not just the problem of one organisation. The solution, they say, will involve people from UNICEF, the Salvadorean Government, the Ministry of Education and the Ministry of Labor, as well as the sugar industry and Coca-Cola. The problem is that Coca-Cola seem to be taking a back seat on this particular example of problem solving. The HRW report made a series of recommendations that The Coca-Cola Company should adopt to play its part in eradicating child labour. Though there is no compulsion for the company to adhere to these recommendations it is worth noting that TCCC has not implemented a single one of them.

COLA-COLA'S REPORT CARD
DID THEY DO ANYTHING THE REPORT RECOMMENDED?

2004 HRW Recommend that Coca-Cola adhere to UN standards on child labour (which they do) and that they 'should require suppliers to do the same throughout their supply chains.'[11] This would mean insisting the sugar mill in turn insists that the plantation does not use child labour and this should be a contractual condition.

2008 Coca-Cola says in its Supplier Guiding principles that as a 'minimum' the 'Supplier will not use child labor as defined by local law.'[12] But does not require the supplier to enforce this through the supply chain.

They therefore do not meet that recommendation.

2004 HRW Recommend that Coca-Cola 'adopt effective monitoring systems to verify that labor conditions on their supplier sugarcane plantations comply with international standards and relevant national labor laws'[13]

2008 Coca-Cola says it is eradicating child labour by being 'part of a multi-stakeholder initiative *working towards hiring* [my emphasis] social monitors to work with the co-ops to monitor against child labour.'[14] So no one has been hired then...

2008 Mark Thomas is currently working towards a positive reaction to the above comment. Coca-Cola do not meet that recommendation.

2004 HRW Recommend 'In cases where plantations fall short of such standards, Coca-Cola and other businesses should assist their supplier mills in providing the economic and technical assistance necessary to bring plantations into compliance.'[15]

2008 The company says, 'Coca-Cola is eradicating child labour by being a part of a multi-stakeholder initiative *working towards hiring* social monitors...to provide education and income streams in collaboration with government and NGOs to divert youth from hazardous work in the harvest.[16]

2008 Mark Thomas is engaged in a multi-stakeholder dialogue that is working towards the eradication of derision of such corporate statements.

There is no evidence that Coca-Cola have met this recommendation.

2004 HRW Recommend 'In particular, Coca-Cola and other businesses should support programs and services that offer children and their families alternatives to child labor, publicly reporting the status of such efforts at least on an annual basis.'[17]

2008 Coca-Cola 'has partnered with TechnoServe, a local NGO working with targeted co-ops to find alternative sources of income for youth 14-18 years of age.'[18]

2008 Mark Thomas asked 'What is the nature of the partnering of TechnoServe? Was there any financial assistance involved? Have there been any assessments made of the results of the partnering and if so, by whom?'

2008 Coca-Cola replied 'We partnered with TechnoServe to financially support the programs that aid children through educational opportunities in El Salvador.'[19] Er, that is it...

The Company have not provided any details of the financial support it gives to TechnoServe, nor have they shown that the work they partnered with TechnoServe is addressing the specific issue of children in sugar cane harvesting. Nor do they show if the children TechnoServe are working with are being offered alternatives to child labour. And they just ignored the question regarding annual assessment.

Therefore, Coca-Cola have not fully and properly met the recommendations made by the Human Rights Watch Report.

Sitting in the front of the van and leaning on the side window, the sound of the wheels' low continuous rumble on the road is comforting and I turn to itemising the day. So far this morning has yielded child labour working on the three fields we visited, two of the boys have tried to hide from us to avoid being seen to work and the Ministry of Labor seem uninterested, at best, in doing anything today. But what this all amounts to I simply don't know. Does what we have seen make child labour on these plantations commonplace? Perhaps what we are seeing represents progress? The only thing I know for sure is that running around plantations filming child labour doesn't make you friends. I couldn't be less popular if I were the UK entry for the Eurovision Song Contest. In fact an outbreak of chlamydia in a nunnery would be greeted with less hostility.

My road-trip meditation is broken as we brake sharply to let a truck out of some gates and on to the highway. This is a *rastras*, a sugar cane lorry, which is essentially a truck with an enormous metal container coupled to it. These containers are almost literally huge rust buckets, 40 to 50 foot long perhaps and when they are piled high with cane they are easily 18 to 20 feet high. They lumber along the narrow roads, swinging from side to side, with odd sticks of cane falling from the uncovered top. So monstrous and unique are these mechanical beasts that it is a small wonder that *Top Gear* hasn't raced them across a conservation area yet.

'Where do these go?' I ask.

'They go to the sugar mill,' says Armando, 'they load up with cane on the plantations and then take it to the mill to be refined.'

'So that lorry has just come out of a plantation then...'

Field four

The gates to the plantation are tall and iron and come with a
gatekeeper, an old man in a battered straw hat who is in
charge of the padlock and chain. As another truck comes out
we act as if we are expected and go through. He shuts the
gates behind us and we are in, on a dirt track surrounded by
tall green sugar cane. Taller than the van, it leans over the
pathway forming a shady lane. This is all plantation land,
behind the gates and away from prying eyes. No one expects
to see a film crew in a van cruising around these tropical
pathways and their expressions of surprise prove to be
unnerving. The first harvest we come to has a group of about
five or six children standing with machetes. They are young
children. Maybe eight years old. One awkwardly puts the
machete down when she sees us, holding it by her side and
then cautiously dropping it, as if she had been caught doing
something naughty. She looks at us and then runs to her
parents working further away. Turning down a fork in the
track we stop alongside a boy who is standing just off the road
cutting. We are so unexpected that he looks up to find the van
practically next to him. He too is underage. Through one
corridor of cane a group of kids on bikes appear, catch sight of
us, drop their heads, lift their backsides out of the saddle and
pump their legs in panic, cycling madly to get as far away
from us as they can get.

Further still we arrive at the main harvesting field to find a
vision of seething toil. The men's vests and T-shirts are
patched with sweat already and the sun is still far from its
midday prime, their hands are black with soot and their faces
smudged with ash too. Predictably the sad regularity of the
scene unfolds. A young boy in a white shirt is in the cropped

area, exposed for all to see, including the foreman who stands watching with his machete in a leather sheaf decorated with tassels slung over his chest. The young boy's older and legal workmates shout to him that we are here. He turns in utter confusion and starts to run, but not towards the dense cane that can hide him, but across the cleared field. He throws a long handled shovel to the ground. Someone shouts for him not to panic, 'Pick it up! Act normal!' they must have bellowed. In his chaos he picks up the shovel again but starts to run. 'Don't draw attention to yourself!' Someone must have shouted, as he slows down and walks to the edge of the field. Trying to gently let go of the long-handled shovel as he goes. He has made it to the path, where older workers are watching. He puts his head down, his hands in his pocket and walks away from us. He goes to turn around but seems to hear an older voice nearby, saying 'Just keep walking kid, just keep walking.'

Through it all, the foreman just stands there with one hand holding the machete sitting on his fat stomach. He has not even bothered to turn a blind eye to it all. He watches the whole thing, down to the kid disappearing into the plantations pathways. Along the pathway at the side a few workers stand watching, and it looks like the owner has arrived, or at least someone with money enough to ride a horse around the plantation with a pair of cowboy boots and a posh cowboy hat. No one talks to us directly, but you could cut the atmosphere with a knife and there are plenty of those around here. They stare at us with poker faces. Then turn back and as one group of men does this one of them spits. I couldn't say if it was out of necessity or with contempt. But what I hear next is definitely shouted for our benefit, as one of the *caneros* in the field yells, 'Come and look at the animals! Come watch the animals!'

Oh Christ, look at us, chasing children as they flounder and flee. Charles Dickens would have loved to have seen us in action, 'the kid hunters', caring beadles with compassionless hearts, terrifying youngsters so they can have a better life. We've been tracking kids like Fairtrade perverts. No wonder the cutters hate us. They hate our presence. Perhaps the landowners do too, but the landowners won't lose one moment's sleep over our visit; we've caused them neither distress nor loss. We have not even reprimanded them nor the plantation managers or the foremen either. But our very presence reprimands the cutters, the families and the children. Just standing by the field, we judge them, our presence alone says, 'you shouldn't be letting your children work on the cane harvest'. But what are they to do, go without money? So we judge them for having to work like this. We judge them for being poor. Intentionally or not, that is what we do. They did not ask us to come. They did not want to tell their story.

For all our discomfort, which is nothing compared to the discomfort of actually having to work in these fields, the fact remains that child labour is obviously present on an unacceptable scale. Our film crew, none of whom know the area, or have had any experience of harvesting cane, have in one morning managed to bumble through cane fields and found, by our reckoning, at least 15 children working. Which goes some way to showing that child labour is still commonplace, and on the plantations that provide the raw materials for Coke's sugar.

It would be glib and wrong to say The Coca-Cola Company don't care about this issue. They do – they say so on their website. 'We care about the plight of these children,'[20] they say. They also say. 'We firmly oppose the use of child labour.'[21] Yet despite this and their multitude of codes and practices there is a glaring loophole. The Coca-Cola Company has a

Global Workplace Rights Policy that says, 'The Company prohibits the hiring of individuals that are under eighteen years of age for positions in which hazardous work is required.'[22] OK, that's fine. They have Supplier Guiding Principles, for direct suppliers like Central Izalco, which state that the 'Supplier will not use child labor as defined by local law.'[23] But some countries do not have adequate laws. Nothing compels either The Coca-Cola Company or the sugar mills to investigate, take responsibility or prevent children harvesting cane on the plantations – no matter what happens further down the supply chain, it is simply not their problem. And until they make it their problem they will be open to the charge of not trying to solve it.

Last night as we filmed the foreman burning the dry leaves in the cane field, cutters told me that the Central Izalco engineers will tell the plantation owners which cane to cut, where, when and how much. The *rastras* have to know where to come to pick up the cane to take it to the mill and the cutters are often driven in company buses to the crops. HRW found that 'Central Izalco directly administers some of its plantations and provides technical assistance to those it does not administer directly.'[24] It is impossible for Central Izalco not to know about the child labour happening under their eyes. But such are the loopholes that a manager from Central Izalco could find children cutting sugar cane literally outside the mill, walk past without batting an eyelid and still comply with all of Coke's codes of conduct and principles. And this is what we witness next.

Field five

Leaving the plantation we tuck behind one of the large *rastras* as it heads to the sugar mill – Central Izalco. There is no other mill in the area but we should double check that the cane cut here is going to Coke's sugar supplier. So we settle into the whirr of the wheels on the road and the warm sun on the forearms that dangle out of the window alongside the van. The lorry sways along the road as it heads to the mill with the cane that children helped cut.

The *rastra* turns off the main highway on to a dirt track that leads to the sugar mill. The truck churns the ground into dust under the weight of its sweet load. The huge lorry turns tightly into an even tighter tunnel that goes under the road it has just left. There is only just enough room to get through and our van follows into the darkness and swirling clouds of dirt, missing the chance to wind the windows up and emerging into the sunlight with an added layer of grime. The truck continues to the mill, while we stop. Just next to this dirt track is a field being harvested, right under the Central Izalco water tower, which is shaped like a turnip on stilts and painted in red and white with the company name in bold: it is impossible to miss. As are the children working in the field below it. Three children, one as young as ten, are working harvesting cane, one cutting, another tying, they all look sheepish and pull baseball hats low over their eyes at the sight of us. And all of this is within view of the sugar mill. If a manager cared to look out of a window they would see the children working outside their mill, right under their noses. You would have to stick pokers in your eyes to miss it. How much more obvious can it get? Outside the fucking company office! For all their codes and PR guff the mill's managers can sit watching the kids hacking cane all day and would still be in total compliance with Coke's 'principles' if they did absolutely nothing. And from what I can see here this is exactly what they are doing.

The Company say 'we have made tremendous progress' on child labour, claiming to have been involved in the removal of 9,000 children from the sugar cane fields.[25] Let us assume this claim stands up to scrutiny: if you have sorted out 9,000 kids, how come there are children are working in broad daylight outside the sugar mill Coke use, and no one does a thing? Not one thing. Coca-Cola – were you so busy with the 9,000 that you missed the ones outside the mill? Until the children are out of these fields and either in school or in legal non-hazardous work then every bottle and can coming out of El Salvador should be labelled: May contain child labour.

THREE THINGS COCA-COLA HAS DONE ON CHILD LABOUR

On its website, The Coca-Cola Company lists ways in which it is helping eradicate child labour in the El Salvador Sugar Industry. Warning – may contain corporate speak. For lovers of the nonsensical, whet your whistles here.

1) 'On Coca-Cola's recommendation, Fundazucar (the Salvadorean Sugar Association) engaged a social compliance auditing firm that helped the Association determine how to detect and control child labour and associated issues.'[26]

Coca-Cola have essentially said – 'oh you should do something about that,' and then listed this as a contribution in the fight against child labour. I repeat: the company didn't actually do anything themselves, they recommended someone else do something. And the something they recommended someone else to do, was hire another someone, to advise the first someone on how to detect child labour.

I would like to recommend that if they want to detect child labour, they look out of the window at Central Izalco. They can have that one for free.

2) 'Coca-Cola has publicly supported the proposal, authored by the World Bank and Business for Social Responsibility, to help position El Salvador as a responsible-sourcing country.'[27]

Oh, publicly supporting a proposal...is that like a petition? Did they sign a petition to end child labour? Hurrah! Now can I put a marker down for ending apartheid? I distinctly remember buying a 'Free Nelson Mandela' badge back in the 1980s...Actually come to think of it I signed a petition against the Indonesian occupation of East Timor and the bastards haven't thanked me yet...

3) 'Nine thousand children have been removed from the sugar cane fields in El Salvador over the last three years through our efforts with the UN and the Sugar Association.'[28]

That is more like it; 9,000 kids out of child labour! Well done. I have asked Coca-Cola how many of those 9,000 were removed from plantations that provide cane for Central Izalco? What was the nature of the work they did with the UN that has led to this?

The Coca-Cola Company replied, 'We have also participated in multi-stakeholder dialogues that have included the International Labor Organisation of the UN to understand and address the root causes of this serious issue in El Salvador.'[29]

7
DODGE CITY

London, UK

'It is not just Corporate Responsibility, it is doing the right thing.'

The Coca-Cola Company

The afternoon sun is hitting the diesel fug in Central London and I am sitting in the visitors' cafeteria of the House of Commons when a woman from Coca-Cola's Human Resources looks at me across the table with earnest eyes and asks one of the best questions I have ever been asked. She says, 'Why are you picking on us?'.

There are few other people in the tearoom and the clink of cutlery being collected just nudges above the low hum of the chiller units that hold the sandwiches and yoghurts. In this setting and with a plastic tray placed on the table between us, the question has a strangely domestic tone to it. Almost as if the woman from Coca-Cola's Human Resources department is going to tug her chair closer to the table and say in a lowered voice, 'You've been seeing other multinationals, haven't you?'

It is a chance encounter, both of us have arrived early for a debate, decided to get a cup of tea and being the only people waiting at the till had got chatting. Her name is Clare, she is in her early thirties and I assume her question refers to past articles I have written along with a TV documentary I had presented all of which were critical of the company. Though I never imagined that investigating them might amount to 'picking on' Coca-Cola. It is tempting to reply, 'Why am I picking on a $67 billion transnational that sponsors the Olympic Games, the Football League and can summon US ambassadors to do its bidding? I guess I am just a bully...'

But actually I am slightly stunned by the question, because the words 'picking on' imply that the company is an innocent victim, blameless in fact; and more than that, not only are my questions to the company intimidatory but I am a flawed person for even asking them.

This is the second occasion where a Coke employee has accused me of picking on them, the first coming in the form of an anonymous email, sent by someone who claimed to work for the company. He also accused me of being a liar and hoped the company would take me to court. So I wonder, is the company's internal response to certain critical coverage to label it as the usual suspects- 'picking on us'? I don't know the answer and in the cafeteria my thoughts are not quite this cogent as I stammer out a response to Clare, 'I don't think I am picking on Coca-Cola, is questioning a company picking on them?'

'No, I mean why us?' she says with a tight face, 'why don't you pick on Pepsi?'

This is indeed an entirely reasonable question to ask, especially were it to come from anyone not associated with Coca-Cola.

'They simply do not have the same amount of human rights allegations lined up against them,' I reply.

Pepsi are certainly no paragon of virtue, they were criticised along with Coca-Cola in India over pesticides found in their products,[2] likewise Pepsi and Coca-Cola were fined over painting adverts on the Himalayas in a conservation area.[3] But while Pepsi may parallel Coke in some instances they come a resounding second in amassing form.

'I suppose we are just an easy target,' she continues, managing to keep a sneer out of her voice, but only just.

'No, you're not an easy target, you're just a big one,' I reply.

At this point a friend who is also attending the debate comes into the cafeteria and my chance encounter with Clare from Human Resources ends, the stairs beckon to the cavernous Great Hall of the Palace of Westminster and from there the committee rooms. It is time to go, we shake hands, smile politely and lie to each other.

'Nice meeting you,' we both say.

* * *

The debate in House of Commons committee room is on multinationals, labour and human rights and it features one of the stars in Coca-Cola's fizzy firmament, a man called Ed Potter who is their Global Workplace Rights Director. He is a cornerstone in the company's Corporate Social Responsibility programme. Let me explain a little. Fashion and fads afflict us all, none of us are truly immune from collective stupidity and corporations are just as prone as the rest of us. Management trends might be more rarified but they are equally humiliating. There was, for example, the mimicking of Japanese company methods, where employees had to endure doing morning exercises with their boss and sing anthems to productivity. The next boardroom fad was the New Age Executive. They never wore a tie to work, played Frisbee during brain-storming sessions and insisted everyone call them by their first name, thus ensuring everyone called them 'tosser'. There was also the obsession with team cohesion and group motivation, this was where managers increased their output as a result of an epiphany during paintballing and accountants bonded by building rafts out of dead okapis, or some such nonsense.

The latest fad is Corporate Social Responsibility where companies construct a series of programmes, projects, charitable pledges, codes of conduct and impact assessments, to show the beneficence of the company. No one working for a multinational listed on the stock exchange can buy a copy of the *Big Issue* without boasting of a contribution to society. For some it is nothing but a PR tool to convince doubters that multinationals are good corporate citizens. However, there are those with a genuine belief in Corporate Social Responsibility who argue that multinationals and transnationals are hugely powerful entities that have the capacity to improve social conditions through the workplace. Globalisation and neo-liberal economics are not just a reality but the dominant consensus amongst politicians, corporations and ruling elites. Thus, supporters of CSR argue, there is a potential for consumers to pressure companies to change, as governments seem disinclined and unable to legislate against corporate excesses. For some Corporate Social Responsibility is the only game in town.

Regardless of your perspective most CSR programmes will invariably do two things. Firstly, it will devise a code of conduct. In turn this will underline the company's aim not to discriminate against their employees on the grounds of race, religion or gender. Considering that it is illegal to do any of the above in the UK, these declarations essentially say, 'It is our policy not to break the law.' And when a company feels the need to publicly promise not to engage in criminal acts, I for one do not feel reassured. Nonetheless, codes of conduct are ubiquitous features on the business landscape and everyone seems to have one. Even the trade association of the Adult Entertainment Industry in America has a draft Code of Ethics for porn makers in which they acknowledge their commitments to employees stating that 'Adult performers are the backbone of the adult entertainment industry.'[4] Surely a fact beyond dispute.

The second item of the company CSR plan will be a pledge to 'go green'; just about every multinational has declared their intent to join in and do their bit to save the planet. BAE Systems, the arms dealers, are seeking to reduce carbon emissions on their munitions, so as 'to impact as little as possible on the environment.'[5] Hurrah! I can hardly wait for a computers-for-schools voucher with every 'precision' weapon! Meanwhile the oil giant BP is 'committed to the responsible treatment of the planet's resources.'[6] Of course they are, who would think anything less. It is now only a matter of time before Hell itself converts to solar power.

One of the central tenets of CSR is the workers' right to join a union and back on planet Cola allegations of union busting have been stacking up against the company. Alongside the Colombians and the Turks, trade union organisers from Pakistan and Indonesia claimed to have been sacked and mistreated for their union membership. Not to mention Russia.

Not surprisingly The Coca-Cola Company embraced the world of Corporate Social Responsibility with vigour and vim: pledges were made, policies and guidelines written, reports commissioned, websites were set up and a new position was created within the company: Global Workplace Rights Director. The chap who got the job was Ed Potter – the man speaking in the debate today. American Ed Potter is an ex-lawyer with a background in international labour and employer issues. He reports directly to The Coca-Cola Company board on 'workplace rights' and oversees the company programme. It is Ed Potter who is responsible for Coke's 2005 pledge to respect trade unions' rights. So he's the man to answer the questions on Coca-Cola and trade unions. Stuck away in Atlanta and with a heavy travel schedule it could prove difficult to engineer a meeting with him. So it is fortuitous that Ed Potter is here in London to address these issues.

The term progressive is a relative term. When governments claim to be progressive they mean out of touch, when musicians claim to be progressive it means they are so skilled and clever that no one actually likes them, and when think tanks claim to be progressive it means they will take funding from anyone. The debate in the House of Commons was hosted by the Foreign Policy Centre, a progressive think tank. Their slogan is 'Progressive thinking for a global age.' They have Tony Blair as a patron and have accepted 'generous support' from British Nuclear Fuels plc, BP, GKN, Nestlé and British American Tobacco. Today's debate is sponsored by The Coca-Cola Company, who join the illustrious names listed above.

The committee room is typical of the House of Commons, but for the fact that it is packed with people. The windows are leaded glass, the wallpaper decorated with heraldic lilies and roses, the ceiling is carved wood and the seats have the portcullis embossed in gold, but all of this merely serves to emphasise the fact that no one does grandeur quite so dully as the British. Somewhere a clock ticks loudly in agreement.

The place continues to fill up with a disparate mix of folk. Students and journalists rub shoulders with company executives, policy wonks and MPs' researchers, who in turn sit alongside non-government organisations and trade unionists, not to mention the smattering of over-qualified graduates hoping for a job. Most of the people from the rarified world of CSR are here: from the great and the good to the average and poor, there are no curious bystanders in this room. Everyone has a view and if you listen carefully, above the clock and the low hubbub you can distinctly hear the sound of axes grinding.

Arriving to the near-capacity crowd someone hands me a programme and I am gently propelled by a series of polite interns towards one of the few remaining seats, which is right in the front row, directly opposite Ed Potter who is sitting at the speakers' table with a little name card in front of him.

The woman chairperson sits in the middle of the four male speakers. At one end of the table is Peter Frankental from Amnesty International sporting a smart jacket and tie and looking like an RE teacher. Next to him is Michael Blowfield who is a real teacher at the London Business School and is a senior associate with the University of Cambridge Programme for Industry. His grey suit is either just from or just going to Oxfam: you don't need a good suit if you're really clever. On the other side of the chairperson is Brendan Barber, who like all previous TUC leaders, manages to wear a good suit badly. Next to him is Ed Potter in a tailored black suit with white pinstripes, a light grey shirt, a darker grey tie and black leather shoes. He has the best suit in the room, anything less would be unacceptable. If you represent the most powerful brand on earth you are not going to show up in tweed and leather elbow patches. It is just not done; it would be like the Pope getting a cock-ring.

The chair, one of the think tank, welcomes us to 'a series on Corporate Social Responsibility in emerging markets, in association with Coca-Cola Great Britain. This programme seeks to explore the issue of Corporate Social Responsibility in developing markets focusing on multinational corporations. It will examine the impact of multinational businesses on the workplace, marketplace and the environment as well as explore how well-designed CSR practices can contribute to economic, social and environmental progress in newly industrial countries...' Somewhere a Business Studies student accidentally snaps the lead point of their pencil on their notepad in tense anticipation. The rest of us settle into our seats.

Ed Potter is trim, with thinning grey hair cut close to his scalp, thin-rimmed glasses and a few liver spots on the back of his hands. He must be in his late fifties or early sixties but I couldn't guess exactly. He is pleasant, polite and not prone to over excitement. He is careful and low key as he stands at the podium and outlines what needs to be done to improve 'global workplace rights'. Not long ago talk of workers rights would be wreathed in the oratory of struggle and sacrifice, today Ed Potter tells us they rely on 'a commitment to global and local stakeholder engagement.' In the word of Corporate Social Responsibility the real battle against worker exploitation needs a 'focus on aligned common business approach' and a 'commitment to get out in front of issues that are systemic in nature.' In the hushed tones of the room I'm sure I hear another pencil lead go...But it might have been the sound of a neck cricking as a slumped head jerks itself into the upright position.

Soft-spoken and mannered Ed Potter might be, but you don't get to be a lawyer in international law and employment for twenty-three years without having a hard streak somewhere.

So when Brendan Barber of the TUC mentions that there are 'unresolved issues in Colombia' Ed Potter doesn't flinch. When Peter Frankental from Amnesty International says 'Coca-Cola has been tainted by association of human rights abuses in Colombia,' Ed Potter seemingly registers nothing. Frankental continues, 'Coca-Cola were exonerated by the district judge in Miami in 2003 on the grounds that its bottling agreement with Panamerican Beverages and Bebidas Y Aliementos did not give the company explicit control over labour issues in Colombia. However, the fact that a company is exonerated by the courts does not mean that it has no moral responsibility.' Surely this is a gauntlet of sorts, thrown at Coke's feet for Ed Potter to pick up. He has to comment on this, doesn't he?

I take a good look at Ed Potter, a mere arms' length away. He is slowly doodling a large picture of a Coke bottle on an A4 pad, complete with curve lines and a passable imitation of the classic script.

Finally the floor is thrown open to queries, observations and comments. Someone from British American Tobacco asks about the forgotten plight of poor farmers in developing countries. And is taken seriously...If ever you want a measuring stick for CSR then this might be the moment, when a representative from British American Tobacco asks about workplace rights and security for farmers and doesn't get laughed out of the room.

The interventions continue apace. Journalists from the *Independent* and *Corporate Age* ask about the effectiveness of CSR and how to improve it. Points are made from the floor about the increasing feminisation of poverty and questions raised about the relationship of neo-liberal globalisation to CSR.

But Ed Potter is still attracting flak and is heckled by members of the Colombian Solidarity Campaign, keen to question The

Coca-Cola Company's response to the murders of trade unionists in Colombia. We are about to learn that Ed Potter's twenty-three years' experience as an American lawyer has made him a blackbelt at avoidance. He deftly draws a line between the bottlers in Colombia and The Coca-Cola Company in Atlanta, the way the Company has always done. 'The situation to which you are describing is one that involves our independent bottlers in Colombia,' he says, that is an issue that Coca-Cola FEMSA [the current Colombian bottlers] can address.'

Amnesty's man picks up this particular point when it is his turn to respond to questions, arguing that human rights and labour rights should be treated as a quality-control issue. If a bottle was contaminated by the bottlers in Colombia, distributed around the world and affected people's health, 'would Coca-Cola have tried to distance themselves from the responsibility? Would they say that it is not their responsibility, it is that of their franchise bottling plants? I don't think they would say that. And they would not be allowed to.' So argued Amnesty's man adding, 'any products we consume that have human rights' violations in their making should be seen as a defective product.' In essence, if Coca-Cola can treat contaminated product as its responsibility then they should do the same for human rights abuse.

And this must apply to everyone The Coca-Cola Company works with, from the bottlers, to the distributors, to the sugar refineries, to the plantation workers – every single man, woman and subcontracted jack of them. It is not enough, said Amnesty, to be 'committed to working with and encouraging them [that is, the independent bottling partners] to uphold the principles in the policy [i.e., workplace rights]'. Amnesty argue that all parts of Coke's supply chain should regard human and labour rights as 'a compliance issue and [there] has to be sanctions against their suppliers, just as there would be if there were any technical defect in the product.'

This seemed like an appropriate point to jump in and try and muscle an answer out of Ed Potter, so I ask 'When are you going to introduce codes of conduct for subcontractors and what measures are you going to bring in to enforce it?'

Ed Potter looks through his thin glasses directly at me. His soft voice gets a rasp around its edge. He stops still and slowly says 'The question you are asking is a question that keeps me up at night.' He said it in such a way that I would not have been shocked if he had pulled put an acoustic guitar and sung his reply Johnny Cash-style. Then in true lawyer fashion he promptly ignores my question and asks the question he wants to answer, namely, 'What is the most effective way that a company can address workplace rights issues not only for ourselves but our independent bottlers and in the supply chain?' And how does Ed Potter answer his own question? He doesn't! He waffles evasively and manages to even dodge his own question. He must have been one hell of a lawyer.

As politicians and celebrities will concur, the distance between the finish of a formal occasion and the start of the car journey home is measured not in minutes or metres but mishaps. It is in this arena that punches and eggs are thrown, knickers and ignorance shown and questions and answers improvised. Here you are not limited to asking one question and waiting for a morsel of a reply, here be dragons, arguments, oaths and curses. Any fool can wander into this unscripted landscape and they frequently do. So as the debate closes and the chair reads out the details of the next event over the sound of scraping chairs, the PR minders are on the alert. Ed Potter stands to pack his briefcase, inserting the doodle of a coke bottle, kept safe for a possible framing at a later date. Or maybe when the board ask him, 'What got done in London?' he can just hold up the picture with a smile.

Ed Potter already has a couple of people vying for his attention

'Mr Potter,' I interrupt, ' I wonder is there any chance we could arrange a time to have a quick chat about some of the issues?'

'Um...well...' he says looking over my shoulder seeking assistance from a minder, 'Well...I...er'

He is interrupted by a woman in her thirties, with long dark hair and a slightly clipped Home Counties' accent. She is Communications Director at Coca-Cola Great Britain and she is professionally polite, by which I mean she is wary, motivated and undoubtedly the product of numerous management training programmes.

'Can I help?'

'I just wanted to try and get five minutes with Ed Potter.'

Her answer is sure-footed and rapid fire, 'I can see if we can sort something out. It might be possible...' she says flicking her hair, first one way and then the next, all the while keeping intense eye contact, giving her the appearance of a barn owl advertising shampoo. Then quickly changing tack, almost urgently she says, 'Look, what do you want, Mark?'

'Pardon?'

'What do you want? What is it you want us to do? I mean you are looking at a company that is trying to change. They want to change!'

'Do they?'

'You are pushing at an open door.'

'Well, the company could try answering my questions to them...'

Another minder is moving towards us, Ed has extracted himself from the gaggle and is heading to the door with one of Coke's PR/security people in tow, but they have been momentarily distracted by one of the crowd and peel off from Ed Potter. Seeing him leaving I blurt, 'Excuse me' and lunge after him.

'Mr Potter I wonder...'

'I have to go...I have a plane...' he says pointing to the door.

I press on, 'You'll be at the company annual general meeting in Delaware in April?'

'Er...Yeah. Yeah I will.'

'Well I'm coming to the States for that too, so maybe we can grab five minutes for a chat?' On his own and with no minders in earshot maybe, just maybe he will say yes.

'Well if it was up to me...you know, back when I was a lawyer I would have said yes...but er....' he motions with his hand at the incoming group of PR closing towards us. They push past chairs, in their immaculate dark clothes, with speed and stealth.

'In principle would you mind?' I hurriedly say to Ed Potter.

'In principle, no, I don't mind...'

'Well, if you don't mind in principle it is just a matter of logistics isn't it?'

The question hangs in the air for a second before a woman with bundled hair and a US accent says, 'Talk to Lauren about it. We'll see if we can sort something out.' She takes Ed Potter's elbow. Two other Coca-Cola people have appeared at his other side, 'He has to go,' says one of them.

The hair flicker appears behind me. 'We'll try and sort something out. Here let me give you my number.'

I turn back and Ed Potter is almost out of the room in a phalanx of Coca-Cola employees. And in the confusion I thought I saw one of the Coke people in a suit and shades talk into the sleeve of his jacket...But I could be making this bit up.

POSTSCRIPT

Ed Potter and Coca-Cola declined a formal interview.

When I returned home after the debate my wife Jenny was helping our daughter with her homework. I interrupted them, telling Jenny of my meeting with Clare from Human Resources and her comment that I was picking on Coke because they were an easy target. My wife looked up briefly from a page of equations and said, 'If they are worried about being such an easy target tell them they shouldn't be so crap.'

8
LET THEM DIG WELLS

Nejapa, El Salvador

'We are commited to working with our neighbors to help build stronger communities and enhance individual opportunity.'

The Coca-Cola Company[1]

The second leg of my visit to El Salvador is far from the sugar plantations and the coastal tides, but it does find the film crew and me once more ensconced in a hire van currently traversing a four-lane intersection somewhere in San Salvador – the capital. All of us are screaming, braced against the seat in front and are wide-eyed with panic as we are just experiencing a 50-mile-an-hour near collision with a six-foot portrait of Jesus. In El Salvador there are few rules of the road and even fewer observances of them. The only traffic regulation that everyone seems to obey is the strict ban on any kind of signalling. Thus it was that a large municipal bus abruptly changed lanes lurching in front of our speeding van with all the calm precision of a drunk staggering for the toilet. The bus is one of the old US school-style buses, it's dented, rusty and looks like it has just escaped from a Fabulous Furry Freak Brothers cartoon. It is also covered in religious iconography, prayers, crucifixes and a life-size Jesus painted in blue on the back of the bus

Suddenly finding ourselves inches away from Jesus and imminent death we all scream 'Fuck!!!!!!!' directly at the Son of God. The van brakes in a haze of tyre-shredding smoke and the battered bus pulls ahead. Jesus looks at us, standing in his robes, hands spread at his sides, almost shrugging, as if to say, 'What can I do about it?' And as the adrenalin begins to subside and we begin to extract our fingers from seat-rests the irony of dying in a collision with the Lord begins to sink in. It occurs to me that in this highly religious country it must be strangely comforting if a pedestrians last thoughts are, 'I've just been run over by Jesus.'

Prior to my arrival all that I knew about El Salvador had been learnt from a T-shirt. Back in the 1980s T-shirts were a major source of information, especially for the Left. If there was a subject you didn't understand, all you had to do was to turn up at a demonstration and read the appropriate garment. Every social movement in the world had a shirt. It seemed as if revolutionaries had given up on seizing radio stations and at the first whiff of rebellion would storm the local flea market and surround the 'Your name or picture printed here' stall.

The particular T-shirt I'm referring to was owned by a supporter of the El Salvador solidarity campaign. Printed on it was a map showing El Salvador to be in Central America, somewhere under Mexico and above Panama. Given that most countries in Central America have been subject to US intervention of sorts, it was almost inevitable that the accompanying slogan was 'US OUT OF EL SALVADOR'. So I imagined the place to be full of armoured cars, goose-stepping soldiers and generals in dark glasses with a penchant for putting jump leads on opponents' genitals. Which at one point it was. The civil war lasted twelve years and ended in 1992. According to the CIA, out of a population of just under 7 million, a total of 75,000 people lost their lives in the war.[2] Others put the number at 300,000 killed, though no one gives a figure for how many of these deaths were caused by buses.

Driving through the city Armando, our translator and driver, is lecturing us on its dangers. 'We have so many gangs here and so many guns. It is terrible. You have to be careful of the gangs it is a real problem. Seriously, this is the most violent problem...' Then as we circumnavigate a roundabout he stops mid flow and says 'I hate this place!'

He is referring to what appears to be a memorial, a plinth and possibly the tallest flagpole I have ever seen, it must be at least five stories high and dominates the whole area. 'What's written on the plinth?'

'"Patriotism Yes, Communism No." It's a very famous quote made by Major Roberto D'Aubussion' He navigates the roundabout pausing briefly 'This guy, D'Aubussion he was the father of the death squads here.'

Roberto D'Aubussion was a charismatic leader for the right wing, and his nickname was 'Blowtorch Bob'. The clue is in the name. Can anyone think of a civil rights leader or progressive figure that has a nickname based on building tools? 'Pliers Luther King'? No. 'Gandhi the Mallet'? No. Basically if your moniker is linked to anything sold by Black and Decker then it is more than likely that you are a cunt. This is a hell of a monument to erect to so recent a war criminal.

Armando sighs and continues, 'So the gangs, a lot of them are armed....'

The one thing for sure about The Coca-Cola Company is that it never knowingly undersells itself. It can't have passed your attention that Coke does love to wrap itself in the cloak of its own benevolence, and one of its proud boasts is the company's commitment to working in sustainable communities. 'As the world's largest beverage company...' so starts Neville Isdell, former CEO of Coke '....we have a presence in people's lives that reaches beyond that magical moment of providing that simple moment of refreshment...'[3] Wow, who would have thought a fizzy pop salesman could have that much self-worth. Neville Isdell continues 'We're also an employer, a business partner, part of the community, a global citizen; and I believe we must play our role in supporting sustainable communities.'[4] Who knew Coca-Cola had so many roles? The only one he left out was 'whore in the bedroom'.

To find out what kind of a role Coke plays in a sustainable community I am visiting Nejapa, a rural town some ten miles drive from the city. I would describe it as having one main street but that is typical of my tendency to exaggerate. Other towns and cities have main arteries to traverse, Nejapa...well let's just say the van jostled along the main capillary. The street is lined with single-storey squat houses, once painted in bright colours that are now bleached by the sun. The shops are essentially people's living rooms containing a few shelves, packs of biscuits, batteries and a Coke fridge. Next to a mural of Che a middle-aged woman sells lunch from an aluminium pot perched on a table. Downwind of her an older woman squats by a rug full of lemons laid out in the street. Opposite and under the shade of an improvised awning boys in black sleeveless T-shirts, baggy shorts and baseball caps listen to Latin hip hop. The speakers sit outside trailing wires across the street through a front door.

The town square is a cultural mix. It has the classic simplistic charm of any decent Western combined with the utilitarian finesse of a 1950s' British housing estate. So opposite an evocative white-walled church with a bell tower and brown wooden doors lies a kids' playground with some creaky swings and a slide. A toddler rocks back and forth on a scuffed plastic chipmunk which is nailed into the ground on a bendy spring, while a father looks on. If Ken Loach ever remade *For Few Dollars More* or Sergio Leone ever remade *Kathy Come Home*, this would be their location. Old men in straw hats sit on benches watching the square while women in shawls head to church. As for the handful of street dogs that stumble in the heat, they look good for nothing but swerving a car around. If I said that not much happens here I would be lying. It is less than that. Or at least that is how is seems, because this is the place that Coca-Cola forgot to sustain; but this community fought back. And won.

The Mayor of Nejapa is a wily fellow and with having won four elections, he's popular too. His name is Rene Canjura and his office is just by the municipal gardens in the square. He is short, fit and dresses like a trade unionist on a Saturday night out – smart trousers and a casual checked button-down shirt. Rene loves football. His office is full of cups and trophies of little silver footballers. But the heart of the room are two pictures on his wall. One of them is the obligatory framed Che Guevara print. Every left-winger in Latin America has one. It's almost religious. I wouldn't be surprised to find pictures of him surrounded by candles and incense, a shrine to Che, patron saint of beret wearers. Next to Che is a framed black-and-white photo. Nine young men, unshaven and smiling, pose for the camera. They are guerillas dressed in khaki and jeans standing amidst tropical palms and plants. One wears shades, one a Che beret, another an army combat hat. They all have guns, some held upright pointing at the air. The biggest man of the group sports a large moustache and has a great metal buckle on his jeans, he holds a belt-fed machine gun on a stand. The confidence of the group is unmistakable. They are happy and defiant.

'These are my comrades' says Rene.

'FMLN?' I ask, using the acronym for the revolutionary front that fought the government in the war.[5]

'Yes.'

This was Rene's guerilla unit. This was Rene at war, these are his friends and it is virtually impossible that they are all alive today. I have a mechanism of dealing with complex emotional situations, especially ones about which I know absolutely nothing and that mechanism is to blurt out ill-considered suburban responses. Today is no exception.

'Gosh. Do you ever have reunions?'

Rene the Mayor keeps his eyes on the photo.

'They are mainly dead. There are only two living now. One is me and the other,' he says pointing a finger at one of the men, 'he lives in America.'

'Right...well...sorry to hear about that...'

'It was the war,' he says with a shrug that seems to cast aside a brief and monumentally crushing sadness.

'Shall we chat about Coca-Cola?'

Rene the Mayor turns from the picture and says, 'Come,' ushering me to a chair.

And there on the wall hang these two photos, one of Che and one of the smiling guerillas – the ideal and the reality. Right next to 'brand Che', the logo of the revolution, is the actuality of the revolution: seven of the defiant men are dead.

* * *

In the run-down world of Nejapa the Coca-Cola bottlers must have ridden into town like a cavalcade. The council were delighted they wanted to open up a bottling plant. 'We welcomed them,' explains Rene, as he places a cup of coffee in front of me. His eager reception of the company is not the predictable response of a gun-toting ex revolutionary footballer but times and needs change. The reason he welcomed Coke was simple.

'Jobs,' says Rene the Mayor sitting down behind his desk. 'It's a poor region, most people here are working class and their economic level is quite tough.'

I tentatively enquire, 'Did it seem odd to you, with your history, to now be working with Coca-Cola?'

'Well…' he says resting his hands on his lap with just the tips of his fingers touching, '…a little. I came from the war. They were a strong company. They had the idea that we couldn't do business. But we got past that stage and as a council we were able to give them permission, even though sometimes they were not meeting all the requirements. As a demonstration of our goodwill we said "Come." Because we wanted the employment they offered the community.'

He flicks a piece of lint from his button-down shirt and sits back.

Nejapa really wanted those jobs, the problem was that the Coke bottlers Embotelladora Salvadorena (Embosalva) did not have a spotless public record when it came to community relations. The previous plant in Soyapango, a working-class area a few miles to the east of San Salvador, was shut down amidst allegations the company had over exploited the area's water supplies whilst residents only had tap water for eight hours of the day.[6] So when Coke's bottlers, Embosalva, came to Nejapa the council had a few conditions. Rene the Mayor explains that the company were told 'There are four conditions you must agree to before opening up here: provide jobs, pay your taxes, respect the environment and provide some funding for the local amateur football team.'

If the company met these conditions it would indeed be fitting for Coke to boast of playing a role 'in supporting sustainable communities'.

So how well did Coca-Cola manage to comply with these conditions? Did they fund the local football team? No. Though as Rene says, 'lately they have taken up the issue again. I hope that it works this time.'

OK. Did they provide employment for the community? Rene says, 'they didn't employ anybody in Nejapa.'

'They have employed no one?' I question.

'No, no one. Absolutely no one.'

Though to be absolutely fair to the company, I later heard a very strong rumour that one person from Nejapa was employed at the new plant...as a part-time gardener. Though this is unconfirmed.

To find out how the company managed with one of the other conditions Mayor Rene has arranged for me to meet Councillor Carlos in the town square at midday. And in a manner befitting the time and place, Councillor Carlos appears with the sun behind him. Middle-aged, trim and sporting jeans, polo shirt and a quiff that any elderly fan of Bronski Beat or

Bros would be proud of, Councillor Carlos has been tasked
with two jobs. Firstly to take us to the community he
represents, who rely on the stream running downstream from
the Coke bottling plant. This hopefully will provide some
insight into how Coke works with sustainable communities.
His second job is to act as our minder. It transpires that
Armando's earlier worries about gangs are not unfounded.
The Coke bottlers are supposed to protect the environment
and the councillor is to protect us. I hope he does a better job
than the company.

We are given directions to the community. The van is to turn
right at the top of the town, follow the road for about five
minutes, keeping an eye out for a dirt track on the right, it
should be obvious as it is directly after a pile of old fridges
lying on their side in a field. Then onwards down the dirt
track, until we reach a standpipe, turn sharp right and we will
have arrived. It is obvious we are not going to the salubrious
end of the neighbourhood. Any explanation of how to get to
someone's home, that involves the directions 'turn right at
some abandoned fridges', tells you the person you're visiting is
pretty much fucked.

By the standpipe lies Councillor Carlos' constituency, a narrow
lane, with overhanging leaves and palms cutting out the light.
The sides of the lane are banked high with dirt and debris
forming walls to create a tunnel wide enough for the van but
not its mirrors. These walls are where roots and scrub entwine
with junk and litter, held together with packed mud. Gnarly
branches are meshed into an old mattress frame, its springs
knotted through with crawlers, which is all propped up by a
tyre set in soil and baked hard. Into these walls of litter and
grime are steps cut in the dirt and the steps lead to homes.
This is the Gallera Quemada Canton of Nejapa.

Kids in shorts crouch on their haunches at the top of the steps. From up there they look straight into the van windows, our faces just feet away from each other. As we slowly rumble down this tunnel of hovels people stop what they are doing, adults stop cooking, girls stop hanging clothes out, kids stop playing; they stop and stare at us.

David our American raises his eyebrows and softly says, 'This is *Apocalypse* fucking *Now*, man.'

Except that it isn't. A foreign documentary film crew has just turned up with a camera that's worth more than three year's wages, so the locals are hardly likely to quip, 'Not another polemic on globalisation, well, there goes the neighbourhood.'

Getting out of the van Councillor Carlos greets a few of his constituents with a nod and a word or two. 'The people here make a living when it's the rice or sugar cane season, they get some building work too,' says Councillor Carlos
   'How much do they get paid?'
   'About $40 a month,'

But the one thing they had in their favour was access to clean water. The stream runs past the community and feeds into the San Antonio River. 'Originally the stream had more water flowing through it and everybody could use it to water their flocks. Within the stream we still had wells and people could use this water.' Poor yes, but with drinking water for themselves, their animals and for washing, they at least had that.

As we walk Councillor Carlos refers to the water in two distinct time zones, Before Coke and After Coke. 'Previously,' he says implying the time Before Coke, 'the water wasn't polluted. People would come and wash and children would get into the stream to have a swim; then as time went by the children would come out of the water with some kind of allergy on their bodies. They were sent to the clinic and that's when they found out it was because of the contamination of the water.' He pauses as we glimpse a field beyond the lane, with one solitary thorny tree and some small grey breeze-block homes in the distance made colourful with the laundry drying in the sun.

'We no longer use the water in the way we used to…People coming to the stream no longer use it for drinking water.'

Two men appear and, smiling, take the councillor to one side, say a few words and then Councillor Carlos explains that we should leave the area and that he will take us to a quieter location where we can continue the interview. The local gang is on their way down here to rob us and take the camera equipment. Apparently they are going to finish their drinks first, then come and get us. Great. Not only are we to be mugged, but we have to give the gang drinking-up time too. Armando the driver fumbles the gear stick gently muttering 'Fuck. Fuck. Fuck.'

'Have we got a security situation?' David the American cameraman asks, adding, 'I want a guard with a shotgun and I want one fucking now.'

Everyone ignores him, the engine revs and we leave. We have been saved by the universal phenomenon of a bloke in a bar saying, 'You can't leave that, that's still half full.'

We drive for a further 15 minutes in glorious and valiant retreat; in situations like this there is nothing finer than the nobility of cowardice. We have followed the stream and charted a course deeper into the countryside, there is no one is sight and we are quite alone. Out here the water sashays along flat plains hemmed in by distant hills and against the backdrop of a clear blue sky. It is easy to forget this countryside is contaminated.

'The gangs will not come here,' says Councillor Carlos as we walk to the stream to set up the camera equipment. 'We are safe here,' he says. But nobody asks how he can be sure of this, no one says 'What if the gang had a car?' or 'What if they drove down the track they saw us leave on?' Or being a rural gang, 'What if they had a horse?' Tattooed gang members trotting along doing a twos-up on a horse might not seem a possibility but this is the countryside – an unfamiliar place in my own land let alone another continent. For all I know the gangs round here could use pigs as pitbulls and pimp tractors. We are in the middle of nowhere, a little shaken up and in need of some reassurance.

The sound of a motorbike revving in the distance is not reassuring. Nether is the vision of the solitary bike heading towards us down the hillside, with billowing dry earth blowing up behind it. A black cop car then screeches to a halt on a ridge, three men step out into the swirling dust, silhouetted in the dirt clouds. The red and blue lights mounted on the roof flash a dull light in the haze. They wait, looking on, as the lone cop on the motorbike drives towards us. The dust and roar gets nearer until the rider guns the engine, brings the bike to a stop, flicks out a stand and dismounts all without taking his gaze off us. He wears reflective shades and is dressed head to toe in black, laced paratrooper boots, combat trousers, short-sleeve shirt, gun belt and holster. Even his jungle hat is black. Perhaps it is a nervous reaction but I get an overwhelming urge to say, 'Fuck me it's a paramilitary goth.' But the words come out as, 'Hi, there.'

We have no idea if we are breaking the law, if we need permission to film here, if he will take exception to foreigners making films that might be critical of his country. He stands tall, legs astride, one hand resting on his belt. Councillor Carlos explains we are filming for a programme about water contamination. The cop removes his shades looks at us and says, 'I'm pleased, especially in view of what's going on.' Then he continues in a deep, serious and sincere tone, 'As a rural police officer we're involved with everything to do with the natural world and the environment. The other forces work within the city, within the urban areas. We ourselves are here for the well-being of the natural world, the rural areas.'

Oh my God, we've just meet our first genuine green cop. He's tough, rides a motorbike, looks as sexy as hell and wants to protect his local eco system. Does he have any idea of how many boxes he ticks? I have women friends who would ovulate at the sight of him...men too.

As if this isn't enough he initiates a brief and succinct critique of multinational corporations. 'Most of the companies, like Coca-Cola, for example – it's a very obvious example, isn't it? – these companies, the waste products which they produce: the only outlet they find is here in our scanty resources.' He gestures to the stream, smiles and says, 'I'm really pleased that groups like yourselves are concerned about rescuing the few natural resources we enjoy today.' And with that he touches the tip of his hat, nods his head, mounts his bike and roars off to fight wrongdoers, hug trees and break hearts.

It's a hard act to follow but Councillor Carlos returns to the matter in hand, telling us the final episode of his saga. The story so far: the Coca-Cola bottling plant dumps waste in the water, kids get rashes, fish die and are found floating belly up, the mayor and the council can't leave the community without water. Carlos says, 'We obtained water tanks...[everyone] gets their water from the water tanks.'

'Where does the water come from?'

'There is a well where the water comes from which by means of piping feeds water to the tanks...so the well water supplies these water tanks for the benefit of the community.'

'Who pays for it?'

'We as a community pay for it. If we get a bill for X amount and 50 people use the tanks then we divide up the bill by 50.'

So the company that was supposed to bring employment to the community doesn't employ anyone, pollutes the stream and causes people earning about $1.50 a day to pay out more money for their drinking water.

Carlos shrugs, 'We fought and struggled so that Coca-Cola would pay for the water tanks, so that they would pay for the consumption of water that we have. Unfortunately Coca-Cola, like the huge company they are, merely came here to take over the resources...'

The question that worrying me is a simple one: how can a company that makes fizzy pop produce waste that kills fish and pollutes drinking water? They are making Coca-Cola in there, they are not Dow Chemicals or British Nuclear Fuels, and to the best of my knowledge they are not the final hiding place for The Mythical Weapons of Saddam Hussein. So how is this pollution happening?

Chemical engineer Daniel Martinez has agreed to meet me to explain. He's a chubby, clean-faced man with an innocent friendliness. A Salvadorean by birth he trained in Canada. 'I used to work for City Hall and was in charge of monitoring how Coca-Cola was handling waste products,' he says while we scramble down to the stream. We are looking for the Coke bottling plants' waste pipe and find it halfway down the bank side protruding on to a brick overflow that cascades into the stream. The pipe leads straight to the plant and is easily big enough for a man to crouch and walk in, Tom Cruise could probably get in standing upright and would do too, especially if you told him L Ron Hubbard was in there.

Daniel stands by the constant flow of water coming out of the pipe and explains how the waste is produced. 'There are two processes, one is the actual production and the other is when they wash the bottles. They use caustic soda to wash the bottles and detergents, that's what gives the water the high PH. The other contaminant is from the process itself, that's sugar mostly.'

Science admittedly isn't my strong point but if sugar is being dumped into the water don't the inhabitants just face very sweet water, surely their problem is calorific at this point?

Daniel develops a habit for dealing with my stupidity, namely he giggles then ignores me.

'The main problem is the biowaste contains too much nutrients. And they are all biodegradable but to be biodegradable they absorb the oxygen in the water.'

Somewhere in my mind a light bulb goes on.

'OK, so when people told us that the fish died when Coca-Cola moved here, it is because this stuff uses the oxygen and there is nothing left in the water.'

'Exactly,' he flashes a quick encouraging smile, 'they suffocate, they drown. When you have these multiple species dead, it's because Coca-Cola had a problem with the plant and they had a dumping...they just opened the gate,' he says referring to the pumps and sluice gates that release the waste, 'and the problem goes away.'

'Except it doesn't go away.'

'Except it comes to the community.'

THE CURIOUS CASE OF CLEAN WATER

Daniel Martinez, the chemical engineer who worked for the council, found curious results when the Coca-Cola bottlers tested the wastewater. He said 'They are supposed to test the water, and because of the quantities they manage, they have to test daily.' So who conducts these daily tests? The Coca-Cola bottlers, that's who, in their own labs. However, once a month, 'They are supposed to send samples to be tested in another lab outside of plant, independent laboratories.... That will help them compare the results with their own results and that will help them to see if their own lab is running properly or not.'

As the man employed by 'City Hall' to monitor Coca-Cola's waste results, Daniel saw the lab results. So did he see anything unusual? What was coming out of the waste pipes at the Coke plant? According to Daniel, the company's results said what was coming out of the pipe was 'almost drinkable...It was pretty amazing, unbelievable, the wastewater was so clean...it was pure clean drinking water.'

'But,' I ask, 'couldn't that be the case? Might it be that the wastewater is drinkable?'

'Look at the colour of the water,' Daniel jumps in, 'look at how people are feeling, look at the discussion about the dead fishes, how can that be clean water?'

Daniel doesn't know how the results came to show this level of water purity but what he does know is that the results on paper do not match the results in the stream. He looks resigned and matter of fact when he says, 'Remember, El Salvador doesn't have the laws that exist in Europe and the US and developed countries. As a matter of fact we don't even have a law regarding wastewater. It is a guideline still...I live in a country that doesn't have the policies to protect the environment and that means big companies can do whatever they want.'

With no resolution in sight it was at this stage that the council took the extraordinary move of taking the company to court over the non-payment of the council taxes. Daniel furrows his forehead and raises his eyebrows, 'To get the taxes they had to go to the Supreme Court to make them pay.' He shakes his head slightly almost in disbelief and smiles, 'I don't know how City Hall won that case, but they did, they actually made them pay.'

Back in the mayor's office, sitting with another cup of coffee, Rene the Mayor reveals how the company fared on its last condition to pay its council taxes. 'They also broke their promise to pay their taxes to the municipality.'

'What were the taxes for?'

'Rubbish collection, for electricity and other things' says Rene.

'Would the taxes include water rates as well?'

'No, the water, they are not paying anything for the water and they should.'

So the council took the Coca-Cola bottlers to court to get their taxes, and the council won.

I ask Rene the mayor and erstwhile revolutionary how he feels to have won in court against such a large company. 'Happy,' he says. Though he isn't displaying a huge amount of that particular emotion at the moment. 'To win against a company of this nature is not easy. They were thinking logically, "well we owe them two hundred thousand dollars, we'll pay one hundred thousand to a good team of lawyers and we'll save half the money and we'll win." They were wrong.' He shrugs the shrug of a stoic.

'After two years we won. They paid us two hundred thousand dollars, and it was a shame that we had to go to court to get them to pay us an amount which is not much for them, but for us it is a lot of money.'

So The Coca-Cola Company's assertion that they have a role to play in helping communities become sustainable is bogus in this case. The water was polluted. The poorest people in town now have to pay for their water. The football team got no support. No jobs came to the town, save the near-mythical part-time gardener. The company did not pay its taxes. Yes, the council won but as Rene says, 'we had to go to court to get them to pay us something which by law...they should have paid.' Which may be why he is so resolutely un-celebratory in this victory.

The ex-revolutionary mayor who welcomed Coca-Cola into town sighs, spreads his hands out and explains how it could have been. 'If you go and live in an area the best thing you can do is get integrated with the local population, look after them, so the place where you live is the best. But they have not done anything...they go to a place, they exploit all the resources and when there aren't any they leave, and they leave the people in the place with the problem.'

Before the *Dispatches* programme was broadcast in November 2007, I put these allegations to Coke. They said they had a certificate to show they met international enviromental standards.[7] They are also keen to promote their water stewardship efforts in Nejapa – which runs to providing two schools with clean water.[8] Which I wouldn't really want to criticise save for the fact that it doesn't really address the concerns raised. But maybe I'm just picky...

* * *

Returning to the capital from the stream at Nejapa the evening track turns to road and the road spreads out from one lane to many. The emerald trees and brilliant pink and peach of wild climbing flowers give way to roadside expanses of dust, inhabited by stalls offering pyramid piles of green coconuts. The open space of the country starts to brim with city clutter. Makeshift bars, handcarts and barrows vie for custom selling sweets and drinks, while people crowd around buses with prayers painted on the doors. The massed throng is as transitory as the dusk that surrounds them. Pick-ups swirl with farm workers who climb on board the back of the truck, and grab hold of anything vaguely stable before speeding off. Barking clouds of black diesel fumes disappear as quickly as they came and the familiar smell of wood smoke haunts the air, promising the dream of home and the distance yet to travel.

As the lanes turn to highways so the twilight turns to night and we glide into San Salvador, where the central strip casts off the mantle of a Central American country, throws its identity to the wind and revels in a downmarket version of LA. Blacked-out windows on Land Cruisers, blasting music, rev at the lights. New model cars compete with each other as to who can cram the most smoking teenagers on the back seat. Here the night sky is torn with a bright glare as every conceivable fast-food outlet proclaims its wares in retina-shrinking light. The mighty yellow buns of Burger King compete with McDonalds' golden arches and the glow fight spills over into the forecourts of Subway and Wendy's. A cartoon chicken waves a friendly cowboy hat from an illuminated plastic shop front – Pollo Campero – 'Howdy partner,' it seems to say, 'I'm cheap, tasty and happy as hell to be eaten!' But KFC outshines them all, it's a two-storey building in the shape of a KFC bucket. Neon strip lights run along the edges of the structure: a bucket glowing in the night. That is what identifies this restaurant, not the food but the receptacle it is served in, a bucket. Didn't anyone at the planning stage of this venture say, 'Isn't using an image of something you can throw up in a bad idea for the food industry?'

'People here love fast food' says Armando in a resigned voice too old for his twenty-four years. 'Pollo Campero that's the favourite, but everyone likes fast food.'

'Is that because so many Salvadoreans fled to America in the civil war that people are really comfortable with US-style junk food?' I ask

'Some people are getting some dollars in their pockets, maybe they spend them here?' ventures Eduardo our minder.

'This, my friends,' I say, declaiming with indignation, '...this is the sharp end of globalisation. This is the future of everywhere.' I slump and sigh in the seat.

'Maybe,' says David the American, 'maybe they jus' like the taste, dude. Ever fuckin' thought about that?'

INTERLUDE: CONNECTING

I feel that Customs Officers do not need to know the ins and outs of my life. A brief who are you, do you match to the photo in the passport, when are you leaving and then a quick check in the bags for Semtex, smack or bush meat: job done. So I am not at my most forthcoming turning up at US Customs when I arrive to get a connecting flight from El Salvador. I step up from the line to see the officer has all the visual requirements he needs for the job: a crew cut and no visible contours twixt head and neck.

'OK, sir,' he grunts, scanning the passport with some kind of blip gun. 'What was the purpose of your trip?'

'In El Salvador?'

'Yes sir, in El Salvador.'

'I was filming, working on a film.'

'You're an actor?'

'Of sorts'

'What kind of film was it?'

Not wanting to say I'm making a programme about child labour, pollution and one of your country's most esteemed companies, I say, 'A drama documentary.'

Without missing a beat he replies, 'What's that, sir? A feature film?'

'Well, sort of, it's live-action drama in real-life situations,'

I say attempting not to stray too far from the truth.

'What is the name of the film?'

'Fizz.' I say, which is genuinely the working title of the documentary.

'Fizz.'

'Yes, Fizz.'

He lowers the passport, cocks his head conspiratorially towards me and in hushed tones says, 'You're not a porn star are you?'

'Sorry?'

'Are you a porn star?'

'No, no. I am not a porn star.'

He smiles and looks at me and says in a slow drawl, 'I think you are.'

'Well, no, erm, I'm flattered that you think I could be but I am not.'

He raises his eyebrows and in a monotone says, 'Of course not, sir.' Smiles, then snaps to officious mode, 'Thank you very much, sir.'

I head off thinking that if I can be mistaken for a porn star, then Coca-Cola is not the only industry that needs to review its standards.

INDIA: A PREQUEL

'The Coca-Cola Company exists to benefit and refresh everyone it touches.'

Coca-Cola Statement to BBC Radio 4's *Face the Facts*, 2003

In the Seventies, while the rest of the world was being taught to sing in perfect harmony, to grow apple trees and honey bees, the Indian government was busy with a new piece of legislation, the Foreign Exchange Regulation Act. The Act required foreign companies to ensure 60 per cent of their shares belonged to Indians in order to 'Indianize' these companies. In 1977, the Indian Government gave Coke two options – sell 60 per cent of your stake or leave. Coke decided to go. It wasn't quite the corporate equivalent of fleeing in helicopters from the rooftop of the US embassy in Saigon but American symbols were poignantly departing from the east. It would be sixteen years before the company could persuade the authorities to let them back in.

In 1993 after several failed attempts, Coca-Cola returned. Its triumphant re-entry should have marked a new chapter in its troubled relationship with the country but Coke was dogged by controversy almost from the beginning and remains so to this day. In the first decade back in India, Coke had three substantial complaints laid at its door:

'Where have the shares gone?'

Coke's re-entry into India through a wholly owned subsidiary, Hindustan Coca-Cola Holdings (HCCH) was under certain conditions, one of which was that HCCH would sell 49 per cent of its shares to resident Indians and was given the not insubstantial timeframe of June 2002 to do so. Did Coca-Cola agree to this mandatory requirement? Clearly. Did Coca-Cola comply with this mandatory requirement? Do bears use bidets? No. In fact, according to Indian news reports at the time, they co-opted the US Commerce Department and the US Ambassador to apply pressure on the Indian authorities.[1] Something clearly worked, because the Indian government agreed to let Coke sell the 49 per cent to private investors and business partners with a small percentage sold to employees' trusts.[2] But most crucially, and rather uniquely, these 'Indian' shares came with no voting rights because the company argued that would be 'substantive and onerous'.[3] So not only did they sell their shares to 'friendly' investors, what they sold was more of an accumulating gift voucher than a share as we might know it.

'Where's the water gone?'
Coca-Cola has shut down two bottling plants in India

In 1998, Coca-Cola bought 35 acres of land around Plachimada, a village in Kerala, Southern India and started building what was to become the most controversial plant in Coke's Indian history. On 22 April 2002, villagers, concerned about the serious drop in water levels and the quality of water in their wells picketed the factory establishing a permanent protest camp.[4] In 2003, the local Panchayat refused to renew Coke's license to operate, citing 'public interest'.[5] And so the David and Goliath battle, as it became characterised, between this small, rural community and the most well-known company in the world was on.

The problem was the very essence of Coke's business – water extraction. Its plant was extracting water from the underground aquifer at the rate of half a million litres a day according to the only official figures there are.[6] Water levels in the area dropped dramatically though Coca-Cola argued that 'the rainfall has been well below average for several years'[7] and therefore the water depletion was not their fault. And although rainfall was indeed below average for several years, it is well known that Plachimada is in a 'rain-shadow' area of Kerala which means that its rainfall is always below average, somewhat limiting the ability of water extracted to be recharged naturally.[8] Not necessarily the best place to locate a water-intensive plant, although the generous subsidies Coke received 'for having invested in a backward area'[9] may have helped in that decision.

When I visited the protest camp in 2004 it was a low shelter made of wood and straw and decorated with banners demanding that Coca-Cola leave. Most of the people protesting that day were women, as having to get the water,

they were the ones most affected. And a drive through the
surrounding villages echoed this point. In each village by the
side of the road a line of pots would appear, sometimes fifteen
to twenty of them bulbous plastic pots for collecting water.
The lead pot sat under the village standpipe and the women
sat opposite, waiting for the water to be turned on for an hour
or so. Coke's response to the villagers' concerns was to
challenge the Panchayat's legitimacy. The leader of the
Panchayat, Mr Krishnan, explained to me that the company
argued the local Panchayat had the right to issue a licence
but did not have the right to refuse to renew it. They effectively
took the villagers as well as the protestors to court. They also
asked for police protection...

As the legal battles raged on, the water levels continued to
drop, so much so that Coke was forced to bus in tankers of
water for the surrounding villages. In 2003, BBC Radio 4
broadcast their investigations into the plant on *Face the Facts*[10]
and Plachimada became a cause célèbre both nationally and
internationally. The programme makers tested both the water
in the village well and the sludge from the factory that Coke
gave away free to farmers to use as fertiliser. The water
unsurprisingly was found to be unsafe to drink but the real
controversy was in the sludge. It contained 'dangerous levels
of toxic metals and the known carcinogen, cadmium'.[11]
Britain's leading poisons expert, Professor John Henry said:

'The [test] results have devastating consequences for those
living near the areas where this waste has been dumped and for
the thousands who depend on crops produced in these fields.

'Cadmium is a carcinogen and it accumulates in the
kidneys. Repeated exposure can lead to kidney failure. Lead is
particularly dangerous to children and the results of exposure
can be fatal. Even at low levels it can cause mental retardation

and severe anaemia. What most worries me about the levels found is how this might be affecting pregnant women.'[12]

Sunil Gupta, Coca-Cola India's vice-president said, 'It's good for the farmers because most of them are poor...We have scientific evidence to prove it is absolutely safe and we have never had any complaints.'[13]

The complaints did come and the company was forced to treat its sludge as exactly what it was – hazardous waste. By March 2004, the company were forced to stop production, later blaming the continued legal wrangling on 'certain misinformed campaigns'.[14]

As to the future, there are serious concerns over Plachimada's water level and it remains to be seen if the aquifer will recover. In 2005, an Indian lab report on water from a well in the village found that it was so acidic that if consumed, 'it would burn up your insides. Clothes could tear in such water, food will rot, crops will wither.'[15]

Coca-Cola's future, however, is altogether more promising – it has offered to relocate to another site, provided the company is adequately compensated. In 2005, it wrote to the Ministry of Industry regarding its offer, saying (I have provided a running translation from the corporate to plain English in the text): 'relocating to the new site would also incur substantial expenditure by us, [*it'll cost us to move*] we request to be provided appropriate compensation in the form of continued and increased sales tax incentives to offset the expense [*so a few subsidies wouldn't go amiss*]...We would like to request that the relocation to the proposed site would entail a confirmed resolution for meeting the infrastructure needs of the company such as water and electricity along with an amicable environment devoid of the problems as have been faced in

Plachimada [*keep the protestors the fuck away from us in future*]. Further, the Company may be allowed to continue with its sales tax incentives and other applicable beneficial schemes for the remaining period [*we're passing round the bowl please give generously*].'[16]

And Plachimada is not the only plant that has been shut down following protests. Villagers in Ballia in Uttar Pradesh launched a campaign against the plant alleging affected water levels and misappropriated community land, as well as calling on the Central Pollution Control Board to investigate chemical waste dumped on agricultural land. According to Coca-Cola, the 'Ballia plant was a co-packing facility owned by a franchise bottler. As part of business restructuring and consolidation, the production at Ballia was discontinued from 26 June 2007.'[17]

'Where's the pesticides...?'
...in the bottles of Coke and Pepsi

In 2003, the Centre for Science and Environment, an independent Indian public-interest organisation, conducted a series of tests, firstly on bottled water and then on soft drinks. The Centre was concerned about the lack of regulations in the food industry and hoped its research would start a debate that would eventually lead to India adopting standards for water quality. On 5 August 2003 it published the results into its soft drinks study[18] and indeed sparked a debate – although not only in India but worldwide. For the CSE had found levels of pesticides in bottles of Coca-Cola and Pepsi to be between 30-36 times higher than would be permitted in the EU.[19]

It is fair to say that all hell broke loose and nothing in the world could have prepared CSE for the backlash. Within hours

of the report being published Coca-Cola and Pepsico held a
joint press conference to denounce the findings and question
the methodology – which is a bit like Iran and Iraq uniting to
say 'the Isle of Wight is picking on us' . Pepsico immediately
slapped a writ on CSE which it later withdrew.[20] And a Joint
Parliamentary Committee (the equivalent to a Public Enquiry
conducted by Parliament) was convened – only the fifth in
India's history. Not to consider pesticides in India's food chain
but to see if CSE's findings are correct. Talk about shoot the
messenger. In the eye of the storm, life was pretty hard for the
CSE – although they expected a fight, they 'had not
anticipated...the sheer power and the virulence of the attack'.[21]
India's secret service even paid them a visit – just to let them
know that anyone who had ever worked for the organisation
was being investigated.[22] Their methodology and motives were
all questioned, their reputation savaged but the CSE held their
ground and in February 2004, the JPC upheld their findings.[23]
They concluded, 'the Committee...find that the CSE findings are
correct on the presence of pesticide residues...The Committee
also appreciate the whistle blowing act of CSE in regard to
alerting the nation to an issue with major implications to food
safety...and human...health...The Committee note with deep
concern that the soft drink...industry with an annual turnover
of Rs 6,000 crores[24] is unregulated.'[25]

But despite this and their recommendations, little changed.
So in August 2006 CSE conducted the tests again, this time
using even more up-to-date equipment. It found Coca-Cola and
Pepsico products contained pesticides on average 24 times over
the prescribed limit.[26]

Coca-Cola's response was to conduct its own tests. Oddly, the
samples provided by Coke showed no signs of pesticides above
EU standards.

So not a great start to business back in India.

I was about to find out how Coke's second decade was shaping up...

9

KURIJI

Kaladera, India

'If you want to know the truth about The Coca-Cola Company: Ask the farmer in India.'

The Coca-Cola Company, 2007[1]

I do like it when companies write stuff like this. 'Ask the farmer in India...' they say, as if inviting all and sundry to drop whatever they are doing, travel to India, drive out to the farmer's place and ask if he will vouch for Coke. Assuming you did mange to get to India with this in mind, you would then face an added hurdle as the company weren't terribly specific about which farmer they meant. That's if they actually did have someone in mind, and hunting representational composites is fiendishly difficult. But I am in India surrounded by farmers and seeing as The Coca-Cola Company did invite me to ask them, I did.

The farmer I chose to ask is Mr Rameshwar Prasad Kuri who is sixty-four and comes from Kaladera in Rajasthan. It is common for Indians to use the suffix 'ji', adding it to a person's name when addressing an elder and wishing to show respect. So Mr Kuri is called Kuriji. This particular linguistic custom was explained to me by an Indian student, who after imparting this knowledge asked, 'What do you have in England like this?'

'Pardon?'

'What do you do to show respect for elders in England?' he earnestly enquired.

'We don't put them in a home,' I replied.

The comment is met with incomprehension.

I met Kuriji in a village called Mehdiganj, the nearest city to which is Varanasi on the banks of the River Ganges, famous for its ghats and funeral pyres. The ghats are the long wide steps leading down to the river where pilgrims flock to absolve themselves of sin. So sacred is the Ganges for Hindus that here in Varanasi you can rent out rooms to die in, so your cremated ashes can be put straight into the river. A friend told me he once saw a tourist sign reading 'Come to Varanasi: a great place to die.'

It bustles with life, markets, crowds and the usual theatre of everyday Indian existence. Indeed, it is not a bad place to die, though my preference would be a violent heart attack in the British Library, just so the last thing I hear on the planet is SHHH!

It is from here that I set out, leaving the city and heading into the countryside for the village. The quick and easy way to get there is by motorised three-wheeler, a kind of tuk-tuk, if you were in Thailand. And travelling for forty minutes in a motorised three-wheeler in India is about the most fun you can legally have outside of Alton Towers. It stops, starts, jumps, revs and swerves its way though a jaw-dropping and beautiful world.

I love these forty minutes. The hot air rushes about you and the driver manhandles the steering like he is in a rodeo. Men scoot past on motorbikes with women riding sidesaddle on the back, clutching their saris demurely. Every village we drive through has a bike repair shop, a cow in the road and if you are early enough a bloke washing from a steel pan outside his home, wearing nothing but a wrapped tight lungi and a lot of soap suds. Temples and schools sit alongside peasant huts, where dung patties shaped like Cornish pasties sit drying in the sun. Top-heavy palm trees and pan wallah shacks sit next to roadside garages where trucks are serviced in the dust, stacked up on bricks while skinny engineers crouch under giant steel frames.

As the three-wheeler twists sharply to avoid imminent oncoming-overtaking-tractor-death, I remember that in India there is a special competition played on the roads called Who Can Transport the Most Improbable Object in a Vehicle. Today's contenders include a very old cyclist with legs like a plucked chicken wing. He carries two very large red Calor gas bottles, one balanced on each handle, and rides unconcernedly on the dual carriageway alongside speeding lorries. He is up against another cyclist doing a sharp left in traffic while carrying half a dozen 30-foot industrial steel rods balanced on his handlebars. It is as if India's Health and Safety Executive is run by Wile E Coyote.

As we drive past the hand-painted adverts which decorate walls, houses and shop fronts I marvel at the way the English language here is laced with the nuances of 1947, the time the British left. Back in Delhi buses have slogans on the side of them proclaiming 'Propelled by hydrogen!' What a wonderful word, 'propelled'! and how brilliant it is that bus loads of Indians can be propelled. And wouldn't you look forward to your commute every morning if you were propelled? Saris are not sold in retail outlets or boutiques but in 'Emporiums'. And out in the countryside adverts, painted on end walls, picture Y-fronts and T-shirts, with the slogan 'Shirts, vest, panties, drawers.' Oh, that we could advertise drawers and panties instead of briefs and thongs. But my favourite word is used to describe the activities of the farmers opposed to the Coca-Cola bottlers, they are not a 'movement' or a 'campaign' nor do they 'lobby'- they take part in an 'agitation'. And that is exactly what they have done, a small group of people has truly agitated Coca-Cola.

The only thing that marks out Mehdiganj from so many other villages is the Coca-Cola bottling plant at one end of it. Apart from that it is an ordinary village that sits on the side of a dual carriageway and collects dust. Which it does very well. I turn down the road that runs between two teashops where the smoky wood fires lazily turn the air blue under the low eaves of the bungalow roofs. The chai wallahs serve up clay cups of scalding milky brew and small plates of home-made sweets. I stand for a moment and see the road snake into the open countryside. Then walking past the open doors of family homes and a tiny shop with boxes of hair colouring pinned to the wall I come to a glade that spreads out to the side of village, on the edge of the fields. This is a natural meeting place, an opening ringed with trees and a low canopy that casts a dappled shade. This is the venue for the National Right to Water Conference and Protest against Coca-Cola, to give it its full title.

Over three days hundreds of farmers and villages from the various corners of India gather to share their experiences of what it is like to have Coca-Cola as a neighbour, as well as to organise how to close those plants that remain open. There are four Coca-Cola bottlers with local agitations running against them. Plachimada in Kerala in the South and Ballia to the East have been shut down. The other two are Kaladera to the West and here in the village of Mehdiganj itself. The glade is set to swell with hundreds of people from these places – villagers, farmers and a smattering of activists and press. Some women and children are literally carted in to attend, on bright red metal trailers hooked up to large clunking tractors with black funnels decorated with gold and pink tinsel garlands. The conference is quickly packed and long trumpet-shaped loudspeakers are hung in the trees, tied up with string and wires run through the branches, so everyone can hear speaker after speaker stand at a podium to decry the company. This is the place to ask a farmer about Coca-Cola.

I spoke to a lot of them. I met Raj Narayan Patel, a fifty-five-year-old from Mehdiganj, a stocky man, with grey hair, black rings round his eyes and orange teeth that come from chewing *paan*. He insisted I look at his well, a brick-lined circular pit level with the ground that descends to a puddle, some mud and a few stones. He pointed avidly at rings in the well, watermarks at various depths, to indicate the depletion. I asked him if he knew of a farmer who might be able to say a good word for the company. He gently led me to a seat in the shade and went off to fetch me a glass of water.

I met Siyaram Yadav, a bearded farmer with five children who, along with his father, sat with us under an awning. While he talked of failed crops and water shortages we shared brown balls of unrefined sugar that he passed around. I called it 'Bootleg sugar'. He too insisted I see his well, which looked like a wishing well that had been in a fight, and had a rudimentary cranked windlass to pull up the water, should any appear.

I met Baliram Ram from Ballia, he was dressed in a matching purple shirt and slacks and had a milky, dead eye where a goat had kicked him as a child. He was straight out of a Tom Waits song. His well is 180 km away but if I wanted he would take me to it. I politely turned down the offer; there are only so many empty wells a man can see. So instead he told me that Indian farmers should be sent to Kashmir to settle the issue, as 'Indian farmers will never give up one inch of land!' Later I retold this to a friend who was also at the conference. He said, 'Mark, what you have to understand is that Indian farmers are not like British farmers.'

'Do they copulate sober?' I enquire.

'Most people in this country live on the land,' he continues, pointedly ignoring me, 'For them the land is everything, it is their worth, their life, their dignity, everything.'

Now I'll confess straight away that I know little about farming. And by little I mean nothing. In Britain most city dwellers tend to love the British countryside but hate the people who live there, leaving a large gap in our knowledge of matters agricultural. Fortunately some of the farmers here were very happy to talk me through the subject and demonstrated as much, if not more, patience in explaining their work as I did in listening about it. And after all their discourse on agriculture it comes down to these two simple facts:

- Farmers need water for crops and villagers need water to survive.
- Coca-Cola's main ingredient is water.

The Coca-Cola Company own and control The Hindustan Coca-Cola Beverage Pvt. Ltd (HCCBPL), which in turn own and operate the Kaladera plant near where Kuriji lives. The plant started running in January 2000 not far from Kuriji's farm and the fundamental problem with the plant is that, well, it's been built in a drought zone. To suggest the community have problems with water is an understatement. Kaladera is in the district which has been in drought for 50 of the past 106 years – 47 per cent of the time.[2] In 1998 the water in the area was deemed to be over-exploited by the Central Groundwater Board.[3]

However, someone at Coke in India decided it would be a good idea to open a water-intensive industry in a drought prone area. For some reason the word that springs to mind is 'D'oh!'

KALADERA AND THE TERI REPORT

I did ask Coca-Cola India if I could visit Kaladera. I also asked them for an interview. They didn't seem very keen. In fact, what they actually said was, '[g]iven the history of biased reporting about our operations by Mark Thomas, most recently in the *Dispatches* programme on Channel 4 that contained outdated and inaccurate allegations, we have decided not to have any involvement in this latest Mark Thomas project'.[4] I took that as a no. But we do know a little bit about how the plant is run from a report by The Energy and Resources Institute (TERI) and it is worth explaining a little about this report. It was commissioned after the University of Michigan suspended its contracts with Coca-Cola in response to student concerns that the Company's actions in Colombia and India violated the University's ethical trading policy. Coke finally agreed to an 'independent' third party study and it chose TERI to conduct that investigation.[5] Finally published in

January 2008 the report, however, did give some interesting information about the operation of the plant in Kaladera, including the following facts:

- The plant pays virtually nothing for the water it uses.
- The plant has four bore wells sunk to a depth of 330 feet that can bring up at least 120,000 litres of water an hour.
- There is a very small charge for the dumping of wastewater: approximately Rs 0.2 per 1,000 litres (the equivalent of about £0.0024 per 1,000 litres).
- The average amount of water extracted in May (peak production month) between 2004-2006 was just under a million litres of water a day, to be specific, 953,333 litres a day.
- During the eight years that Coke has been operating, the water tables have gone down by more than a metre each year and about three metres in 2003/04.
- On average it takes 3.8 litres of water to make 1 litre of pop.[6]

Did I mention they pay virtually nothing for the water?

The conference in the glade is in full swing. Speakers are in full cry, the crowd cheer appreciatively and if there are any gaps in the programme the local band jumps in to perform protest songs – ripping out the lyrical innards of popular ballads and replacing them with a more suitable polemic. So Kuriji and I look for a quieter place to sit and have a chat. We cross the road and smile at the barber who has set up shop under a telegraph pole, walk through the mango orchard and out on to the fields, coming to rest at the edge of a grove of trees.

Even for a farmer Kuriji is a self-contained man. Balding and grey he is not a large person, either in height or weight, and he carries himself with the gentle gravitas of age. Two ballpoint pens are clipped into the top pocket of his shirt. His family have farmed in Kaladera going back to 'my great-grandfather's grandfather,' he said. His wife and son ran the family farm when he worked as a civil servant for the state government of Rajasthan. As the assistant director of agriculture, his job was to find ways that farmers could practically apply the latest research into farming methods and would tour farms explaining and helping. On retiring in 2002 he took to working full-time on the farm and in turn agitating. Sitting, he produces a large notebook, this is his journal of Kaladera's struggle for water, detailing each twist and turn in the saga, including each journalist he has ever spoken to on the subject. I suppose you can take a man from the civil service...

Kuriji begins with Coca-Cola's arrival, 'As soon as it started, the water level went down drastically. This is the main problem. Second problem, earlier we used a three-horsepower motor. But immediately after Coke arrived we had to replace it with a five-horsepower motor.'

'Is this because of Coke?'

'Yes. The water level went down. We had to dig the wells deeper and to pump water from such depth, five-horsepower motor was needed.'

He might well have the civil service knack of itemising the issues, but he has a farmer's concerns. Having listed depleted well water and pumps, he comes to 'Thirdly, earlier we could irrigate around fourteen–fifteen acres of land with the water available but now the water is sufficient for only ten-twelve acres of land. The fourth problem is that yield also reduced. Water is required for a good harvest...'

It is only after working his way through pumps, yields and irrigation he comes to the fifth and last problem, at the bottom of the priority pile. 'Fifth problem was that water for the hand pumps dried up. In some parts they have stopped working, have become dry. There is no water.'

Problem number five means that people in the village have no drinking water from the local pumps.

'People realised that it was because of the plant. The villagers started getting together. The people were involved not just farmers. So in February 2003 we started this agitation.'

Kuriji and others visited other villages in the five-kilometre radius of the plant, organising and campaigning, urging people to agitate. They did everything they could from demonstrating to writing to the state government of Rajasthan and members of the legislative assembly. 'Through this agitation we are trying to tell the government that the plant has used up all the water and there is a shortage and want the plant to shut down, so we can have sufficient water.'

As the agitation got under way Kuriji found himself approached by Coca-Cola. According to him they had asked, 'Why are you wasting your energy in this? You support us, we'll do a lot of good work if we're together.' I put it to him that this was a sign that the company wanted to work with its critics but Kuriji disagrees: 'They asked me whether I need a hand pump or a tube well. I told them I already have a tube well. Why do I need you to make me a tube well?'

'When the Coca-Cola people came to you offering to install a new hand pump or tube well did they say anything about stopping the struggle or supporting them?'

'Yes, that was the main thing that they talked about.'

The term Kuriji gave to describe Coke's offer to him was 'manage': Coca-Cola wanted to 'manage' him. He was not the first that the company sought to 'manage' either. A close relative of one of the campaigners was suddenly offered a job working at the plant, and that particular campaigner dropped out of the agitation.

The leader of the Panchayat (village council) was a slightly more spectacular turncoat, according to Kuriji and the agitation organisers. He had taken an oath in front of them vowing to fight Coke, 'He took some water in his hand and promised he would remove the plant from the village. He said that if he became the Sarpanch [leader of the village council] of this village, he would support us and try to do his best to remove the plant, and then what happened? He became the Sarpanch and within fifteen days he changed completely.'

Coca-Cola uses letters from the Sarpanch on their website to indicate the level of support they have within the Kaladera community.

Out by the grove, with the music and speeches of the conference wafting in the background, we chat for an hour or so: about how the police create a three-kilometre exclusion zone around the plant on demonstration days, about local politicians politicking and the shenanigans of local skullduggery but mainly about Kuriji's farm.

'If you come to Kaladera I will show you.'

'Thank you, that would be great.' I say.

'I will even show you the empty land in my farm.'

'Fantastic,' I say, hoping the language of raised eyebrows is not international.

It is not often that I get invited to someone's home to see an empty field. I suspect that the invitation is just an excuse, he wants to get me to the farm and then he'll do what all the farmers do around here: show me his empty well.

* * *

Four days later Kuriji leads us through Kaladera. A village by Indian standards, but with a population of 12,000 to 13,000 people, it would constitute a small town in the UK. This is a farmer's village to be sure, every other stall is piled with fruit and veg and every other shop sells sickles, similar to the old Soviet flag-style ones but much straighter. One trader has theirs laid out on a table next to the hair grips, and I envisage a shopper holding up some rupees tonelessly saying, 'Just the sickle and the hair grips, thanks love.' Here the cattle seem to aimlessly lollop down the roads, their hides as parched as their soft bellows. Lethargic and thin, they have more ribs on show than London Fashion Week.

In the centre of the village cool narrow alleyways bustle with shoppers and traders, where the milk-sweet sellers pick pieces of *barfi* from stacks piled on trays and hot fresh pastries are scooped out of pans of bubbling oil. Chai sellers and pan wallahs line the outskirts of these pathways where men sit spinning an eternity out of a tiny cup.

Kuriji chivvies us along, worried we are late. He looks old and smart today in his white pressed shirt and grey slacks. We arrive at a white building that looks like a small fort complete with mini battlements, the kind of place the Oompa Loompas might billet in times of war.

'Come. They are waiting.' Kuriji points to the door, clutching his ever-present notebook. The entrance is a shaded archway beyond which lies a small courtyard, partially covered with a low awning of metal sheets, propped up in the middle by a single pole. This is the local primary school, and the rug laid in the shadow of the awning is where the children sit for lessons, taught out in the open and out of the sun. Classroom charts and pictures are pinned to the back wall next to a blackboard with spellings hand written in Hindi and English and an adult-size bench sits at the front. Today the school doubles as a meeting place for the village resistance to the Coke bottling plant and twenty farmers sit waiting patiently on the large rug as we arrive. The farmers greet us with smiles and deference to Kuriji. These men form the Committee for Struggle, which is exactly what it is – a committee engaged in a struggle; an entity that marries India's twin loves of social movements and bureaucracy.

After tea, Kuriji sits to one side of the assembled group, notebook at the ready. It is not merely for my benefit that the men are gathered here, there is to be a planning meeting after I have chatted to them. In the meantime one of the farmers decides that the best introduction to the assembled group is a story, which he proceeds to tell. Kaladera has just celebrated Holi the festival of colour, where people mark the occasion by painting each other with coloured water. It is, I am told, advisable to wear old clothes around festival time as no one is immune and the administering can range from a polite face smearing, to throwing coloured water to using super soakers full of paint. The bolder and brighter the colours the better: reds, purples, greens, all collide leaving an end result that can be a tad LSD. With this in mind the farmer begins, 'We had a programme called Holi Milan here in Kaladera,' explaining this is traditionally a party where grudges and ill will are set aside. 'And for this Holi Milan, all the people contributed some money. We made arrangements for food and drinks for everyone. The manager of Coca-Cola, he was also there. Since it was open, anyone could come.' He pauses and looks around the gathering in the courtyard. They smile knowingly, already anticipating the punchline. 'The villagers thought that everyone would contribute, have some good food and have a nice get together... but the villagers had a problem. The villagers' biggest enemy had come to be a part of their celebrations. Everyone was furious.' What were they to do? They couldn't ask the Coca-Cola manager to leave as it would be impolite but he was spoiling the party by being there. So as it was Holi 'one of the oldest members of the committee he took some photocopying ink in his hands and applied it on the manager's face. He blackened his face.' Amidst the bright colours of Holi the Coke manager stood covered in jet-black ink and left shortly after that. The farmer telling the story pauses, looks around at his friends and then to me before saying, 'There has been a lot of tension since then.'

This story is carving its way into village memory already, everyone seems to know it and have probably told it themselves. And the farmers smile, happy to hear the tale told once again. Its ending is my cue to ask the question I have asked in countries halfway around the world: 'What was it like before Coca-Cola came?'

Mukut Yogi squats leaning against a side wall half, he's thirty-six, with a pink shirt, a neat side parting and a moustache.

'We were all self-sufficient in those days,' says Mukut.

And when Coke came?

'It was only when the water level fell, that we realised what was going on.'

His younger brother Mahesh, shakes his head ruefully, 'You could never imagine the speed at which the water level fell.'

'Earlier,' says Mukut talking of the time before Coke, 'there was water at a depth of thirty-five feet. Water could be pumped into the fields using a motor of three horsepower.... Now the water has to be pumped out from a depth of 125 feet. It is done with the help of a ten or fifteen horsepower motor.'

The farmers don't have an exact measurement for the water loss (amongst other factors the water level varies with the seasons) but they do know they have to dig their wells deeper and get stronger pumps to bring the water up. You don't need a tape measure to know the well is dry.

Everyone acknowledges the water situation here is bad, and it depends on who you are as to how you describe it: Coke call it 'a highly water-stressed area', the farmers call it a crisis. Water is being drawn out of the ground at a rate that is at least 35 per cent greater than what is being recharged by rainfall.[7] It's a Doomsday scenario.The impact has left farmers unable to grow their crops as they once did and leaves them fearful for their futures.

'People are unemployed now,' says Mukut

'Financial condition has worsened,' his brother adds.

Crossed-legged and leaning forward Mukut calmly explains, 'People from this village now go to other cities in search of work. There is no water here. A person cannot do farming. He has to look after his children. What will he do? Many villagers have gone to the cities.'

Few would argue that Coke is solely to blame. And Coke is right when it says 'agriculture remains the most significant use of water in the watershed'.[8] But by agriculture they mean the men sitting in front of me, the small farmers and their families. Here between 60-80 per cent of the population lives on the land, so by agriculture the Company means Indians growing food. Not surprisingly, when I put the Company's statement to them the agitators get very agitated. At the front of the group is Sudher Prahash, the thirty-year-old teacher at the school and a farmer with just under a hectare of land. Sitting on his haunches and with the eager disposition of a pupil he nearly leaves the ground in outrage at Coke's suggestion. 'I can explain this in a minute. In every man's life, there are a few basic necessities like eating food. What will the people of this country eat? If the farmers consume water, it's for growing crops. It is for sustaining life. But what are these people doing? You will neither live nor die by drinking a bottle of Coca-Cola.'

Perhaps the most surprising criticism has come from Coke's own report. The TERI report, published in January 2008, does something quite incredible: Coca-Cola's own report suggests that Coke should consider shutting the plant down!

It is not often a company like Coke hires a consultant tasked with giving them the once over and the consultant says 'you're so shit you should think of shutting' – though the report didn't actually use these exact words.

The report examines the Coke plant's activities saying, 'the water withdrawals by the HCCBPL [Coke], Kaladera, need to be viewed in the context of the already overexploited condition of the aquifer.' The impact of the Coke plant on the water is such that TERI say 'the plant's operations in this area would continue to be one of the contributors to a worsening water situation and a source of stress to the communities around.' To this end TERI concludes:

'TCCC has to evaluate its options for HCCBPL, Kaladera, such as:

- Transport water from the nearest aquifer that may not be stressed (could be at quite a distance from the existing plant)
- Store water from low-stress seasons (may not exist!)
- Relocate the plant to a water-surplus area
- Shut down this facility.'[9]

Please note the whole of that statement is in quotation marks...

So let's look at the options. As Jaipur is a drought-prone area the chances of a nearest aquifer under no stress and with a population willing to let Coke grab it is about as slim as the chances of storing enough water without rainfall. Thus eliminating the first two options. Leaving option three, 'Relocate the plant to a water-surplus area.' Or take option four, 'Shut down this facility.' The only viable options the plant has is to: shut down and move or shut down and not move. The company chose to continue its operations in Kaladera. Referring to the TERI report, Deepak Jolly the company Vice President said, 'It doesn't blame us even once,' adding 'It blames the farmers and agriculture.' In fact Mr Deepak Jolly goes on to say, 'It also does not even once suggest that we should pack up and leave those areas. It says that there are four or five options for bring up the water levels and if nothing is possible then alone we should go. Anything but closure.'[10] Deepak Jolly is also the holder of the Public Relations Council of India's 2006 award for Communicator of the Year.[11]

* * *

In the school that looks like a fort the farmers prepare for battle, sitting on the rug and planning how to persuade one of the biggest multinationals in the world to take option three or four. It is time for my questions to end and the meeting to start. Speaking nineteen to the dozen in Hindi, Kuriji explains the TERI report and its significance, that Kaladera's case was so strong the report couldn't help but condemn the current running of the plant. His audience listens rapt as Kuriji sits upright on his knees, notepad in hand resting on his lap. Sudher the teacher is still at the front, keen-eyed and coiled. Mukut leans against the wall with his brother next to him.

In the Land of Ignorance my knowledge of Hindi is infinite, in reality it is nil, all I know is that Kuriji has lowered his voice in dramatic significance when my mobile phone rings. My body assumes the 'oops' position as I reach hurriedly for it. With my hand cupped over the mouthpiece I whisper 'Hello?'

A friend from home wants to know if I can come to a party.
    'I'm in India,' I hiss.
    'Oh sorry, is it Coca-Cola?'
    'Yes.'
    'Oh, you poor thing it must be horrible for you.'

Speaking as a person who has said so many stupid and inept things in my life that I stand a good chance of being elected Mayor of London, I like to think my friend said that out of surprise and shock. But instead of uttering the hissed mantra of the inappropriate phone interruption, 'Call you back later, bye', I impulsively reply, 'I am in the middle of a meeting of farmers who are plotting how to take on one of the biggest multinationals in the world – it's not horrid at all, it's brilliant. Call you back later, bye.'*

Guiltily I lift my head, pocketing the offending technology. No one has noticed my blathering, they are listening as Kuriji

* *This conversation really happened.*

finishes with a flourish. They nod emphatically and murmuring breaks out. I edge over and ask one of the crowd, 'What did he just say?'

'He said "Are you ready to agitate?"'

* * *

Kuriji's son Mahendra jumps from his cot where a second before he had lain unaware of the impending visitors. Patting down his hair he hurries into the house and emerges moments later with a jug of water and a low bow. The first thing a farmer does when guests arrive is offer water – the second thing he does is show them the well. Groups gather around it, peer into darkness, point to old tidemarks on the wall and tut. In good years a farmer might have shown a guest his cattle or full crops, but these are dry years, so everyone comes to the well with a quiet lamentation, to plead, curse, and sigh. Farmers show their wells like bruises, as evidence of injury.

'Here,' says Kuriji gesticulating with an outstretched arm. Mere metres from of his home lies the dry and dead well. The top courses of its brickwork have been exposed to the elements and are blown and puffy with erosion. 'Initially it was thirty feet deep. So where the pigeons are sitting, that was the depth of the well.'

Leaning precariously, holding the top of a metal ladder that descends into the well, I can see a circular shelf of concrete that is home to the birds; four nesting pigeons who inhabit the ledge, cooing in the shade amidst the caked bird crap and feathers.

'That was the depth of the well, dug in 1990,' says Kuriji enunciating the numbers so there is no confusion. From where the pigeons sit another smaller hole drops into total darkness, this was the second well, that went down to 80 feet.

'Dried. Dried.' he says, with a tilt of his head. 'I have this tube well after this,' he points to a couple of pipes that run across his yard to a metal cylinder which houses the pump. This tube well was dug in 2002 and goes down to 205 feet. That is the depth he brings the water up from.

'It cost me 1 lakh rupees.' Which is about £1,200. And as if this were not indignity enough, he can use the pump for only a few hours a day. The state decided to allow farmers four hours of electricity every twenty-four hours thus limiting the amount of water they can bring up. A decision that has caused considerable bitterness as the bottlers are not subject to the same measures. Coke can pull up water when it likes.

We walk along the side of a barley field that is home to a small temple, a stone affair with a peaked roof barely a metre in height. This is a temple to Hanuman, the monkey god who owns and protects the well. Not a task the primate god has excelled at in this instance. Before us is a large field that remains unplanted, the promised empty field. It is stark in its absence of plant life, it is a large patch of tilled earth. Where the blackish trunks of the trees are set out against the insipid brown of the earth. Kuriji speaking in English explains slowly, 'Out of seven hectares two fallow.'

'Why is this left fallow?'

'Due to lack of water, sufficient water is not available for us, that's why.'

We turn back to face the planted land, opposite the barley is the small family vegetable patch where white garlic flowers sit on thin green stalks and coriander bunches grow close to the ground.

'Usually we cultivate all the land, it's all irrigated but now because of the scarcity of the water...two hectares are left.'

'So nearly one third of the farm is gone?'

And with that we walk back to the home away from the barren dirt in silence.

* * *

Before I leave I ask, 'Can we take a photo of you and your grandchildren in front of your home?'

'Yes. Of course.'

He calls for his two grandsons, Subham and Nishant, who are seven and ten, and they stand under the porch in front of the wooden cot their father had lain in as we arrived. The grandsons stand quietly, impassive and polite. Mahendra, their dad suddenly remembers he is wearing only a vest. He rushes inside and comes out doing up the buttons on his shirt. The children's hair is sorted with swift parental hands and someone must have said, 'Tidy yourselves up,' as the two boys tug their shirt bottoms and brush down their sleeves. Then with a herding shuffle and one arm gently around each child, Kuriji allows his chest to swell a little. They stand straight and confident, looking at the camera with a happy pride and I ask, 'Kuriji, do you hope that one day your grandsons will inherit this land?'

'Yes. They will. Automatically.' He answers instantly, without a second's hesitation, not taking his eyes away from the camera. He seems so sure. So painfully sure.

10
GAS

Kaladera, India

'The Coca-Cola Company
has invested more than
US $1 billion...[and]
employs approximately
6,000 local people...indirectly,
our business in India creates
employment for more than
150,000 people.'

The Coca-Cola Company[1]

The Company's ability to take credit for positive news is
monumental. In fact it is inversely proportionate to their
ability to distance themselves from the negative. Not
surprisingly they talk up the jobs they create and the benefit
they bring to a community. TCCC say they employ 6,000
people directly and 'indirectly, our business in India creates

employment for more than 150,000 people.' Which sounds intriguing, who are these 150,000 people who benefit from the Company largesse? When pressed Coke said their 'positive economic impact is multiplied by the employment generated through our chain of distributors and retailers, through our vendors...[and] point of purchase.'[2] So the Company are taking credit for shopkeepers and street vendors who stock Coke...Now I have dealt with quite a few Coca-Cola PR and press people over the years and under these rules I would just like to make it clear that I am indirectly responsible for the creation of those people's jobs.

To put Coke's economic benefit to India into perspective, consider the Company's claim to have invested over $1 billion in just over a decade. The money that comes into India from foreign transnationals comes under the category of Foreign Direct Investment. But another source of money coming into India is remittance flows: very simply, this is workers leaving the country, working abroad and sending money home. The economist and analyst Kavaljit Singh estimates that, 'In India, remittance flows are nearly four times larger than FDI flows.'[3] This means that hard-working ordinary folk looking for a better life for their family and sending the money home put significantly more money into the Indian economy that foreign-based transnationals like Coca-Cola. And by significantly I mean four times as much money. Every year.

* * *

A potent image of the benefit the company has brought to Kaladera was shown to me early on in my visit and it happened before I went to Kuriji's farm and met the farmers' struggle committee. The day started with an encounter that was as sudden as it was unexpected and it began in a fertiliser supply shop in the village. This is the place I was to meet up with Kuriji; it is off the main drag, past a row of barbers in wooden huts lathering customers' chins and on a corner of a network of tight alleyways stuffed with traders. The shop is very small, with two doors, one opening at the front, the other to the side street. Instead of walking around the corner of the shop, you could walk in one door and out of the other and cut an entire second off your journey time. But somehow the place is packed with sacks, barrels, boxes, bottles, a couple of toilet seats to one side and a smell of ammonia that indicates the organic movement has yet to gather strength here. Pride of place in the shop, pinned to the wall, is the Indian flag covered with the slogan 'Pepsi Coca-Cola out of India!' Hanging a foot away by some seed packets, is its polar opposite: a Coca-Cola calendar with a picture of a chipmunk drinking Coke through a straw.

Helping me out with the translating is Amit Srivastava from the Indian Resource Centre, an NGO that has worked a lot with grassroots groups on the issue of Coca-Cola. Amit is an Indian non resident and a US citizen, so working on Coca-Cola's practices in India means he can attack the rapacious standard bearer of American capitalism and visit his mum in Delhi at the same time. He is about my age and has a West-Coast style ponytail, which is two years past its wear-by date.

'Good to see you. Hello,' Kuriji greets Amit and myself in English. 'Here please. Sit,' he says ushering me to a fold-out chair in the one remaining bit of space.

'Water?'

A copper metal pot with a spout is passed round, Amit holds it away from his lips and the pours water straight into his open mouth.

'Chai? For you?'

'Yes, yes please.'

I sit back and Kuriji explains today's itinerary. 'I will take you to my farm. And you will meet the farmers who are organising the agitation to talk with them. This afternoon I have arranged it.'

And with the business part of the morning over we get down to the hard work of sipping tea. I must have been there all of three minutes when an old man, with cracked NHS glasses and goggly eyes appears in front of me. Wearing a traditional big red turban dotted with tiny yellow and green flowers, his magnified black eyeballs hold me in his gaze, as he unleashes a torrent of Hindi gushing from him nonstop, as if gasping for breath might prove lethal. The village grapevine must be on broadband, because he had heard I was in the shop. It is me he has come to see. Well, not me exactly, he had heard a foreign journalist was here and how was he to know any better?

When he finally comes up for air Kuriji explains, 'He wants to show you something.'
   'Show me something?'
   'A well,' says Amit.
   'Oh.'
   'He wants to show you a well.'
   'A Coca-Cola well!' adds Kuriji.

The old man tilts his head and looks at me. Through the lenses his pupils look so large that if he ever took MDMA his eyes would end up bigger than his face. He cocks his head one way and then the other awaiting a response.

Taking a deep breath I say, 'Right then,' before reluctantly and unknowingly stepping off into an unscheduled revelation.

The old man leads us through the market, down the shaded alleyways and out of the centre of the village, out past the stalls and homes, out to where the shacks and shanties stack up in rickety regularity. This is a *basti*, a slum, home of the landless labourer, the Dalits, the lower caste. Out here the roads are wider, the tarmac thinner and the dust thicker.

The old man arrives at the edge of the *basti*, excitedly turns to us, refocuses, declares 'Here. Look!' and presents a large pothole with an outstretched arm. I've never seen a pothole get such a build-up and introduction. I should give it a round of applause but I'm a tough audience when it comes to potholes. I live in Lambeth, south London, we're connoisseurs. We classify potholes as something that an Invacar can't climb out of, anything less is a divot.

Amit, Kuriji and I stare at this metre-wide hole with a bit of tubing poking out above the soil.
   'This what he wants to show you,' says Amit.
   'A hole?'

The old man with the bushbaby eyes smiles in triumph, his one skinny arm outstretched waving at it like a tourist guide.
   'A hole?'

He grunts and points again. I remain singularly unimpressed. But the crowd forming a circle around us obviously views this with slightly more significance.

People seem to gather easily in India. Even in the smallest village an argument over parking can over draw many more spectators than the average English County Cricket match. The throng here has assembled quickly, it's three deep already with kids pushing past grown-ups to get to the front and getting slapped on the head for their trouble. Already there is shoving at the back and shouted comments – this is a proper crowd, a mere scapegoat away from a rabble. Someone screams the words, 'Coca-Cola!' which is the trigger word for the old man to begin.

'This is the well Coca-Cola built for us,' he says with a flourish. 'Coca-Cola came. Coca-Cola drilled this well.'

'Useless,' shouts a man from the crowd.

'Not deep enough,' says a man in a grey T-shirt in the front row. 'They don't drill deep enough.'

The old man shakes his finger in the air and shouts to regain his position as chief storyteller, 'Soft soil! They only drill in soft soil not to rock.'

'Too shallow,' says grey shirt.

'It fell in,' the old man says.

The well had worked fine for a few months but once the moisture in the surrounding soil was gone it dried up and Coke's well collapsed in on itself and died. However the cave-in had only occurred at the bottom of the shaft, thus allowing one of the less sure-footed village goats to tumble down it and die too.

The old man starts, 'When the goat died, the community thought this is dangerous and a child will fall in and die too...'

'So we filled in the rest of the well,' says grey shirt nipping in to finish the story.

The old man glowers at him then turns to the hole. And for a moment the old man, grey shirt, the crowd, Amit, Kuriji, and I stand over the small crater of detritus that once was a well in respectful silence. Had I a lily about my person I would have cast it at that moment.

'The public of this colony are all distressed because of the shortage of water,' says the old man.

Wonky well aside, the bigger issue is the scarcity of water. It is normally women who bear the brunt of this, as they are the ones who have to fetch it. There's a group of women in the crowd so I try striking up a conversation by saying 'Hi' and holding out my hand. At the front of the group a small lean woman sticks a hip out, one arm folded and the other pulling her yellow and green headscarf across her face. She glares at me and there is no need for a translator to know that she's saying, 'Who does he think he is?'

Amit shoots me a prompting stare, brings his hands together and mouths 'namaste' at me.

'Namaste,' I say bowing slightly awkwardly.

With a tiny movement she pulls her chin up in contempt. Someone declares, 'He's a reporter.'

She retorts to the crowd while holding me in a hostile gaze. 'It's not going to bring any difference to our situation. The water problem will remain.'

I do what I do best in these situations, which is smile and bumble, and she agrees to speak though will not give her name. I nickname her The Stare.

The lack of water here has many consequences. Drawing it from the hand pump can take a long time and there may not be enough for the 200–250 families here. If a woman wants to make sure her family has enough water she has to work harder.

'What time do you get up for water?'

'We get up at four in the morning.' She replies, in a slightly less hostile manner.

'How long is the queue?'

'It is as crowded as it is now.' Which is very crowded. 'A lot of women end up with bruises. The children end up fighting.'

This is quite common as others confirm. A second woman in a green skirt joins in, telling of how she and her son go to collect water in the morning. 'Sometimes we end up fighting.' To avoid this her son 'goes on a bicycle to a different place to get water...it's very far away.'

Women and children are literally fighting for the remaining water.

Over a series of questions and curt answers The Stare explains she has to draw water for fifteen people in her extended family and five cattle. Then she makes breakfast, walks the three to four kilometres to work, fetching stones from eight in the morning until five in the evening. When she gets home there is no water. 'I have to fill water in the evening. By ten o'clock we have our meal.'

One of the kids, maybe five or six years old, takes her hand and looks up at her. The Stare has let her headscarf fall from her face and has tossed it over her shoulder.

'It's because of the shortage of water that my child looks like this. I don't even get time to bathe them.' She says pulling at her daughter's jumper to show that there is neither water nor time to wash their clothes.

This is not the only impact on the children either, the woman in a green skirt says. 'We have four daughters and one son. All of them have stopped going to school because of the water.'

Because both parents are out working the children have to fetch the water and the shortage means they don't have time to get water and go to school. Green Skirt's youngest daughter Neetu is eight years old and she appears on cue.

'Namaste,' I say to Neetu.

Embarrassed at having been spoken to she tucks herself into her mother's skirt and then peaks from the folds to flash a grin Hallmark could sell a million cards on.

'When there is no water she stays back,' says her mother, one hand around Neetu. Her son is a few metres away and she nods towards him. 'Because of water, even our son has stopped going to school. If there is water he will go to school tomorrow.'

So the women get up early, fight for water, have no time to bathe their kids and the children are taken out of school so they can get water for the family. What was it like before the Coca-Cola plant came? A voice from the crowd responds, 'There was a lot of water then.'

'So do you ever buy water?'

'We don't have money to buy water,' says The Stare.

The voice from the crowd calls back, 'No, we never bought water before.'

'Then, there was so much water here,' says The Stare and with that she tugs her headscarf firmly over her face and moves away.

A group of men stand by the collapsed Coca-Cola well, the older ones are in their late twenties, the younger ones are barely out of their teens and some are clearly not. They lounge with easy familiarity, leaning on each other's shoulders and dangling their arms around a friend: a vision of a stage gang in a West End musical. They all clearly have something on their minds, though it might be a dance rendition of 'Greased Lightning'. They lazily follow our activities and as the women walk away a male voice calls. 'Workers are always crying for employment. They are not given any jobs. Coke gives them employment.' This is no defiant cry, this is a sad statement of fact.

So I ask, 'Is there anyone who works for Coke?'

Nudges and looks are exchanged and then, 'Yes, I have,' says a young man.

'Yes,' adds another.

'I worked for three years,' says a confident voice. He's in his early twenties with swept-back hair and in a thin jumper with equally thin stripes. He stands in the middle of the group, framed by two lads behind one resting on each of his shoulders. The confident voice belongs to Rahis, he worked at the bottling plant, though he was employed as a casual worker by the contractor.

'They never made us permanent. One day you are working the next day you don't have a job. It is not just me. They do this to everyone.'

The group don't say a word but nod quietly as Rahis continues, 'Sometimes they take us, sometimes they don't. At times they remove us from the job. We are all troubled by this.' He says, indicating the crowd around him.

'How do you know if you have work that day?'

'At times they give us a phone call. Sometimes we go and stand in front of the gate. They chase us away, asking us to come the next day.'

It is a relatively common complaint of the temporary worker that the contractor holds out the promise of a permanent job if they do longer hours. And by Rahis's account this plant is no exception. 'They used to always say that we would be made permanent. They used to tempt us and make us work even harder'

This time the nods are more emphatic. It dawns on me that they all seem to have some experience of working there, so I ask if there are any more Coke workers in the crowd. They nod and put their hands up. About eight have worked at the plant at one time or another, though some like Rahis no longer do so.

'Has anyone got a permanent job?'

The 'No' that comes from the crowd is more confident now and the youngest-looking of the group pipes up, 'When the contractors are in need of workers, they make all kinds of promises,' he says, ' they promise but they chase the workers away after a while.'

The cocky member of the group is a young lad in a vest with chains around his neck and an Elvis mini-quiff. He stands leaning on his mate's shoulder, who is the drabber of the two in a plain brownish shirt and a scruffy mop top. They look to be best friends. Elvis Quiff nudges Best Friend, and says something to the group who burst out laughing. Best Friend drops his head, when he lifts it up a moment later his face has reddened, this proves even more hilarious to the group who laugh even louder. Best Friend laughs too and shrugs; Elvis Quiff pats him on the shoulder. It is obvious they are somewhat of a double act.

Amit explains to me that Elvis Quiff had told the story of how his best friend had been working in the water treatment plant – this is where the water is purified and cleaned ready to be used in drink production. Best Friend had passed out with the fumes of the chlorine, this, Elvis Quiff had joked, was because Best Friend was weak-brained, thus prompting the laughter and minor moment of shame. But when they stop giggling others acknowledge they have suffered too.

'While you were working were a lot of chlorine fumes emitted?'

'Yes, in huge amounts.' says Best Friend. 'They never did anything for our safety. If people from audit came over they would give us something for our safety just to show them and took it back when they left'

'What did they give you?'

'Safety clothing.'

'What kind of safety clothing did they give you?'

'Something to cover our face,' reports Best Friend.

'Masks?'

'Gas masks,' says Elvis Quiff joining his friend.

'Gas mask. Gloves,' adds Best Friend.

'Could you describe the masks?'

'There were strings to tie it to the back of the head...but this was only to show them they never did give us these masks.'

'What did they make you do?'

'They gave us chlorine,' shrugs Best Friend.

'They used to give us chlorine,' says Elvis Quiff, backing him up.

'There were people to give us instructions and we used to do accordingly...they used to tell us what to do.'

'What did they chlorine look like?'

'It looked like white powder, it came in sacks,' explains Best Friend.

'Plastic sacks,' says Elvis Quiff, who for some reason, probably mischief, points to the boy who looks like the youngest in the group and says 'He still works for Coke, he still works in Water Treatment.'

'Yes,' Youngest says looking at the ground and holding his folded arms high to his chest.

'Do you mix chlorine with water?'

'Yes,' Youngest replies.

He is a temporary worker like all of them and he gets 86 rupees for an eight-hour day.

'Did they give you anything for safety?'

'They have only given us this T-shirt,' Youngest scoffs lightly, indicating the dark blue collared T-shirt he is wearing.

'Yes, just a T-shirt,' joins in Elvis Quiff, 'Show him your T-shirt'

'No,' says Youngest giggling and hunching, pulling his arms to him covering something on the breast of his shirt.

'It's a Coke shirt,' laughs Elvis Quiff and one of the group playfully pulls Youngest's arm away to reveal the Coca-Cola logo on his shirt, the shirt that will protect him from the chlorine fumes. And they laugh.

With this I sense they have said what they wanted to, so I ask one final question. 'When you are working, when you see the result of what Coca-Cola does, when you see the water going here, does that make you feel conflicted?'

'It is necessary to fill our stomachs. We have no choice. We need to meet the expenses of our family,' says Youngest.

'If we don't go, they will bring workers from other villages,' Best Friend states with a shrug, and for once Elvis Quiff doesn't chime in.

* * *

So the men will line up outside the gates waiting for a chance to work in the chlorine fumes for a company which is pumping millions of litres of water out of the ground while the women fight each other for pots of water and the children are taken out of school. Like Coca-Cola's well this village is falling in on itself as the water runs out. The question that keeps recurring is the simple one, why did Coca-Cola set up in a drought-prone area? Surely when the company conducted its environmental assessments before opening up a plant, problems with water levels would have been identified? Surely any report would have shown that there was not enough water for them and the community? Exactly why the company chose to open there is a mystery. Who knows, perhaps it was the result of drunken chief executives playing dares: Exxon had to spill oil on the Alaskan coast, Enron had to turn the lights out in California and Coca-Cola had to open up in the worst possible place for bottling their product.

While no one but Coke knows the full reasons why they built their plant in Kaladera, we do know two key facts thanks to Coke's own report by The Energy and Resource Institute (TERI). Unsurprisingly, as they were conducting an assessment of Coke's plants, the organisation asked to see various documents, including the Environmental Due Diligence reports for the plant. These would show Coke's appraisal of the water situation before starting production and might shine a light on how the company thought they could operate in India's driest state. Stunningly, Coca-Cola simply refused to hand them over, 'due to reasons of legal and strategic confidentiality'[4] thus denying the assessors vital data with which to complete their work. But TERI did manage to elicit one vital piece of information. The TERI report states 'in response to queries from TERI, Coca-Cola representatives explained that the company's requirements do not explicitly necessitate the assessment of the effects of HCCBPL, Kaladera, bottling operations on groundwater in the region of operation but focused on ensuring a sustained supply of water for business operations.'[5]

TERI describes this situation by saying the 'focus of TCCC... is on business continuity – community water issues do not appear to be an integral part of the water resources management practices of TCCC.'[6]

In lay language this means the company only checked if there was enough water for its own use. Coca-Cola did not consider at any point if there was enough water for the plant *and* the community. They simply didn't give a fuck.

11
THE FIZZ
MAN'S BURDEN

India

> 'We are a user of water in a highly water-stressed area, and the burden of proof is on us to demonstrate that we can reconcile our operations with local community and watershed needs.'
>
> **The Coca-Cola Company, 2008**[1]

I have simple rules for my life that apply to wherever I am and whatever situation I am in, but in particular they apply to India, and the rules are: I don't do joss sticks, chanting or naked. Yoga, yogis, gurus and inner journeys can fuck themselves as far as I am concerned. And the same applies to anything in the vicinity of the word 'tantric' – I can't think of anything worse than an hour-long orgasm – it sounds exhausting, pointless and showy. I do not want to find my inner self – I've found more than enough of myself already and what I've found so far is distressing enough. Furthermore the answer is 'no' to the question 'Do I need a fat bloke with a beard selling me meditation tapes and mantras?' Nor do I want anyone helping me reach enlightenment by teaching me breathing exercises. I have been breathing for forty-five years without a single lesson. Frankly when I want to expand my consciousness I'll read a book, thank you very much.

Having stated these simple rules, believed in them and indeed led my life by them I am somewhat bewildered to find myself in a Gandhian ashram in the middle of the desert having spent the early part of the evening sat on a rug at the top of a mountain having tea with a 'Holy man' dressed in a lungi.* Frankly it has all gone a bit *Donnie Darko*. Furthermore I am not calmed by the fact that it is midnight, a thunderstorm is breaking overhead, the lightning has brought down the electricity, the place is in total darkness while the window shutters slam and bang and there is no one else in the

---

* *I had trekked up to the top of a mountain to see a dam that had been built by villagers to conserve water for the wildlife. The holy man lived in a tent at the top of a ridge. It was a tiring trip and he had offered a cup of tea. Sitting on the rug with him it had seemed rude to ask, 'so what are you about then?' So I did a lot of grinning, and bowing. His tent had grabbed the best spot, as it looked out across the long valley, green and lush from the dam water, and this scene rolled back as far as it was possible to see with the human eye. I did at one point say to the holy man, 'you've got yourself a lovely view here, haven't you,' but somehow as the words came out of my mouth it sounded like I was talking about Littlehampton.*

dormitory. If it were not for the two frogs and one mouse I would be completely alone. The bed is wooden with a straw mattress frame and the pillows have so many sweat stains that I wouldn't like to guess at how much DNA is soaked in them. I am sitting under a mosquito net that has been deployed more out of a need to erect a barrier of some kind between me and whatever else is out there than to stop me from getting bitten. I'm all for protecting the environment and minimalising our reliance on industrial-based consumerism but I am currently inhabiting a world that has never smelled the simple chemical pleasure of pine-fresh cleaner and I am not sure I like it. So holding a Maglite between my teeth and writing in my notebook I try and make sense of the past 48 hours and how I got to be here.

It started as usual with The Coca-Cola Company. The Company gave little credence to the fact that their own report recommended serious consideration be given to shutting down the plant in Kaladera. It had been the threat of a boycott by the University of Michigan that had led to Coke commissioning TERI, so when the report was finished Coke sent a copy to the university. In the seven-page covering letter Coca-Cola failed to mention that TERI had suggested the Kaladera plant be shut down. Instead they claimed the plant in Kaladera was responsible for putting *more* water into the ground than it took out,[2] despite the farmers, the workers and Coke's own report saying the opposite. I am not suggesting this is a comparison but if I ever get caught shoplifting my defence is going to be, 'Actually I was putting stuff on the shelf!'

Kaladera, like most of Rajasthan, relies on groundwater – getting water from a well. Coke claim that they are replenishing (recharging) the groundwater using 'rainwater harvesting schemes...In Kaladera the rainwater harvesting systems we have installed have the potential to recharge about fifteen times the amount of water the plant uses currently...Even in recent years when rainfall has been below average, *actual recharge has been more than five times the amount of water used for production of our beverages*[3] [my emphasis].' This appears to be an amazing assertion; it is not often you hear of water-intensive industries putting five times the amount of water they use back into the ground. And considering Coke normally charges for its water, I have to say nice of them to donate for free too.

The next line of the Company's letter to Michigan does qualify it somewhat, 'we will install measuring devices that will verify the amount of water recharged'. Now some might sneer at the fact that the Company can make such specific claims without bothering to actually measure and record the quantities of water involved. But I say shame on you naysayers! We are witnessing the birth of a new scientific era where companies can state facts without having to fall back on the outdated and tiresome concept of collated scientific data.

When I pressed Coke on this technicality, they told me that 'The company, along with community/NGO, tries to take water table readings before and after monsoon, keeps historical data, conduct community interviews, facilitate media visits to understand the efficacy and impact of such projects besides site visits by its own high-ranking officials'.[4] Oh where to begin...Firstly, I ask the Company how they monitor their scheme and they reply saying the company 'tries' to measure water. Secondly they say they keep historical data but of what? Old train tickets are 'historical data'. An Enron financial report is historical data. A stalker's trophy cupboard is 'historical data'. Thirdly the company say they 'facilitate media visits', so how does this relate to monitoring the schemes? Am I to assume that the paparazzi finish with Brad and Angelina and then nip over to Kaladera with their hydrology kits? Fourthly, the company says they get visits from 'its own high-ranking officials'. Well done – your boss looked at it. So to conclude: The Coca-Cola Company, the company that put their own products in space with a device that enabled astronauts to drink their fizzy pop in zero gravity, when asked how they monitor their own rainwater harvesting schemes replied, 'We do try...I've got some cuttings...the boss looked at it and a photographer took a photo.'

Assuming Coke's claim is based on a paper calculation, let's make one of our own. According to Coca-Cola the Kaladera plant extracted nearly 88 million litres of water in 2007.[5] If Coke's statement were to apply to this data then the company would need to be putting at least 440 million litres of water into the ground through their rainwater harvesting structures to replace the 88 million it took out. I wanted to find out how and if Coke are putting these amounts of water back into the ground, which is how I ended up at the ashram.

To be honest, I know a little more than nothing about rainwater harvesting but substantially less than anything of worth. If we were measuring ignorance in units I would assess mine to be about a *Daily Express*'s worth of stupidity; despite which I have a very strong negative opinion of rainwater harvesting. I have judged it to be a little tie-dye and lurking near the borders of pseudo-science. However, if Coca-Cola are basing their continued existence in Kaladera on a claim to be a net contributor of water in a drought-prone area, based on their rainwater harvesting projects...well it makes sense to try and understand a bit about it. Which is why I made contact with the man credited with pioneering water management and community rainwater harvesting schemes in Rajasthan, Rajendra Singh. He is referred to as the Rainwater Man and knows enough about the subject for Coca-Cola to try and get him on board for their schemes. Something he took exception to.[6]

* * *

Rajendra Singh is staying in Delhi at the Gandhi Peace Foundation.

'Have you been before?' asks the taxi driver as we weave for dear life.

'No, never.'

'Do you know anything about it?'

'Well it's run on Gandhian principles...it's educational and they have rooms you can stay in...other than that the only thing I can tell you is I would be surprised if they have a mini-bar service.'

'You are meeting Gandhi followers, yes?'

'Yes, though I wouldn't recognise a Gandhian if they hit me in the face...'

This was apparently a faux pas.

The driver resumes talking when he stops to ask for directions at the next lights and we re-enter the fray of Delhi's traffic with a firmer sense of where we are going. At one point a big banner on the side of the road reads 'Make every day safety day. 37th National Safety Day 8 March.' At least I think it was the eighth, it was hard to tell as we were swerving to avoid a cow in the middle lane. I have chewed my nails in many cars around the world but Delhi beats them all for sheer fear, here a driver's horn will wear out quicker than the brake pads; the experience is like playing Grand Theft Auto with four million people connected to the same console.

The front of the Gandhi Peace Foundation is a big building that looks like a university done in the style of a Soviet apartment block but without the frills. The walls used to be white and the strip lights used to work without flickering. Rajendra's room is bare save three camp beds with slim mattresses, two painfully hard wooden chairs built by comfort-hating carpenters and a portrait of Gandhi. Undoubtedly Gandhi was one of the most important political leaders of the twentieth century but he could have encouraged his followers to accessorise just a little bit. Frugality may well be the moral cornerstone of their philosophy but they manage to make the Amish look decadent.

Rajendra Singh leads me to the seat and smiles. He is nearly fifty with a black beard and a face that runs with emotion, his expressions letting you know the tone of the next comment before he opens his mouth. Shifting the folds of his kurta that hangs loosely on his stocky frame he sits on the seat, with an easy and relaxed manner that belies the austerity of the chair. And with a wave of his hand to signal the start of his story, he smiles, leans backs and says, 'I started this work in 1984 in Rajasthan in a place called Gaoloura village, in the Alwar District. This area is semi-arid with hardly any rainfall annually.'

He had originally gone there as part of an educational programme but became immersed in creating rainwater harvesting structures when a village elder taught him about the traditional ways of capturing water. Rajendra smiles as he tells me about the physical work he did. The first structure he made was a *johad*, a concave pond, he worked on it by himself and it took four years to make. Which probably explains his ability to luxuriate in the wooden chair; after spending four years navvying on your own I would imagine he could nap on concrete.

'In '88 we had very good rainfall, which collected and recharged the underground aquifer. You can see water in the wells that were old and dry before.' Though his English is infinitely more advanced than my Hindi it occasionally requires minor mental adjustments to get the flow of it. 'So in the beginning,' he says, 'it is a little hard, because in the beginning nobody believed, nobody trust it, but when you can show some visual impact, people come...and the next year thirty-nine villages start rainwater harvesting structures.'

Over 4,000 rainwater harvesting structures have now been built within this region, with the help and inspiration of Rajendra Singh and the non-government organisation Tarun Bharat Sangh. The work is done on the Gandhian principle, shunning development money, government aid and grant assistance, preferring instead community work and self-reliance. 'In my country the water is not the asset of the government, it is not the asset of any one person...the responsibility for the drinking water, for agriculture, for industry is the community responsibility.'

It was when Rajendra and his structures started to make old rivers run again that people began to notice him outside the district. I ask him about this story.

'The river come after twelve years, the river was dry, and river come back in '98.'

'What was the name of the river?'

'Arvari river.'

'So this river was once dry...'

'Dead and dry.'
'And it is flowing?'
'The river is perennial.'

Using a series of dams built by villages along the length of it, the river started to flow again. Not surprisingly he began to attract press attention, articles appeared and awards quickly followed. Rajendra became known as the 'Water Man of Rajasthan'.

I am not exactly sure of how rainwater harvesting works, from the sound of it, you build dams and ponds in a place where water can collect and then it seeps into the ground. But maybe I am oversimplifying it and more to the point if it works and he can do it, can Coca-Cola? But this question is given short shrift. 'I am saying they can't give back to the region, the water they are taking is from the underground water. They can't, they are not doing recharge water.'

'But their publicity says "look at the rainwater harvesting we're doing", they're in the papers yesterday saying we will be water neutral by the end of the year, what do you make...'

'This statement is a big lie, this is not possible, I can say that they are not doing what they are saying.'

'OK,' I say uncertainly.

'It is impossible. They can't do the water harvesting because they have no right on the water, so they can't do. The water can only be harvested through the community. They can't do it.'

'You saying that technically they can't do it?'

'I'm saying technically they can't do. '

But I have heard nothing that proves this point and I worry that Rajendra's Gandhian ideal of community self-reliance has become too dogmatic. I don't quite understand why Coke can't do what he has achieved? So I press the question home again, but he replies 'My dear friend, we have a community doing water conservation, water harvesting and water management. I request you tomorrow go there and see where the community is doing these things. You will understand.'

'Great.'

And with that I take the next step towards the ashram.

* * *

Twelve hours later the car wheels whirr with the familiar dry sound of motion along a fair to middling tarmac. The low noise leaves me feeling contented, it is the sound of connections having been made, people met and a journey underway. It is the sound that all is well. Quickly the trappings of the city fall behind us. The ashram is three hours' drive north of Jaipur and its famous Red Fort.

Lumbering lorries grinding through the highway to the desert replace the congestion of cars. The garish billboard hoardings hawking perfumes, burgers and pop stars gradually fade, and as their number diminishes so the number of camels increase. Nearly all of them have patterns shaved into their flanks, angular cuts in their coats creating a kaleidoscope pattern of flowers near each camel's backside. Intentionally or not this is the ultimate act of optimism, to stick such a scented image so close to a camel's arse.

Devayani Kulkarni sits in the front passenger seat. She works with Tarun Bharat Sangh, Rajendra Singh's NGO. She's a small wiry woman of about forty with long black hair in plaits, jeans, gappy teeth and a cough, she is taking me to visit rainwater harvesting projects. Sitting in the back next to me is Kanhaiya Lal Gurjor dressed in a neat, pressed kurta, trousers and a set of glasses that make him look like a Fifties jazz intellectual. Kanhaiya worked on his first rainwater harvesting structure in 1989, a check dam: a traditional dam used for rainwater harvesting.

'How many structures have you worked on since then?'

'Forty,' says Kanhaiya, answering the question as if he had just been asked how many combat missions he had flown.

Gazing out of the back window I try to pick out distinguishing marks in the scrubland. 'This is all semi-arid,' says Devayani, indicating the surrounding landscape. Semi-arid is an understatement, I never knew there were this many shades of light brown.

Although he's not driving, Kanhaiya keeps his gaze fixed firmly on the road as he explains how the state's annual rainfall can fall in just three days. 'In Rajasthan sometimes you can get ten centimetres of rainfall in one hour.'

'What? Ten centimetres an hour? That is huge!'

'Sometimes it happen,' says Devayani leaning over the front seat to tell me. 'If we don't construct any check dam or rainwater harvesting structure that rainfall goes. It does not go inside the ground, it goes...' and with that she shoos imaginary water away with her hand, '...when we arrest this water with a check dam the groundwater recharges and that goes in the wells.'

So that is all there is to it, build a dam in a strategic place which stops the water, the water then soaks into the ground and this fills up the wells.

Stopping halfway up a hillside we step out on to a scrubland that is called Darugula Ka Bandha. The hills climb behind us with a few bits of brush over the slopes, and these knotted little skirmishes seem to be the only plant life in sight. It is only when Kanhaiya shows me, 'There. This is where the water comes,' that I begin to notice the gullies. They are cut into the earth, lightly scarring the ground and streaking downwards. At a second glance tiny signs of life become a bit more obvious, piles of stones dislodged by once rushing water have tumbled down only to re-lodge at a lower point, making untidy altars where they gather. 'Water comes down quickly, here and here and here,' he says pointing. Then smiling for the first time he says, 'Shall we see the structure?'

A short walk downhill leads to a dam made of earth about five metres high, its sloping sides and flat top make it look like a Toblerone that has had its tip filed off. 'This fills with 3.5 metres of water when it rains,' says Kanhaiya pointing at the dry pit behind the dam. Then he strides along a pathway on top of the earthen mound. As we follow him Devayani explains that the villagers collect money for the materials but use their own labour to build each pond or dam. We catch up with Kanhaiya looking downhill, and with small gesture of his hand, he points us to the other side of the dam and a wooden hut, a well with upright supports and a winding rope but most remarkably a garden – a vegetable garden. In the middle of a landscape Neil Armstrong would feel at home in there are tomato plants. Kanhaiya and Devayani point in turn.

'Mustard.'

'Wheat.'

'Black gram.'

And to crown the scene a young papaya tree stands upright in defiance of its surroundings.

The rest of the day is full such moments but my favourite was the village of Palpura, where the local rainwater harvesting structures culminate in a pond area. Climbing over a low wall we set off towards clumps of bright green tall grass.

'This is elephant grass,' laughs Devayani.

'Elephant?'

'Yes, because it is tall enough for an elephant to hide in.'

Kanhaiya is ahead of us again and, turning into the grass, he disappears. We find him walking carefully along an overflow, slippery with algae and a slight but steady cascade of water. Walking out after him on to the concrete I look up the pond, about a hundred metres long and maybe forty wide in places. Gulls swoop on it. Egrets emerge by the bullrushes, dragonflies hover and fish peep from under small lilies. A white temple sits on one bank where a troop of monkeys roam under the sound of the peacocks yowl.

'Sorry, what was that?' enquires Devayani standing next to me on the overflow.

'Oh, it's just an expression. It's very colloquial, very hard to translate. It means this is very beautiful.'

I had not realised she was quite so close behind and had overheard my muttered words of awe, 'Fuck me! I'm in a Yes album cover.'

As we stand on the overflow, listening to the burbling water I decide to mention the C word and say, 'Coca-Cola claim they put more water into the ground than they take out, is that possible?'

'How much they take out?' says Devayani.

'Well, it varies, but a million litres a day at some points.'

'Does the company protect the water that much every day?' she says in contempt and disbelief that the company can put an equal amount of water back into the ground.

'They say they do...'

'That is not possible, it is impossible.'

'Why?'

'Because you don't get that much rain every day.'

'But they say they do put more water in than they get out...'

'Only a local community can protect, maintain and manage water resources properly. If you hand over water resources to a big company they could not think about the local situation, of how to protect these resources. So if any company construct a rainwater harvesting structure it is not enough for conservation.'

Undoubtedly Kanhaiya and Devayani have performed small miracles and I am looking at one right now, but there is just not enough science in their answer.

* * *

I am not sure where these past days have led in regard to Coca-Cola. Everyone has said Coke can't recharge the amount of water they claim to, but no one has proven this. No one has factually explained their claims. So have Coke's critics got it wrong? I don't know. The only thing I know for sure is I started as a sceptic, believing rainwater harvesting to be a pseudo-science and find myself lying on an old mattress in an ashram with a sense of genuine wonder. I curl up and sleep the sleep of a convert.

Having managed to stay here without being reborn, changing my name, getting a henna tattoo or even playing hacky sack with Dutch travellers recovering from dysentery, I bid farewell to the two-frog chorus in the dormitory; whom I have grown rather fond of and have nicked named Paul and Linda. Travelling south to Kaladera I arrive with genuine trepidation at Coke's rainwater harvesting structures.

'Hindustan Coca-Cola together in Development' reads the wind-blown sign by the side of the track, announcing we have arrived at one of Coke's much-vaunted projects. 'Kaladera a dream', it reads, sounding more ambiguous than the company's statements on the matter. If my dad had seen the sign he would have said it was 'on the piss' as it leans heavily to one side. However, according to the information on the board Coke has dug seventy filtered boreholes to a depth of 103 feet to recharge the local water supply. Apparently this benefits not only the farmers but the local area as well. This sounds simple and practical: rainwater trickles down through various thicknesses of gravel in the hole and percolates into the groundwater, instead of running off or evaporating.

These holes are laid along an old dry riverbed in the middle of an expanse of barren scrubland, where the sandy soil crunches underfoot, clear and crunchy like walking on stale crisps. A few trees make the effort but I've seen more flora and fauna in a builder's yard. It is hot, dusty and virtually featureless, exactly the kind of place you'd bump into Ray Winstone while filming a Costa del Crime caper. The first borehole is a metre wide concrete circle, about half a metre deep before the first layer of gravel starts. It is surrounded by a few bits of rubble and a plastic bottle. The second hole is every inch as glamorous as the first, except this time a three-course brick circle has been built around the hole. Someone later took exception to it and kicked some of the bricks over. Possibly fans of the first hole gripped by inter hole rivalry.

There are another sixty-eight to go...

Across the way is a concrete road leading to the home of one Kaladera's politicians, an ex-Panchayat leader. They must have got along very well with Coke as the company has installed a metal hand pump just outside their home, for the community obviously, though in this case the community seems to be mainly the Panchayat leader's family. A man from the village emerges from a palm leaf shelter by the side of the old Panchayat leader's home and offers to crank the groaning handle up and down to illustrate the pump in action. After five minutes he is hotter and thirstier than when he started. 'It's useless,' he says, 'sometimes you can get water but it can take half an hour to bring it up.' It is Coca-Cola we have to thank for this thirty-minute wait, after all they have alleged they are a net contributor to the groundwater, so without their help there would be even less water and it would take even longer to draw the water. The villager walks back to the shade of the shelter muttering – possibly a hymn of praise to Coca-Cola.

The TERI report – Coke's commissioned work – noted that field visits to randomly chosen external recharge shaft sites 'revealed that all the shafts were in a dilapidated condition.'[7]

From what I can see out here I would agree. The place is dilapidated. Frankly, Pompeii looks in better condition and that was buried under volcanic ash. Coke claim they do the maintenance work just before the monsoon.[8] I suppose it doesn't matter what it looks like if it does the job, though at this stage I am convinced of nothing.

* * *

Someone has to know something about the veracity of Coke's claim and that someone might well be Professor Rathore, a Senior Fellow at the Institute of Development Studies in Jaipur, whose data is quoted in the TERI report. The professor specialises in water resource management and the fine academic tradition of vertical filing systems. Stacks of reports, articles, notes and statistics form tall ordered blocks around the room. So prominent are these piles that if ever a map were to be drawn of it, this would be the first study to require contour lines. The walls are covered in hydro porn, pictures of large bodies of water, bare-arsed reservoirs and cheeky lakes. And stuck in one corner a board has term information, phone numbers, timetables and official pronouncements tacked on with drawing pins. I find the room strangely reassuring, it smacks of the twin pillars of academia: obsession and overwork.

The professor sits behind his desk between two more literal pillars. He is somewhere in his fifties, and has (like many Indian men) innate trust in his ink pen's durability and craftsmanship, as it sits neatly in the top pocket of his spotless white shirt. He peers over his glasses before taking them off and exudes the demeanour of an educator, that is an air of quiet and calm exasperation, a man who has had to explain the obvious too many times.

'It is the rainfall pattern of Rajasthan which is important,' says the professor. 'If the rainfall is low, then the withdrawal is much more than the water that is being recharged through the rainfall. So it's a perpetual depletion of the groundwater.'

This much everyone seems to agree on. What I want to know is can Coke put up to fifteen times the amount of water they use in production back in the ground, so I start to ask my question, 'The company are saying that they are using rainwater harvesting projects to recharge...'

'It doesn't work,' he says shaking his head sadly.

'But,' I begin again, 'one of the rainwater harvesting projects which they've got is on a dried riverbed, they've got seventy bore holes—'

'That's the wrong thing,' He interrupts flicking his hand dismissively.

'Why is that the wrong thing?'

'Ask them how many times that river flowed, you will be shocked to know that in a year, in five years...OK, I'll have to show you something.' And with that he rummages in a pillar and plucks out a single piece of paper, showing the number of times the Jaipur area has been in drought. These are the figures that show that the area has been in drought for 47 per cent of the last 106 years.

Jaipur district frequency of occurrence of drought and its intensity since 1901-2006

Number of years district of Jaipur over past 106 years

- 56 years normal
- 10 years light drought
- 17 years moderate drought
- 12 years serious drought
- 11 years very serious drought

Source: Professor Rathore, Institute of Development Studies Jaipur

After staring quietly at the piece of paper I look up at his expectant face and say 'So there is not enough rain...'

He affords a brief smile, 'There is no run off,' he says, referring back to the dry riverbed that won't run without rain. 'So you build a structure and it doesn't work. It will work only when there is a run off. OK? That run off only takes place one or two years, and how much is that? Very small, so these rainwater harvesting structures are to bluff people, and the state.'

'And it doesn't work because the riverbed...'

'Because of these reasons: the rainfall is very meagre; rainy days are very limited; droughts are a perpetual phenomenon, and where is the run off? Where is recharge? Where's the water going to come from?'

The professor makes the simple point that you can't do rainwater harvesting without rainwater. But I still can't quite believe Coke's credibility rests solely on this, so I try and sneak in one more attempt. 'Is there a way the company could do rainwater harvesting in a meaningful way in the area?'

'No, it's just not possible, it's not possible.' He holds his hand up and sighs. 'Coca-Cola also have a right to do business, we don't contest that but we contest that you can spoil the lives of so many people. You may have Coca-Cola or any brewery industry, but the source of water should not be groundwater, it should be surface water.'

Then looking out from between his two pillars of statistics and reports, unprompted he says, 'If I am chief minister in charge of this, I will stop today the industry, and ship it from that place. I will give them choice. Go to Kota Barrage, go to Indira Gandhi Canal, or quit, there's no other choice. Go to Namada, if you want, but not here, don't have groundwater as your source.'

* * *

So I'm left with Coke's claim that 'even in recent years when rainfall has been below average, actual recharge has been more than five times the amount of water used for production of our beverages.'[9]

I asked Coke if they would show me their figures and assumptions on which they base that claim. After a bit of a wait, they sent me a document compiled by a retired chief engineer that detailed each structure and its expected annual groundwater recharge. And unsurprisingly, it calculates that with normal rainfall the structures can recharge ten times what Coke takes out. In the case of less rainfall, that figure drops to five times. Which is still very impressive, and surely worthy of a little celebration. But before the corks are popped it is worth remembering that these figures are not verifiable.

There are no measuring devices. And around here no one's celebrating. Not the farmers, not Rajendra Singh, not the people who made the river flow again in Alwa and not Professor Rathore. Even TERI say, 'Water contingency measures as adopted by the plant seem to rely heavily on rainwater recharge structures, which in turn depend on rainfall in the region. Since the rainfall is scanty, the recharge achieved through such structures is unlikely to be meaningful.'[10] Everyone except Coca-Cola and their retired engineer says, 'no rain, no recharge'.

Perhaps it's too obvious a solution that maybe Coke could just actually measure the water its collecting, rather than merely 'trying' to do so. So I offer a different solution: if, Coca-Cola, you are so very sure in your historical data and attempted measurements that you harvest so many times more water than you use, why not just use the water you harvest instead of extracting it from the aquifer? You could store your harvested water and extract it at your leisure. Then, when you give back the five, ten or fifteen times more than you need, everyone will see exactly what great guys you are.

I agree with The Coca-Cola Company when they say the 'burden of truth is on us', their trouble is no one around here believes them.

* * *

Professor Rathore smiles politely and looks at his watch, by way of ending our chat, fortunately I am socially inept so I plough on.

'If it carries on, what will happen, what do you think will happen?'

He raises his eyebrows in concern and says, 'Very soon they'll realise that industry has to close. It cannot survive, not more than four, five years definitely. Because the water quality will deplete, it will be so bad they cannot use it.'

Of all the answers I did not expect, this was about the most unexpected.

'So you're saying that industry has got four or five years here, and then it's finished?'

'Yes, it's definitely finished,' he says stretching slightly.

'What happens then to the communities?'

'Ruined...There'll be no drinking water available to them.'

INDIA:
A POSTQUEL

When I asked the Hindustan Coca-Cola Beverages Pvt Ltd if I could come and see their plant in Kaladera they refused saying I was 'biased'.

I reply using The Coca-Cola Company method of issue resolution and advanced rebuttal techniques.

'We are proud of the Mark Thomas system of objectivity and are appalled by these unfounded allegations levelled against him. Only recently Mark Thomas became the proud winner of the prestigious Emerald Eagle Award for Unbiased Reporting, the judges cited his even-handed dealing with The Coca-Cola Company as a case in point. But perhaps more importantly Mark Thomas has launched a bold and innovative truth harvesting and trading scheme initiative, where journalists in truth deficit can purchase unused truths on the open market, with exciting possibilities in the expanding markets in truth developing regions of Russia, Italy and the *Daily Express* news desk.

'Even in "truth drought" regions he has managed to recharge the equivalent of five times the amount of falsehoods extracted.

'It is a journey, he is not there yet, but it is one that Mark Thomas is committed to making and he aims to become completely bias neutral by 2011.

'Mark Thomas's book will create over 10,000 indirect jobs.'

12
SECOND FATTEST IN THE INFANTS

Mexico

'You know the bottom line is that we welcome competition... if the Pepsi company didn't exist we would have to invent them...but we welcome the increased competition because the voice behind the industry is, y'know, a rising tide floats all ships.'

Neville Isdell, The Coca-Cola Company Annual Meeting 2008

Mexico is *the* Coca-Cola country. This is what the landscape looks like when Coca-Cola invades and occupies a country, this is the view as the smoke clears from a marketing blitzkreig. Mexicans drink more

Coca-Cola products than anyone else on the planet, on average over 135 litres of stuff every year. Per Person.

And it is beginning to show. Mexicans are among the fattest people on the planet and are piling on the pounds at a rate that would alarm even Robbie Williams. In 1989 less than 10 per cent of Mexicans were overweight.[1] That figure is now over 68 per cent and rising.[2] Perhaps it is no coincidence that in the last fourteen years, the consumption of soft drinks has increased by 60 per cent;[3] it is also perhaps no coincidence that Coke spends a fifth of its global advertising budget in Mexico alone.

But despite controlling over 70 per cent[4] of the $6.5bn Mexican soft drinks industry,[5] Coca-Cola wanted more. This is the story of how Coca-Cola and its aggressive marketing were exposed by the determination of one working-class shopkeeper who wouldn't be bullied.

* * *

Arriving in Mexico City I start by visiting a man who I hope can explain the basics of why Mexico is plumping up. His name is Alejandro Calvillo and he founded El Poder del Consumidor – the Power of the Consumer – which runs a campaign called Dump the Soda. He has spent some time and thought trying to answer the question 'how did they get to be so big?' The 'they' in this case refers both to Coca-Cola and its drinkers.

Alejandro operates out of a shared building set in a quiet cobbled alleyway along the road from a squat church. Other NGOs work here too and Alejandro has his office set in the communal garden. He used to work for Greenpeace before leaving to form his own campaigning group, taking the compulsory environmentalist beard with him – though it is trimmed enough to reveal a lean and kind face. When he started El Poder del Consumidor he went back to basics. 'We began with a review at the office of information. We had a shock. It's terrible what's happening in Mexico. We found Mexico is the second-highest country in the world for obesity.'

But it isn't just the adult statistics that are alarming. More worryingly, the number of children between five and eleven who are obese or overweight has increased by 40 per cent in seven years. And El Poder del Consumidor lays the blame for Mexico's obesity problem on the soft drinks industry, 'Sodas have become the main source of refined sugar intake among the Mexican people and therefore the main responsibility for the current intake that has led to overweight problems and obesity.'

'So what we've seen here is a quite big explosion, ' I say.

'Yes.'

'In quite a short time.'

'Yes...and in this panorama Coke sell 12 per cent of all their world sales in Mexico.'

And Mexico makes up just 1.65 per cent of the world's population.

Alejandro explains that one of the factors in the popularity of soft drinks is Mexico's lack of clean available drinking water, 'water fountains in schools in particular. If children can't have water they buy sodas.' And this is a country where 80 per cent of schools have no drinking water.[6] For the majority of children, soda consumption isn't a choice.

Coke's dominance of this market might be...well, how can I put this sensitively...it can't hurt to have the ex-President of Coca-Cola Mexico as the President of Mexico. Vicente Fox was the man who did that very thing, rising through the Coca-Cola system before branching out into non-drink-based politics.

FOX FACTS: From President of Coca-Cola Mexico to President of Mexico, Coca-Cola Country

President Fox's six-year term was between 2000-2006. According to Coca-Cola's own figures Coke sales increased 56.5 per cent between 1997 and 2007 - a period that coincides with Fox's Presidency.[7] It's not conclusive proof that he helped the company but he was seen selling cans of Coke during toilet breaks in the Mexican Parliament.*

During the Fox administration several things 'happened' that might be seen as beneficial to the company.

The first involves an artificial sweetener called cyclamate, banned from use in the USA and Mexico as it had been linked to cancer. One of the last acts of Fox's administration was to lift the ban on its use. Coke appeared to jump at the chance to use cyclamate as it is massively cheaper than aspartame and launched Coke Zero containing the sweetener in Mexico almost immediately after the ban was lifted. A massive backlash followed - led by El Poder del Consumidor and Alejandro - and the Ministry of Health even issued warnings over its consumption. Coke bowed to consumer pressure and removed cyclamate from the ingredients.[8] It is a well-known fact that during toilet breaks in the Mexican Parliament President Fox was seen using unsold Coke Zero containing cyclamate to clean the toilets.**

The other major helping hand Coke received during Fox's tenure was a change in the law that allowed Coca-Cola to bag generous twenty-year fixed-rate water concessions from the National Water Commission (CONAGUA). The man appointed to head up CONAGUA is an ex-Coca-Cola man Cristobal Jaime Jaquez.[9] Fox exchanged these concessions for cigarettes in the toilets in the Mexican Parliament where he smoked, a habit he kept secret from his wife.***

But the big reason Coca-Cola has got such a hold here is the combination of advertising and aggressive marketing practices. Coke spends a fifth of its annual advertising and marketing budget in Mexico alone,[10] or if we 'do the math', that's US$4.54 for every Mexican man woman and child to persuade them to consume kilos of sugar every year. Let us pray heroin dealers never get an advertising budget.

Just as Coke's advertising budget is huge, so its sales teams are trained to work aggressively – to the extent of illegality. The Coca-Cola Export Corporation (a wholly owned subsidiary of the Atlanta-based Coca-Cola Company) and its Mexican bottlers have been found guilty of unfair monopoly practices by the Mexican Federal Competition Commission and fined the maximum penalty thanks in large part to a small shop owner called Raquel Chavez and a cheeky newcomer into the Mexican cola market, Big Cola.

When Peruvian drinks company, AjeGroup launched its star product in Mexico nobody, least of all Coca-Cola, predicted its success. An explanation for which can be found in its name, Big Cola – it was sold in really big bottles for a similar price to its smaller rivals and was a cola, two things that were bound to appeal to a cash-poor, sugar-hungry people. Within two years, it had captured 5 per cent of the market. Not a killer blow for Coke and in actuality more threatening to Pepsi but Coke's response was to hit back and hit back hard. And one of the things they did was cut off the supply of Coca-Cola to shop owners if they dared to stock their Peruvian rival, which

---

This is apparently not true but only in the sense that I have no facts to prove it.

** *This is absolutely true in the lying sense of the word.*

*** *Once again a truth waiting to happen...but technically a lie.*

is what they did to Raquel Chavez and her small shop. However she took the company to court and won, and along the way exposed a vicious national campaign of intimidation and coercion.

The lawyers from Big Cola have agreed to chat about the case so I head out to their offices in a newly developed business district – although the rate of development in Mexico City is so fast by the time you read this, it will probably be referred to as 'the old town'. Around the sculpted plains of these high-rise business parks there is a competition among companies to see who can put the most people into ill-fitting guards' jackets and place them around the building entrance. Here the parking lots seem full of black company cars still smelling of their new paint parked alongside enormous 4x4s, which for some reason all contain a single sports bag in the boot. But despite the conspicuous company culture the more lumpen branch of entrepreneurialism is evident all around, as along the street the irrepressible food stalls have sprung up like a crop. These makeshift wooden frames and their tarpaulin coverings are held together with bull clips big enough to trap a poacher, and under them Calor gas burners roar and frying pans the size of car tyres smoke with oil. Delivery boys and secretaries huddle around to stare into pots heating purple black beans and at grills turning corn breads brown. A police van has pulled up too, the cops get out, order *toastas* wrapped in napkins and then eat them leaning forward away from their uniform, for fear of dripping chilli sauce.

In one of these new company high-rises is a meeting room belonging to La Arena Trevilla Hernandez Y de la Torre, a legal firm who represented Big Cola. The room has the type of intense air-conditioning that can induce nosebleeds, and the walls hold a plasma TV and a presentation screen. To the side of a long desk, by the best chair in the room, is a pentangular conference call phone, with a big light underneath that flashes when it rings – it looks like a plastic electric starfish bought in a pound shop but it passes for flash around here.

Seated on the other side of the table is a lawyer, he might represent the people who sell big cheap cola but he sips small expensive bottles of water. He has requested that I do not name him, somewhat bizarrely given that his work has hitherto not been anonymous, so let us refer to him by the pseudonym 'Dan'.

Dan leans back in his chair and says, 'In Mexican culture a person who goes to buy a soft drink will never go to a big shop, they will always to got the corner shop...small shops where the owner is a family and the whole family depends on that shop to make ends meet.' There are 700,000 such shops in Mexico and 80 per cent of all soft drinks are sold through them. 'In mid 2002 a new soft drink called Big Cola was introduced. It started in the market offering a product, which is cheaper, and of better quality,' continues Dan, 'the company got 3 per cent of the market share in a year.'

In the lucrative soft drinks market this represents a major prize and one that Coca-Cola was not willing to give up easily. Dan explains that by April 2003 'Big Cola started to realise that the small shops had stopped buying their products.
    'Why?'
    He pauses.
    'Because Coca-Cola were using their muscle to stop the small shops selling it...' I say answering the question that wasn't intended for me to answer.
    'In mid-2003 Mrs Raquel Chavez together with other five shops denounce Coca-Cola to the Federal Competition

Commission because Coca-Cola had stopped selling Coke to her.'

'So they stopped selling to her because she sold Big Cola?' I chip in.

He nods.

The FCC found that Coke had been conducting a widescale campaign against Big Cola and so 'concludes that these are monopolistic activities which are aimed at removing Big Cola from the market. The authority imposed the biggest fine ever known in Mexico of $50,000,000 on Coca-Cola. This is the first time that a fine like this has ever given in the country...Everything was started thanks to Raquel Chavez.'

'Did you represent Raquel Chavez?'

'No, I was the lawyer of Big Cola. Mrs Raquel Chavez and the others did not have a lawyer. They are very poor people.'

We chat about the case and he gets some papers for me, but it is Raquel Chavez I want to see. I have been having problems trying to track her down. So I ask the lawyer if he knows has a current address for her.

'Have you got an address for Raquel?' I ask.

'She lives in Itzapalapa.'

'Oh, I should go and see her, she sounds great!' I say, reigning in my over-enthusiam for meeting Raquel that is clearly not shared by the present company.

'It is very difficult to get there and it is very dangerous, ' says Dan, though the assessment of danger by a man thus cloaked in anonymity might not be the most accurate.

Dan's parting gift had been a telephone number for Raquel Chavez, so all I had to do was phone her to arrange a visit to her shop and a chat. Unfortunately the line is dead and no pleading with the operator will bring it back to life. A journalist working in Mexico City says he has another phone number for her, different from the first. But that too does not work. So as I head towards the Metro station I call all the contacts I have once again to see if any of them have any new leads in my hunt for this elusive woman. The messages I leave on these poor people's answer machines are increasingly desperate – a mixture of begged favours, twisted arms, and promises I can't keep. But someone must have a working phone number for her. As I descend the stairs I can only wait and hope it comes through.

* * *

I am getting to that age where I find travelling by foreign public transport to be quite exciting. I actually believe there should be an intermediary Freedom Pass for people like me, who are not technically in retirement but have adopted some of its attributes early. Nonetheless I love the fact that the Mexico City Metro stations not only have a station name but they also have their own pictoral representation – an individual logo for illiterate travellers to guide themselves by. Which also has the incidental benefit of enabling ignorant tourists to use them too. On one journey I boarded the train at the station of the 'jug of water with wavy lines' then zipped past the 'wasp' changed at the 'two snakes wrapped around a sword', stayed on as we went by the 'white cross' and then the 'cannon' too, finally getting off at the 'silhouette of an army bloke'.

Charles Dickens would have loved the Metro, all forms of urchin life are here. The carriages are packed but somehow the tide of hawkers runs a path around the cramped bodies: men selling peanuts, women waving packs of Chiclets chewing gum, a line of blind beggars and a woman selling Superglue. Who would have thought that there was a commuting market for Superglue? But here there must be.

My favourites are the home-made CD compilation sellers, playing their tracks on a portable player wired into a loudspeaker strapped to their chests - they look like jihadist DJs. One minute the carriage is filled with the sounds of salsa, the next it is dance music; one man's CD was so good I nearly missed the 'two snakes wrapped around a sword' and only just made it through the doors in time. On the platform the station's own speakers forlornly played 'I'd rather be a hammer than a nail' on pan pipes.

While feeling a tad despondent that no one had called me with Raquel Chavez's phone number, something rather remarkable happened. I got a source. Someone from inside Coke, willing to talk on condition of anonymity and this time there really was good reason not to name this person. Woodward and Bernstein had 'Deep throat'; I have 'Coke Throat'.

What can I tell you about Coke Throat? Well, essentially not a huge amount except that I was passed a piece of paper with a phone number and a time to dial it. I waited and dialled. A voice answered and asked me 'Are you having a good time in Mexico Mr Thomas?'

I said, 'Getting a stranger's phone number is often the way a good time starts.'

Coke Throat laughed but only just.

'I think you might want to talk to me.'

And that was the beginning of a beautiful friendship.

Coke Throat sang loud and long. So did Nana Mouskouri. But this stuff wasn't Greek to me.

Coke Throat knew all about the big trouble with Big Cola and was keen to tell me how it started. Instead of using sales staff, distribution warehouses and a fleet of delivery trucks, Big Cola opted for a more innovative distribution method and caught

Coke on the hop. The Peruvians simply said anyone who has a truck or even a car can come to the warehouse, pick up crates of drink and go and sell it on commission to the 'Mom and Pop' stores. These 700,000 'Mom and Pop' stores account for 80 per cent of soft drink sales in Mexico, so Big Cola were able to simply bypass the normal practice of setting up a sales force and delivery system and still get their product into the market. According to Coke Throat, the sudden arrival of Big Cola in these stores, 'gave them a huge massive presence that Coke never expected so that, combined with the nice pricing they have, almost 40-50 per cent cheaper than us, was why a lot of low-income consumers switched their preference to Big Cola and it started to hit us...we underestimated that product and it came and hit us in the face.'

Mexico offers soft drinks companies an extremely lucrative profit margin and with so much money at stake Coca-Cola decided something had to be done. 'The idea was to start blocking them at the point of sale,' Coke Throat explained. 'It was like that at the very beginning.' Coke assembled its sales force with the simple tactic. 'The name of the game is availability, if Big Cola was available, Big Cola has a winning formula that can sell. So the idea was to remove them, and if you are a salesman and if you have a hundred stores you should not have more than five stores selling Big Cola [in your area]. That was the benchmark.'

The operation against Big Cola even had its own name, 'The ABC plan – Anti Big Cola plan.' Local comedians were hired to appear in training videos for the sales forces, 'training them how to remove Big Cola from the point of sales and the consequence of not doing that. So less income, less job security and not having their nice house at retirement.'

Coke's assault was a well-coordinated strike at the 'Mom and Pop shops' that stocked Big Cola, Coke Throat called it 'the red wave' and they used a variety of tactics.

'There was the direct change of Big Cola products for Coca-Cola products.'

'You take Big Cola out of the shop physically?' I enquire.

'Physically, yes.'

'You swap it bottle for bottle...'

'Bottle for bottle...I'm the salesman I see this Big Cola bottle I switch it for a Coke and throw the other to the garbage or throw it in the street so the shop doesn't sell it now.' In some cases the sales force would empty Big Cola down the drains in front of the shop.

'But why would a shop swap?'

'You offer two for one.

Coke Throat goes on to describe how the sales force would issue a 'direct order to remove Big Cola from any Coca-Cola cooler in the shop. [They would tell the store owner] that they would be losing the cooler if they have one Big Cola available either in the cooler or even in the store.'

Just to be clear I go over it again, 'So you would say to them if you have Big Cola in the fridge here, it's a Coca-Cola fridge, get the Big Cola out or I'm taking the fridge.'

'Exactly, or get Big Cola out of the store or I won't supply you with Coca-Cola.'

It all sounds slightly Al Capone with carbonation, going round to stores and intimidating or cajoling shopkeepers to get rid of Big Cola and I say, 'That's almost like Mafia tactics isn't it? '

Coke Throat affords a smile, 'Well, let's just call it protecting my market share.'

The big question is who sanctioned this?

'Very clear, from top to bottom, it was a well-organised army going into war.'

'So was this the Mexican bottlers...' I begin.

'It was Coca-Cola who coordinated it with bottlers, [we're] the brain power and the mastermind behind everything...we bring a lot of practices from other countries, we put them on the table and we find strategy with local knowledge, that might be the bottlers, we define it and then we go to war.'

'We wanted to get out of this saying to people "we do not sell Coca-Cola and we didn't do anything, we just sell concentrate" but the reality – and that's why the competition commission brought us down – was that we have the brainpower and are the money behind everything and we are the ones that make everything work in a synchronised way.' The FCC investigation visited various shops to examine the claims against Coca-Cola and found that Big Cola was either not available or was placed way at the back of the shop, away from the Coca-Cola fridges at the front, in 500 instances that they examined. The 'red wave' had struck across Mexico.

* * *

On 4 July 2005 the FCC fined the 'Coca-Cola system' $157 million pesos (approx USD$13 million) for monopolistic practices, as Coke's conduct contravened Article 10 Part IV of the Federal Law of Economic Competition. The fine was levelled at the bottlers and distributors FEMSA, Contal, Grupo Peninsular, Grupo Fomento Queretano as well as The Coca-Cola Export Company (Mexico) which is a subsiduary of The Coca-Cola Company. They were also ordered to immediately stop putting conditions on the sale of Coke products. The decision was appealed by Coke. But on 17 November 2005, the CFC ruled upheld the earlier decision and threw Coke's appeal out.[11]

As for Raquel Chavez the search was not going well, the six degrees of separation theory – that we are all but six phone calls away from the person we need to reach, the very theory that had worked its bizarre charm in Turkey – was failing to find her. True, it had turned up some interesting and charming folk along the way, including a former guerilla, a workers' co-op and someone who knew someone who knew someone that could summon up the ghost of Leon Trotsky, but no Raquel Chavez. Not even an address for her shop. I trawled the internet looking for clues and found a couple of pictures of her from when she won the case. She was forty-nine in 2005 and photographed sitting in her small shop amidst its grilles and crates. She had black shoulder-length hair and a flowery top – that was all I could make out.

The part of town she lived in was called Itzapalapa and it quickly developed the status of a desolate moor, as every time I mentioned the place in the presence of a Mexican – be it a receptionist at a hotel or local folk I was meeting up with – they would pause significantly, adopt a Cornish accent and say, 'You don't want to go up there sir, not on a night like tonight.'

'Why?' I would ask.

'Why sir, the last tourist that went up there by 'em self never came back...though they do say on a dark moonless night you can hear the pages of a Rough Guide book a'rustlin' in the breeze.'

I was beginning to think somehow I missed the boat. Everyone I asked seemed to know someone who might know how to get to her but then never did. And time simply ran out. Or it nearly did. A telephone number was found at the last minute and although I didn't get to see her I did finally speak to Raquel Chavez over the phone.

She does indeed live in Itzapalapa and it is indeed a tad...
er...Moss Side. Some have called it impoverished, others worse
but Raquel says 'We are a working-class area. This is a
difficult area,' then adds, 'as everywhere is.'

'I wanted to meet you personally but I have only just got
your phone number,' I explain, ' all the numbers I had for you
were dead.'

'I had to change all the telephone numbers. After I won the
case against Coca-Cola people thought I had won thirteen
million dollars. But the fines go to the judicial system I had
not won any money. So people phoned. I got death threats, I
got blackmail attempts, people phoned up just wanting me to
give them money. But what could I do with all these people
threatening me? I had to make ends meet. I still have to go to
work – I just had to change the phones.'

Then she told me her story. Raquel wanted what many
working-class parents want: for her children to have a better
life than her own. 'My biggest dream was to give them a
professional career and get them to go to university. I was in a
economic bind, so I started the shop and I started with all my
energy and enthusiasm in 1992.' It was on the corner of mall
but it was a 'Mom and Pop shop'.

Then in 2002 her Coke salesman came by and politely
asked 'Why don't you swap your Big Cola bottles for Coca-
Cola? I will give you two bottles of Coke for every one bottle of
Big Cola you give me.'

Recounting the moment to me she explained, 'If I accepted
they would give me the Coca-Cola and would take away the
Big Cola but the condition was that I could not sell Big Cola
any more.'

'What did you say to the Coke salesman?'

'I said "No. My shop is free. Even if it is only one customer who wants Big Cola I have to offer him the best service." He was very upset and annoyed.'

The Coke salesman had obviously seen one of the training videos that Coke Throat described, as Raquel's initial refusal didn't deter him. But Raquel kept saying no.

One day the salesman came into her shop and started again, 'Mrs Chavez, come on, I will give you two bottles of Coca-Cola for every bottle of Big Cola you give to me.'

'No,' said Raquel ' Not even if it is ten bottles of Coke to one of Big Cola will I do it.' And the salesman left.

A little later he came round again, this time arrogant and cocky, 'OK,' he said 'We will give you ten for one – I will give you ten bottles of Coca-Cola for one for Big Cola.' I suspect he even afforded himself a little knowing smile. He simply did not expect Raquel to say 'No. I won't let you buy me.'

So it began. At first they refused to give her any promotional presents or offers; the other shops had them, but not hers. Then they wanted to only allow Coke products in the Coke fridge in the shop. She said to the salesman, 'You can take your fridge away. I can buy one myself.'

The Bank Holiday in March is a big day and lot of drinks get sold. So Raquel placed her orders with 'Pre-sales – there is a person who comes round the day before and asks what we need and the following day the truck comes and brings the drinks. But they didn't bring any to my shop. They left me during that important Bank Holiday without a bottle.'

The following day when the truck came around she rushed out and gave them a new order on a handwritten note.

'Why didn't you deliver my order?' She said and started back to her shop.

The manager came after her holding her order in his hand and waving it in the air.

'Are you going to bring my order now then?'

But he kept waving the paper in the air. Smirking.

'You are not allowed any of our products any more,' he said.

'What? Why not?' She said, dumbfounded.

'Because you don't support us and because you won't stop selling Big Cola.'

'This is unconstitutional!' said Raquel, not knowing if it was or it wasn't.

'No,' he said, 'Coca-Cola does what they want...You can do whatever you want. Coca-Cola has too many lawyers and too much money. No one can touch them.' He waved her order in the air, 'If you want this you know what to do.'

'No, thank you,' she replied.

And with that they stopped bringing the products for good.

The trouble is people drink a lot of Coca-Cola in Mexico and if the shop doesn't have it then that shop loses a lot of custom.

'People are too used to buying Coke so people stopped coming to my shop and I didn't see them any more. I was completely alone. I had to start to work long hours into the evening and try to recover what I hadn't sold during the day. I lost a lot of money, I think I lost 50 per cent of my income at that time. Fridays and Saturdays I shut the shop at 2am,' she sighs. 'Too many hours for too little profit. Even my husband was upset with me.'

'How dare you do that against them,' he had said. 'You know they are very powerful, they will ruin us.'

On one rare day when she was away from the shop she asked her husband to mind it and on that day the Big Cola salesman came around. Her husband promptly cancelled the Big Cola orders. They did not stay cancelled for long. Raquel returned to her shop, and just as promptly reordered the Big Cola. Her husband simply didn't understand, he kept asking, 'What is it you want? What is it you want?'

Finally Raquel went to Federal Competition Commission to denounce Coca-Cola and ask them to investigate. 'I asked them "What can I do?"'

'What can we do?' they retorted.

'You are the Federal Competition Commission!'

'What can we do when no one will denounce them? When there are more people in the same situation I will talk to you.'

So Raquel went and found others.

Her husband became unhappier still. 'He kept putting a lot of pressure on me because of The Coca-Cola case.' But Raquel said to him, 'I would prefer to close the shop, and go and wash clothes in other people's houses in order for my children to have an education, but I won't let Coca-Cola humiliate me. I will never let them humiliate me.'

And she didn't. The FCC found The Coca-Cola Export Company, a direct subsidiary of The Coca-Cola Company in Atlanta, guilty along with the bottlers and fined them in November 2005. As Raquel said she gets no money as the fines go to the state. So why did she do it?

'Although economically I didn't win anything I wanted to have the pride of winning. My motivation was my pride... Raquel Chavez will always be a sour name for Coca-Cola and it will always be like that. I am very proud of myself.'

* * *

Recently a student came to visit Raquel and she lent him the papers from her case, showing the verdict in her favour. He was doing a new course on monopoly practices in business and wanted to study her case. There is a certain joy that a woman who fought so hard for her children to go on to higher education should finally have her story being taught at university.

13

BELCHING OUT THE DEVIL

San Cristóbal, Mexico

> *'San Cristóbal is my Tara of Gone With the Wind. It's a place I go back to. It's the place where you get strength, where you get strong.'*

Vicente Fox, Interview with *Larry King Live*, CNN, 8 October 2007

I t was the city of San Cristóbal in the southern Mexican state of Chiapas that hosted the unlikely relaunch of the balaclava. Who would have thought a fashion comeback was ever on the cards? I for one thought its long association with peeping toms and the IRA had finished it off but it bounced right back into the limelight with Subcomandante Marcos of the Zapatistas when he boldly started to accessorise standard revolutionary army fatigues. Out went cigars and berets and in came balaclavas* and tobacco pipes. Through

---

* Balaclavas are referred to as ski masks in the USA but there is a major difference between these two items – namely, a British grandmother would never knit a ski mask.

the power of the internet Subcomandante Marcos, the enigmatic spokesman and poster boy for the Zapatistas Army of National Liberation or EZLN (Ejército Zapatista de Liberación Nacional), became a world-wide phenomenon. The Zapatista 1994 uprising was primarily the indigenous Mayan people's struggle against poverty and racism but they became synonymous with anti-globalisation and opposing neo-liberal economic changes. And for a while the picturesque city of San Cristóbal became the epicentre of Zapatista activity and it was to this city that the solidarity groups, sympathisers and curious lefties flocked to witness the struggle. These supporters became quaintly and quickly know as Zapatouristas.

San Cristóbal is somewhat quieter these days. The town square has a gentle pace to its colonial colonnades, the narrow side streets in pastel shades are lined with gift shops, all seemingly packed with crystals and small animals made of wood, sold to the tune of non-stop Manu Chau. It is the only place in the world I have been comfortable enough to wear my WOMAD T-shirt in public – an act I wouldn't normally do, even at WOMAD itself. The local artisans' market is predictably rammed with things made out of brightly coloured woven thread, hammocks, belts, wrist bands, bags, hats, plant pots – probably driving jackets and slacks too. Rows of stalls covered with canvas sheeting to keep the sun at bay, offer rugs, jugs and shoulder purses on string, next to necklaces and woollen reptiles, not to mention the endless array of small percussion instruments, flutes, pan pipes and wooden armadillos with a shaky tail. You can even get a balaclava with EZLN, the Zapatista acronym, sown in red over the brow – which must be the anarchist equivalent of a Kiss-Me-Quick hat.

The place is stuffed to the gills with arts and crafts crap – or as we like to call it in our house, 'ethnotat'. There are even

Zapatista dolls on sale, small woollen figures wearing balaclavas, riding donkeys and armed with rifles.

'Who buys this sort of shit?' I ask Laura, an American friend who lives here.

'Probably the same people who buy the Subcomandate Marcos pipes,' she says, then pointing to a display of carved beasts and metal trinkets, warns, 'Don't buy anything from that stall. All that stuff is made in China.'

These days even handcrafted, locally produced indigenous produce seems to be subcontracted. Later I wander past two cooing German tourists bent over the Chinese goods and I sneer in superiority, before heading home clutching my two Zapatista dolls and a pipe.

* * *

Laura is a twenty-four-year-old American student living in San Cristóbal. She is tall, with short black hair and very clever. She is working on a master's degree and her thesis is on the local Coca-Cola bottling plant: together we form a Coke obsessives' support group. Friends of hers find us huddled in cafés hunched over laptops, swapping documents and data or chuckling over an in joke about borehole capacities and water extraction rates. The pair of us are a research paper short of an identifiable dysfunctional condition.

The situation here is unlike India. To the best of my knowledge Coca-Cola has not opened up a plant in a drought-prone region of Mexico (although if anyone knows different please write). Chiapas is water rich; what it lacks is not rainfall but publicly available clean water.

The local bus service is a fleet of white battered combies with wooden seats in the back and a couple of rails to cling to when it gets too cramped – using these and the odd taxi Laura and I set off on a whistlestop trip around San Cristóbal.

Our first stop is San Cristóbal's water board, where I ask the receptionist if there is any chance that I can talk to someone about the city's water situation. She mutters in a phone while nearby a fan on a stand rattles loudly as it manfully loses the battle with the hot air. From behind an office door a head pokes out and beckons to us to enter. Jorge Mayorga is a cheery chubby chap with an obligatory moustache and dressed in a pale blue water board shirt.

'Please,' he says, pulling out chairs. Sitting behind his desk, hands clasped together, Jorge beams a smile in anticipation, waiting to be asked a question. He is either someone working for an organisation that wants to promote its activities to foreigners who might pop in with a few queries or he doesn't meet many people interested in his work. He is so impulsively friendly that within five minutes he is offering to give us a tour of the water pumping stations and treatment rooms in the area.

'I just wanted to get an overview of the city's water situation,' feeling my inner nerd flinch at his awesome power.

'OK,' he says and starts to explain part of the cause of the city's problems. 'There has been a big increase in the population of San Cristóbal.' He points out that back in 1991 the water board had 13,867 families on its books, now they have 34,900 families - and these are just the ones connected to the water supplies. He gets out a data sheet to illustrate the increase and even helps me understand the water distribution by drawing concentric circles in my notebook. The inner circle represents the centre of San Cristóbal where the hotels and bars are – in the tourist area tap water is available twenty-four hours a day – the middle circle represents households that get water for twelve hours a day and finally the outer circle have their taps working for six hours a day.

'That's a very good day if they manage that, ' says Laura,
'I live in the area that should get water twelve hours a day
and often that water doesn't come on at all, and when it does
you have to boil it for at least twenty minutes before you can
drink it.'

'When do you know it is OK to drink?

'You get this white powder, really fine grains that falls to the
bottom. God knows what it is but it ain't water. So when that
falls to the bottom I know I can drink the stuff on top of it.'

'What happens if you don't boil it?'

'You don't want to find out.'

Two days later I didn't and she's right – you don't.

* * *

San Cristóbal's Coordinator of Epidemiology in Sanitary
Jurisdiction No. II of the Highlands Region of Chiapas
has an office that is only marginally bigger than his
title. His name is Cuauhtemoc Zapata Cabrera and he is
another eager and smiling official. The building he works out
of is just by the abattoir, which is a bit too open-air for my
liking. The less brutal environs of his cosy office are cluttered
with papers, books, folders and kids' toys, which I assume is
to make them as happy as the physical state that drew them
here allows. Over the next half hour he explains that gastro-
enteritis is one of the top five sicknesses in the highlands of
Chiapas. In his district in 2006 there were 9,998 cases
involving intestinal amoebas, intestinal non-specific
organisms, giardia, paratyphoid, food poisoning due to
protozoa and the like. The infection rates are higher in the
indigenous communities and there is a focus on teaching the
importance of boiling water and how to soak food in iodine
and chlorine.

The lack of water, clean or otherwise, is a common story too. We bump into a friend of a friend of Laura's, a Spanish teacher called Yasmina who lives with her husband and children in an area that should get water six hours a day. In reality they get it 'Two or three times a week and maybe for three hours, sometimes four...We never know when it is going to come on, so we have a storage tank.' The next day her water went off and didn't come back on for two weeks.

And actually Laura and Yasmina are both relatively well off when it comes to water. Consider the situation the Comunidad 5 de Marzo, (5th March Community) found themselves in. The community squatted on an area of land, which was to have been developed into a hotel golf course, and for that alone they will have my undying love. As far as I am concerned the situation could only have been bettered if a Bush family member had been playing a few rounds at the time. Although initially a Zapatista community, it opened its doors to all comers and has expanded over the years. The water board, after refusing to run taps into homes, charged people instead for the standpipes they ran in. Javiar, one of the community's inhabitants said, 'They didn't give us even public fountains...and because we didn't pay they say "well we are not giving you any water".' So in a land that is water rich and in a culture that relies on taking water from springs, rivers and wells this refusal to pay for the second rate was met with petty punishment. In 2007 the water board issued locks for paying customers – so they can slip the small metal cap over the standpipe and padlock it after they are done, to ensure no free water for these golf-hating ingrates.*

---

* *The community are running their own water project with the help of Berkeley College to create a water system independent of the water board and without need of stand pipes.*

Meanwhile the Coca-Cola plant sits on top of the best water source around, the Huitepec aquifer. The plant has a twenty-year lease to extract water and is legally entitled to withdraw 500 million litres of it a year.[1] And in academic research conducted with the anonymous assistance of a senior plant official it was revealed that in 2003 the company extracted 240 million litres of water and paid $320,000 Mexican pesos-about 1p per 150 litres – which is not bad for a main ingredient.[2] The concession at Huitepec is one of twenty-seven that Coca-Cola has negotiated with the CNA (Comission Nacional del Agua – the National Water Commission)[3] – the body run by the ex-Coca-Cola man Cristóbal Jaime Jaquez, who had been appointed by another ex-Coca-Cola man, President Vicente Fox.[4]

Up on Huitepec mountain above the Coke plant one of the community representatives or agente municipal, says the water level has gone down. He sits in his zip-up mauve jacket and flicked-back greying hair like an elderly member of the Soprano family about to take a driving test, 'There has been a lot of depletion but that is understandable. There are more of us, there is global warming so we have less water and obviously as water flows underground Coca-Cola has an effect.' Further along the hill Martin, an ex-agente municipal and farmer is wearing split shoes and no socks. He has worked on the land so long that his huge, gnarled hands look like something could take root on them. His hands tell the story behind his impassive face. When I ask says about the well water on his land, 'Yeah it has gone down,' he says and then adds, 'The thing is they [Coca-Cola] have a very deep well that sucks up a lot of water.' The situation is not critical in terms of supply but he worries for the future.

There is no allegation that Coke is directly responsible for the lack of clean available water through San Cristóbal, but this is the situation they operate in and one they can take advantage of. Even the guidebooks say 'Don't drink the tap water, buy bottled water' – such as Coke's water brands. As Yasmina says 'It is the worst thing...There is a shortage for basic needs, no electricity, no water but everywhere Coca-Cola.'

When I ask Martin what he would say to the CEO of Coke in response to the company claim that they support sustainable communities he said 'Really, he should realise, instead of helping, how much Coke helps fuck communities over.'

Perhaps it is not surprising that there is some bitterness felt towards the company and later that evening when Laura and I sit among her friends in a café in the centre of town, they laugh as they tell the tale of Coke's gift to the community. Each year the company donates a thirty-foot high plastic Christmas tree covered in baubles decorated in the Coca-Cola logo and topped off with a large silver star. It stands in front of the church and under the tree is the classic nativity scene, Joseph, Mary and a large Coca-Cola polar bear – the type used in their adverts. In fact it is quite close to the baby Jesus, perhaps not surprisingly Joseph stands further back and Mary is behind him, there is absolutely no sign of the three wise men. Though the bear has a smirk on its face – a smirk and a resentful demeanour, as if to question its Arctic presence in Mexico.

A few years ago in the middle of the night miscreants, set fire to the tree, its thirty-foot plastic leaves momentarily shooting a pillar of fire under the star of Bethlehem. In the morning a sharp odour of molten plastic lingered in the air and a pile of black shrunken gunk was all that was left of Coke's gift to the community. The local businesses condemned the act, some blamed the Zapatistas, others blamed troublemakers and some blamed drunks – though a polar bear was spotted fleeing the scene.

But it takes more than a burnt Christmas tree to intimidate the Coca-Cola bottler and the very next year a new plastic tree rose from the ashes in all its majesty. And the baby Jesus was placed in its hallowed and traditional place under the Coca-Cola bauble. Mary and Joseph had obviously received some trauma counselling as they too stood strong under the protective plastic boughs. Though this year, the tree did have barriers around. And an armed guard. To enforce peace on earth.

* * *

Back in Mexico City right at the start of this trip, Alejandro from El Poder del Consumidor had said, 'I think Coke is inside the consumer habits of a great part of this society, and it's stronger in the indigenous communities and with the worst case in Chiapas, Coke is part of the rituals.' Which is why Laura and I are on a tourist bus bound for Chamula – a Tzotzil Mayan town, where the indigenous community allow visitors in to see their religious ceremonies. Here they use Coca-Cola to help remove bad spirits and nightmares by way of a gaseous emission. Now I have heard of Coca-Cola being used for many different purposes from a misguided anti-spermicidal douche to the LAPD using it to wash blood away at the scene of car crashes,* but I have never before heard of Coke being used in an exorcism. So there are a host of anthropological and cultural reasons to go and witness this event, there are questions to ask of the company regarding their marketing practices, as well as an appraisal of the economic and nutritional consequences. Though I have to admit a significant

---

* *This is an urban myth.*

part of the appeal is the sanctified burping in church. Why they do it and quite how Coca-Cola managed to muscle in on an ancient tradition, are important addenda, but the assault on the mannered orthodoxy of the church by the release of belly air at the altar is too alluring to miss.

Bizarrely this is one of the things that got Laura researching Coca-Cola. As an anthropology graduate she lived in the Highlands of Chiapas and became fascinated by the way the drink had become so ingrained in the religious life of the community. Laura explains her research and interviews with indigenous Mayans on the subject. 'Basically people say that Coke came to the Highlands, the indigenous communities, when it came to San Cristóbal in the 1950s. It was very much the advertising of the time, they used promotions, free gifts, they sponsored film shows in neighbourhood squares or had loudspeakers on a cart which went around town telling everyone to drink Coke.'

Laura told me the first man to run a Coke concession in Chamula started in 1962 and brought the bottles into the Tzotzil Mayan town on a horse. His wife recalled that no one really knew of Coca-Cola but Coke's businessmen said they could sell their product and they did very well doing just that. Indigenous people would come here from communities as far as forty kilometres away to buy it.

The tour bus potters through the mountain splendour, leaving the city centre of San Cristóbal behind us in the distance. And as we get nearer to Chamula our tour guide, a thirty-something bearded fellow, runs through the dos and don'ts of the trip like a flight attendant: 'You must respect the traditions of the indigenous people. You must not take photographs unless I say. You must not give money to child beggars, it encourages them stay from school. You must not stare at the people in the church. Remember this is a mix of ancient beliefs – the worship of the sun and the moon and the earth fused with Christianity. It might seem strange too that they drink alcohol in church, indeed some people may be a little drunk but this is their religion and you must be respectful.'

I chime in wanting to demonstrate my understanding nature, 'Well, the Catholic church serve up wine at the communion rail, so they accept the principle, it's just the size of the glass that is at issue here...'

But the bearded man turns to me for a second in blank disapproval, then turns back to the group in the bus and starts again, 'You must respect the traditions...'

* * *

The population of Chamula is Tzotzil Mayan – it is an indigenous town, whose peaceful surroundings are constantly pierced by the loud screeching bangs of home-made fireworks and rockets that are set off as part of the religious rituals. And glancing around the surrounding hillsides and the stark blue sky you can see puffs of black smoke popping in the distance before the speed of sound catches up with a crack. Pitched on one side of the square the church of San Juan dominates the town, it has a high bell tower and large wooden doors – the kind that hunchbacks can gratifyingly bang on while calling for sanctuary.

'Stick close to me please,' says our bearded guide as we enter.

From the bright light of the cloudless sunny day we pass into the dim church. There are no pews or seats but there is an intense smell of smouldering resin and scattered fresh pine needles that cover the ground. It is a big spacious building but already the grey smoke has filled its entirety. Groups of worshippers clear a space of the green needles to sit, and drip wax on to the floor to stand their rows of burning candles upright. Some sit at the altar, some in the nave, some by the walls where row upon row of glass boxes house effigies of the saints. Some have a small band of drummers, guitars and singers with them.

'When you walk around, do not intrude on the worshippers,' says the guide.

'Is that a chicken in the bag there?' asks one of the tour party pointing.

'Yes, that is a live chicken which will be sacrificed for a healing ceremony.' Then, turning to the group, he says, 'Please, a few of you can walk around.'

'But don't stare, right?' says one of the group.

'Do not stare, just be quiet and if you are lucky you may see a chicken being killed for the sacrifice.'

There are plenty of Coca-Cola bottles, and Pepsi too, set out on the floor, and their metal caps mingle with the pine needles, as families and friends gather in groups sitting, drinking, lighting candles, praying and singing. One family sits with bottles around them and a wicker bag, while the mother and father pray, a grandmother holds a small child on her lap with a bottle of Coke in front of her. This is an image I particularly warm to and think of the memory of my own nan smoking and singing songs.

Wandering here it occurs to me that the Pope has about as much control here as he has over the Presbyterians and the sense of individual ownership here is quite moving. The models of the saints are gaudy and slightly disturbing – as they should be in a Catholic church – but the figure of Jesus is jaw-dropping. In a glass cabinet near the altar the prone figure of Christ is being borne down from the cross by his followers. But Our Lord is not wearing the traditional loincloth. Our Lord is wearing a spangled powder blue glitter flower frock that comes up to just under his nipples, making Jesus look like a Thai transsexual fainting at a wedding.

And no matter how much I want to respect the Tzotzil families here, I find it hard to feel comfortable amidst high camp, low poverty and liberal tourists trying to sneak a peak at a chicken having its neck wrung.

* * *

Searching for a line of enquiry that involves a little less poultry and voyeurism we follow the curves and crumpled hillroads back to San Cristóbal. From the tourist centre of the postcard homes and tiled roofs, we step from the raised pavements away from the bars and hotels, past the markets and the stalls of Zapatista dolls, out on to dust tracks that all seem to have a single Toyota pick-up truck lunging from side to side as it trundles in a cloud of dirt; and then on to narrow lanes lined with ditches and weeds, where bulrushes sprout by wasteland ponds and plastic bottles collect around them at the edge of the mud. Out in the sun we wander to the shanty towns through the packed soil corridors and alleyways of wooden boards, with lone standpipes and packs of barking dogs, past the open family huts and homes, on to a long car-less street where children play chase in its empty lanes, twisting and turning from each other's flailing arms, while their parents sit by stalls watching and waiting for customers. And above, looking down on us from the distance are the newly built mountainside hovels, a hill of blossoming shacks and sheds on stilts. These are the newcomers fresh from the frontline of penury sprawling across to spread to the upper reaches, searching for a foothold to cling to, searching for a moment's respite.

Under this gaze we arrive on the outskirts of San Cristóbal at the Mayan Medicine Museum. The compound houses not only a museum but is also home to the Organizacion de Médicos Indigenas del Estado del Chiapas the Organisation of Indigenous Doctors in the State of Chiapas), where, amongst other things, they organise Mayan midwives for the communities in these hills. The front steps of the museum are under the cool shade of a porch which proves a tempting place for folk to squat and chat. This is where I meet Miguel, a member of staff who works on the committee for the indigenous doctors as well as in the museum as a youth worker. He is going to talk me through the significance of the Coke in the Tzotzil church.

'You can see Coca-Cola being used in the rituals and ceremonies of traditional doctors as it happens in San Juan in Chamula. But these happen everywhere, in communities, in small chapels, here in this museum...' In the religious healing ceremonies each component represent an element: the candles represents fire, pine needles the earth, prayers represent air and Coca-Cola symbolises water. 'In this case the ritual process, the drink has another element, the gas,' he says, explaining that burping throws out the 'bad energy, negative energy'.

'Some people say it is throwing out bad spirits?'

'It's all the bad energy, the ghosts, the nightmares, everything bad in that spiritual part.'

Considering parts of these ceremonies go back hundreds of years, it begs the question how did Coke muscle in on an ancient ritual?

'Before the famous soda was introduced there was atole which is made of corn. You have to leave it to ferment for eight days. After that you grind it and you make sour atole.'

This was the original burp juice. However, people began to realise you could get the same effect with Coca-Cola or Pepsi, and you didn't have to ferment corn for eight days. According to Miguel, 'Step by step Coca-Cola has started to be involved in religion and the indigenous communities and it started at the beginning with very cheap prices [for a bottle of Coke].'

This is a practice that carries on today: the price of a Coke in an indigenous community is half the price it would be in San Cristóbal, because in this poor community they can only buy what they can afford. Miguel looks up at the shantytown on the side of the mountain. 'Even in the small shops on the tops of the hill – they transport it up by donkeys.'

Some of the men sitting on the porch have listened to us talking and take this opportunity to pipe up, 'You can have a healing ceremony conducted for you here.'

'Oh really?'

'Yes, if you want,' says Miguel.

'A healing ceremony,' repeats one of the men.

'I'm sure it is very good but there is nothing physically wrong with me.'

'That is what you think but this heals your spirit.'

'Do you think my spirit needs healing?'

There is silence. Then the man nods. 'Yes – you will see how much better you feel after it.'

'OK, then, I would like to do this...' I clap my hands together and smile awkwardly while mentally rationalising, 'It's all OK. It would be rude not to. I should respect this culture and after all what is the worst that can happen?'

I turn expectantly to Miguel, who says, 'First you will need to buy some big bunches of basil and an egg.'

* * *

Fifteen minutes later a shaman is instructing me how to order the rows of lit candles on the floor while he places the egg and a cup of water next to them. Our spiritual guide for this particular healing journey is a stocky small man with a paunch and cropped hair, dressed in a blue denim shirt. Although I didn't have a fixed image of a shaman in my mind, I somehow did not expect him to look like a night watchman at a Parcelforce depot.

This ceremony does not involve Coca-Cola and burping, so my bad spirits are staying put, but a couple of local folk are having the same healing ritual and tell me as we line up in the small chapel that this is a protective healing ceremony. Figures of the saints inhabit the alcoves, including the Virgin of Guadeloupe in crown and gown, Saint Anthony looking lost in the corner and John the Baptist with his head still on his shoulders. There is one figure that stands out from the rest, a cross, chubby man holding a stick in the air wearing a frock – though it could be a toga – and I wonder if John Belushi has been canonised.

The stocky shaman sits upright on a small stool, rocking back and forth with his hands on his knees, intoning place names and saints in a sing-song monotone. Rising with a laboured breath he motions for me to come forward and he starts walking the length of the chapel chanting in Tzotzil, brushing the basil against the saints, evoking their names each in turn, before arriving at the corner where I wait by my egg and candles. The stocky shaman stands before me, coming up to my nose in height and as he intones his prayers he brushes the swatch of basil over my face, first once, then again. Then he taps my shoulders with basil, first one side then the other – all the while continuing his chant. Next my stomach and sides are hit, each time harder than the first. Bending down he starts working on my calves whacking them with such force that he is beginning to pant with the effort of the blows and the chanting. The air is now thick with a peppery smell and as he returns upright he starts all over again, with even greater energy – smacking my shoulders with such vigour that leaves begin to fly off the branches. As he hits my stomach the air becomes a blizzard of basil and I want to shout, 'This isn't healing, this is seasoning!' but I am speechless in the face of the serious conviction held by everyone in the room. Suddenly he stops and stares as leaves flutter to the ground. Stooping he picks up the egg waves it over my body, breaks it into the cup of water which he holds to the light to examine the floating yolk. Then he says: 'All the jealousy people have towards you is gone – you will return to San Cristóbal one day.' And with that he motions it is over and I to return to my seat.

Outside one of the local folks walks with me back to the city centre.

'Well?' he asks expectantly, breathing in deeply to show his own contentedness 'Did you see the way the plant turned black?'

'The basil?'

'Sí, it turned black. It is the plant taking your bad energy. Some things science cannot explain.' He nods wisely, breathes another deep sigh of contentment and says, 'So, how do you feel?'

'I feel like I have been beaten up by pesto.'

* * *

As an atheist son of a family of preachers I have a bastardised version of the supposed Christian credo, 'Love the sinner, hate the sin', namely 'Love the religious, hate the religion'. It is impossible for me to fault anyone for wanting to buy a bottle of Coke over brewing maize for eight days, and believing basil takes away bad energy is no more bizarre than thinking a wafer turns into Jesus' body when it hits your tongue. But Coke and Pepsi have managed to inveigle their way into a ceremony that is an intrinsic part of these people's identity. They have once again become woven into the fabric of ordinary lives and special memories and I wonder if the children in the church will remember drinking Coke with their grandparents on the pine-needle floor. In these circumstances it is entirely possible to 'Like the drink, loathe the company'.

14
WE'RE ON A ROAD TO DELAWARE

Wilmington, USA

'If the communities we serve are in and of themselves not sustainable, then we do not have a sustainable business.'

Neville Isdell, The Coca-Cola Company, 2008[1]

The city of Wilmington in the state of Delaware is about ninety minutes and three decades south of Brooklyn. The best thing about the place is that it is effortlessly forgettable. This is not where I envisaged ending my journey. Having stood on the banks of an oasis in the desert of Rajasthan, watched cane fields of fire turn the sky orange in El Salvador and marvelled at the mountain mist tumbling down the steep hillsides of Bucaramanga and into bustling streets of the city itself; Delaware is not the geographical dénouement I was hoping for. I have travelled thousands of miles, through squalor and splendour, meeting people with courage and tenacity searching for the political equivalent of what Spalding Gray would have called a 'perfect moment'.

If I was on daytime TV I would call it 'closure', if I was a lawyer – a 'resolution', I suppose I want to know what the fuck this has all been about and I have a niggling feeling that Wilmington is a resolutely 'epiphany-free zone.' I am not doing down Wilmington, I just didn't know that IKEA did a flat-pack town. And as soon as someone finds that Allen key this place will tighten up just nicely.

The Coca-Cola Company has its annual meeting of stock holders in Wilmington because the company is registered not in its southern home of Atlanta but up here in the north in Delaware, along with half the Stock Exchange who take advantage of this on-shore tax haven. The meeting is to take place in the Hotel du Pont, 'the best hotel in town' a policeman tells me, which may be the case but a hotel owned by DuPont – the second-largest chemical company in the world – just doesn't conjure an image of pampered luxury. To be fair it does look like the kind of place that hosts a lot of corporate events, a place where managing directors pick up industry awards and trophy wives.

Back in London I had taken Coca-Cola's PR people up on their offer to try and arrange an interview with Ed Potter, the company's Global Workplace Rights Director, who I had seen at the House of Commons. The likelihood of the company sanctioning such a meeting was never high, still I went through the process with the same grim lack of expectation with which my mum buys her lottery tickets every week – knowing it is not going to happen but still being slightly disappointed when that turns out to be the case. 'It's a No right now' said the mail from the company, as if this were only a temporary state of affairs.

Nonetheless this is the only chance I will have had of seeing the corporate titans of the world's most famous brand and I'm curious how they will handle the criticism levelled at them. But more than this I wanted to see if the company was changing, if all these campaigns and lawsuits, struggles and fights were having an effect. In the House of Commons debates one of the PR people had said, 'You're looking at a company that wants to change.' And if that is the case here's the place to see it.

* * *

Ray Rogers has been described as a 'legendary union activist' and has been campaigning against Coca-Cola since 2003. He founded and runs the Corporate Campaign Inc who coordinate Stop Killer Coke.[2] Ray is making the now-annual pilgrimage to Delaware to challenge the company at the annual meeting. With him is Lew Freidman, a retired teacher who coordinates the websites, and the pair of them gave me lift from Brooklyn. Arriving at Wilmington, Ray runs off ahead of us while Lew and I chat as we amble over to the protest line opposite the hotel. This comprises primarily of clean, well-groomed, polite people in their early twenties who look a bit like market researchers for a Bible college as they smile and hand out seditious balloons with anti-corporate slogans on their innocent oval shapes.

'Mark!' shouts Ray as he runs across the road, momentarily disappearing behind a large truck. 'Mark!' he shouts again. Passing, the truck reveals Ray running toward a smartly dressed man who stands on the wrong side of the hotel's covered colonnade, adrift from the mass of shareholders milling towards the meeting. And I suddenly realise that Ed Potter has been caught in open ground.

When properly motivated I can multitask like a motherfucker. By which I mean I can cross a road, extract a digital recorder, turn it on, check the sound levels, pop a pre-interview breath mint, grab a blast of Ventolin and reach Ed Potter before he can get to cover. Behind Coke's Global Workplace Rights Director a group of scaffolders work overhead, with mandatory hard hats and obligatory work belts, a few wear high-visibility orange vests and the place is covered in safety signs and warnings. It is under the appropriate sound of their hammering and sawing that I manage to interview Ed Potter. He smiles wanly as I wave the digital recorder at him and dive straight away into the case of the Indian workers in Kaladera being forced to work in dangerous conditions without the proper safety equipment.

'How are you going to sort it out?' I enquire.

'I don't know the circumstances of India so I can't really comment directly on that but just like other issues that are, what I'll call systemic issues, we're working to resolve those,' he says.

Ed Potter's voice is slightly thin, pitched at the tone of a man trying to clear his throat, so every now and again he has to go up a decibel to be heard above the building noise.

'How would you deal with it?' I press.

'If you email it to me we will definitely look into it.'

'Is there a procedure that you have for looking at this?'

'Do we have a written down procedure?' He repeats, eyebrows raised with his voice, 'No...if you bring me a situation and location x, depending on what it is, we would put in an audit team...'

'...But they say the only time they get given gas masks and gloves to work in the water treatment plant is when the auditors come round.'

'You know,' he says shaking his head ruefully, 'we have the

same challenges as any national government will have with respect to people who may want to manipulate the outcome.'

But the real issue is not just tracking down these abuses but how the company acts to solve them, so I ask what the sanctions are for bottlers who commit this kind of labour rights' abuse.

'Well, in the case of the supplier, a supplier who fails to take corrective action is subject to not being a supplier any more, that's the sanction.'

Assuming that this is the case, that bottlers have their franchise removed, how will it work in this instance? Coca-Cola is the bottler. Or at least it is a direct subsidiary – the Hindustan Coca-Cola Beverage Pvt Ltd is owned by The Coca-Cola Company.[3]

From under the hotel covered entrance a Coca-Cola man has spotted Ed Potter talking alone and unguarded and has come over to keep an eye on things. The man introduces himself as 'Tom, Head of Public Affairs'. To be fair to Ed Potter he stays and answers the questions, his thin hair blowing slightly. I am keen to get some action taken on the situation in India and press Ed Potter once more on the course the company will take.

'These guys are going in, and not working with the proper safety equipment, is this serious enough to investigate?' I ask.

'Well, of course! Health and safety is one of our...things.'

'So if I come to you and say this is happening here...'

The Public Affairs man nods firmly, 'We'll go and look.'

'You'll go and look.'

'Yeah, of course,' says Ed Potter.

* * *

Days later I emailed Ed Potter asking how we might proceed on this issue. The reply I got reads:

Ed Potter has referred your email to me. You can find information about our workplace practices on both cokefacts.com and on www.GetTheRealFacts.co.uk.

Sincerely,
Kari Bjorhus

Which seems a long way away from the response of 'we'll go and look'.

* * *

Overhead the casual yells and hollers of building work continue as metres away the shareholders start to gather around the hotel entrance while police officers with Secret Service earpieces watch over them. So before time wears our encounter to a close and we too must herd inside I say, 'Colombia. Isidro Gil. I spoke to people who saw him killed – someone was shot and killed on Coca-Cola's property.'
Tom from Public Affairs says 'We understand that.'
'We get it,' joins Ed Potter.
'We understand that he was an employee. We understand that he was shot there...It's a very difficult area, it was a very difficult time. If we can come to some resolution, we'd like to help that family and move on.'

But it quickly descends from that compassionate line into the usual company statements, hiding in the mire of the 'Coca-Cola system'. Ed Potter describes the dead as men who 'were not current or ever Coca-Cola employees'. He parrots the company mantra, seemingly oblivious to the fact that the refusal of the Company to acknowledge they have a responsibility over 'the Coca-Cola system' is the very thing that gets them into so much grief. People don't much care for the lawyerly lines of separation between legal entities – if your name is on the label you have got the responsibility.

When I mention the breakdown in negotiations between the company and Sinaltrainal, Ed Potter takes a breath and realigns the furrows on his brow. 'All I will say is, and this is a personal opinion – I honestly don't believe they want to resolve this.'

'You don't think that Sinaltrainal wants to resolve it? Why not?' I say incredulously.

'That's something I...It's a personal opinion, I frankly...I mean as soon as it goes on that recorder...' He nods at the digital recorder, implying he doesn't want to talk of this publicly. But it seems that Ed Potter thinks a group of people who collect death threats like Nectar points and have been specifically targeted for organising workers in Coca-Cola bottlers want to prolong the situation.

Alongside other campaigners, Ray Rogers of Stop Killer Coke has caused the company some considerable discomfort. To Ray, arguing comes as natural as breathing and the idea of just allowing Ed Potter to get past without lambasting him is just too much for Ray to bear so he strides over to us, calling out 'The ILO investigation is a scam!'

Let me explain the back story here. The International Labor Organisation is a UN body that exists to promote labour and human rights. It is made up of representatives from government, employers and trade unions.[4] After coming under pressure from the University of Michigan student body (the folk who put pressure on for the TERI report in India) Coca-Cola agreed to approach the ILO with the International

Union of Foodworkers to ask that they conduct an assessment of workplace practices in Coke's bottling plants in Colombia. The ILO announced their intention to do so on 24 March 2006.[5]

The problem with this is that the Company have somewhat used the promised ILO assessment as a fig leaf to hide behind when questions are raised about the assassinations, when in fact the ILO is only assessing *current* labour practices and will not consider the assassinations or any of the allegations of complicity by the bottling plant managers. Which is why Ray is claiming, 'The ILO investigation is a scam. You know it, I know it, The Coca-Cola Company knows it.'

'I absolutely disagree' says Ed Potter emphatically.

'It's a scandal,' decries Ray raising his hands to the heavens, oblivious to the fact that the passing shareholders are turning to stare at him. 'There is no investigation being done.'

Ed Potter replies, 'Well we've never represented that the ILO was going to do an investigation.'

This is an unfortunate thing to say, as inside the annual meeting, just metres away from where we are standing, staff are issuing a printed company statement on Colombia, in which The Coca-Cola Company describes the ILO assessment as an 'investigation' on three occasions in five lines of text. This, they claim is 'fulfilling our commitment to an independent, impartial third-party investigation and evaluation,' though it fails to mention Ed Potter is the US Employer Delegate on the ILO. The body that just happens to be conducting this particular 'independent and impartial' assessment.[6]

Unfortunately Ed Potter is also contradicted by his boss the current chairman and former CEO, Neville Isdell, who said at the Company Annual Meeting for shareholders in 2006:

'We have a document. From the ILO signed by the ILO...We have a document. We have an agreement and they are going to investigate past and prior practices...We think we have gone to the most credible people that can possibly be found in this world to look at what has happened in Colombia.'[7]

Just to further clarify matters I talked to the General Secretary of the International Union of Foodworkers , Ron Oswald – this is the person who negotiated with Coke and then the ILO to get the assessment. Ron reacted to Neville Isdell's statement saying, 'Well, he was wrong, and they know he was wrong, but clearly once that cat's out the bag, that cat's out the bag. Our proposal to the ILO was very clear: we did not ask them to do an investigation into criminal or murderous events in the 1990s...I don't think they've got the competence to do that, frankly.'

In case there is any lingering doubt Ron Oswald says 'there are still calls for Coke to agree to an independent investigation of those incidents and that's something we thought Coke should have agreed to many years ago.' So obviously the ILO assessment is not that 'independent investigation'.

There was never going to be an investigation into past practices of Coke bottling plants in Colombia by the ILO. So I asked Coca-Cola if they would publish or let me see the document Neville Isdell alleges the ILO had given the Company, to see how such a prominent captain of industry could be so confused. After all it is probably not a good idea to tell untruths and give false information to shareholders at an annual meeting. To my surprise the Company reacted positively to my question to see the ILO letter and invited me to their HQ in Atlanta providing a private jet with in-flight entertainment from an acoustic set by Joni Mitchell...OK, I'm making it up, but they started it. They ignored my question.

* * *

M ood music is piped into the Hotel du Pont rendering the lobby's grand piano just a symbol of good taste. But saunter past this soundless wooden box of strings and hammers, past the check-in desk, between the pair of welcoming signs and their attendant police officers, and at the bottom of the carpeted stairs and their polished handrails stands the company fridges in all their glory, lit up like a petrol station at night. These are the new HFC-Free fridges, which the company call Climate Friendly Coolers. Each is packed with Coca-Cola products in branded blocks and shareholders are invited to enjoy the company's produce. I don't want to take anything out of their fridge, though I do wish I had a bottle of Big Cola to put in there. The meeting hall is cavernous and ornate, with two chandeliers, all brass and glass, hanging from the ceiling. The columned walls are painted with flowers, flutes and fat cherubs dancing and the alcoves house gilt-framed mirrors; around these edges staff and plainclothes police officers stand in an obvious display of authority.

Walking into the hall I immediately bump into the friendly smile of B Wardlaw. B Wardlaw dresses in grey tracksuit bottoms, trainers and a driving jacket which, along with his scarecrow grey crop and Southern gentleman-style goatee beard, give him the appearance of Colonel Sanders with a hangover. But despite his appearance, B Wardlaw is heir to a large number of Coca-Cola shares which he uses to help finance a homeless shelter in Atlanta: 1,000 people drop by in the day, 600 sleep there at night. The homeless repay this charity by giving B fashion advice, which he appears to have accepted today. He comes from an old Atlanta family and his grandfather was involved in the financing of The Coca-Cola Company so B knows many of the board and the Atlanta elite.

The first time I met B was outside of Washington. I had heard of him through a network of anti-Coca-Cola campaigners, who helped set up our meeting. I had been told to get a train to Tacoma Park and phone his number.

'Hi is that B Wardlaw?'

'Mr Thomas?' I heard a Southern gentleman's drawl.

'Yes.'

'Walk along the platform. Come down the escalator not the elevator. Walk through the barrier...'

'And...'

Almost in a parody of Southern manners he said, 'Ah will make myself know to you.' And then he hung up.

I did what I was told and on leaving the station B popped out of a coffeeshop doorway and shot a wave at me. He was dressed much like he always does and was wearing a sweatshirt emblazoned with the slogan 'Celebrate Freedom: Read a Banned Book!' During that first meeting I asked him what he thought The Coca-Cola Company should do to address the many issues it faced and he had replied in his charming drawl, 'Stop making Coca-Cola.' He was serious, 'I don't think it is a good product and we shouldn't be conditioning children to it.'

'But this is the source of your money which goes to the shelter...'

He shakes his head with a smile, 'I know it's a paradox,' then with mock seriousness he confides, 'I call myself the Coca-Cola anarchist.'

'Seriously, what should the Company do?'

'Well, when I mentioned the Colombia issue to people involved in the...er, shall we say, upper echelons of the company,' he said with an edge of irony in his voice, 'they said "we just sell the syrup – it's the bottlers".'

'That is the standard line...'

'Well, we should take responsibility or we should not do business.'

* * *

B Wardlaw is here in Delaware to propose a shareholder motion that the company should create a Board Committee on Human Rights, which would consider and advise on the consequences of its actions on these issues, including sponsoring the Olympics in China.

'Do you mind if I sit next to you?' I ask.

'I would be honoured,' he says.

A company's annual meeting is one of the rare times activists and opponents of a company get the chance to question the board and all they have to do is buy one single share to gain admittance. So the room is beginning to feel like the gathering of the clans, just behind me is an official from Amnesty International who wants to second B's proposal; next to him is a representative from Reporters Without Borders. Ray Rogers has entered with Lew Freidman, though they split up and sit in different sections of the room as they stand more chance of both getting called on to speak if they are apart. Behind Ray is a contingent of Tibetans who have just seen the brutal repression of democracy demonstrations by China, the host nation for the Olympics and Coke's most precious emerging market. Teamsters walk into the room smartly dressed but still managing to swagger like they are part of Rocky Balboa's training camp. There are Campaign for Corporate Accountability folk dotted around, plus the environmental and human rights groups like the Polaris Institute and Canadian water rights campaigners. Amit Srivastava is back from India and looks suitably unimpressed by his surroundings, though he nips over to say hello with a hug. There are even a couple of nuns who have come along to protest Coke's policies.

Most meetings of this sort start with a chairman clearing his throat, welcoming the room and calling the session to order. Coke's begins with a hymn, the lights go down and they play one of their adverts – the ultimate song of praise to the product. A video screens the commercial in which enormous inflatable figures from a parade break away from their tow ropes and a cartoon toddler and a superhero dog do battle in the skies for the prize of a large inflatable bottle of Coca-Cola. B Wardlaw tucks a conspiratorial head in my direction and in his Southern lilt chuckles, 'They would appear to be over-carbonated...too much gas.'

The ad finishes, the lights come up with the applause of the room and Neville Isdell, the outgoing CEO, rises to the podium.

In the world of CEOs some are born elegant, some achieve elegance and some have elegance thrust upon them. Isdell falls into the latter category. Strip him of the suit and he would look like a balding referee at a Sunday morning football match. 'Good morning, and welcome to The Coca-Cola Company's 2008 annual meeting...'

Isdell is the model of competence, delivering his opening remarks and then introducing the board members who are up for re-election. These folks sit at the front of the meeting in a cordoned-off area for executives with the riff raff kept firmly at bay, a sort of mini Dubai. As Isdell calls out their names in turn they stand and wave to the assembled mass behind them. There is a director of Delta Air Lines brandishing his hand in the air like it doesn't quite belong to him, the President of Hearst magazines graciously gesturing and a chap touted as the outsider for the vice-president's slot on the Obama ticket grinning like he has messed himself.

Muthar Kent,[8] the incoming CEO, sits next to his outgoing counterpart. As Isdell is tall and lean, so Kent is squat and square, between them they possess the classic shape of a double act.

Muthar Kent takes his turn at the podium and says as CEO elect he is 'humbled' and 'honoured to be part of this great legacy...' and thunders that we all have 'good reason to be excited' in the future of the company. 'I believe,' he cries from the podium, 'there is no better packaged goods consumer business to be in, today or in the future, than the non-alcoholic ready-to-drink beverage industry.' It is noticeable that he never refers to Coca-Cola as 'pop', 'fizzy pop', 'sodas' or even 'carbonated sodas' – Muthar Kent describes Coca-Cola as 'sparkling beverages'.

His speech is littered with sentences like 'Our sparkling beverage growth is achieving its highest rates in almost a decade!' and 'Sparkling beverages are the oxygen of our company.' In fact he uses the phrase 'sparkling beverages' eight times so he obviously isn't taking the 'golden stream'. It is out with the old soda or pop with its image of sugar-laden fizz and in with the calorie-free phrase 'sparkling beverages.'

But it is Isdell's speech following Kent's that proves to be the more intriguing, and he begins by saying, 'We're transforming our business very simply because the world in which we operate has changed. Our planet and its resources are facing increasing pressures.' As an opening it is standard fare for business leaders to stress changes they are bringing to keep the company at the top of its game, but he continues, 'We have a presence in people's lives that reaches beyond that magical moment of providing that simple moment of refreshment. We're also an employer, a business partner, a part of the community, a global citizen; and I believe we must play our role in supporting sustainable communities.'

Having just seen some of those communities that have not been sustained by Coke, I crane my neck around the room searching out other small scowls of disbelief. However, it becomes clear that alongside the business journalists, the investment fund managers and the vested interest groups there are ordinary shareholders here; not rich people, just folk with a few dollars and a will to invest. Behind me sits a family on a day out. On one side of the family group sits the father, in a green check shirt, his back bolt upright with his hands on his knees. At the other end of the line a twelve-year old-boy wearing a baseball hat sits slumped, dangling his rucksack between his knees. In between them is the mother, in her forties, knitting a red, white and blue jumper.

'Last year,' says Isdell, 'we set a very aspirational target: a goal of becoming entirely water neutral in our operations on a global basis...In the past, some of you have expressed some concern about our business in India that primarily revolved around water and water use. I can tell you not only have we listened, but we've taken action. For starters, there are over three hundred rainwater harvesting structures across seventeen states in India.' This is Isdell in full CEO as Indiana Jones mode, leading a company that faces criticism and triumphs. From here he deftly moves through the emotions of contrition, struggle and hope.

'People have talked about our transparency in India, so

we agreed to an independent assessment of our water management [by TERI],' says Isdell, underlining the idea that the company has risen to the charges of its critics. 'There were some areas that they identified where we can make some improvements; these were just recommendations, and of course we will proceed with those.' Without scrutiny this looks like a company that have looked deep into their corporate soul admitted imperfection and embraced change. The knitting mum is still working on patriotic woollen wear but the checked shirt dad is nodding vigorously in appreciation at the scale of Coke's challenge.

However, with scrutiny Isdell's comments reveal a sleight of hand and quite a good one too. The improvements the company is going to make are small ones, relating to waste water improvements and compliance issues. These may be necessary but they are not the major recommendation of the report, which is to shut the plant down. So the inclusion and acknowledgment of some of the TERI report's criticisms is a masterly stroke, humbly admitting to minor errors while ignoring the major indictments.

Isdell lunges into the climax of his speech. 'The challenges facing our planet are too urgent and complex for governments alone, business alone, or NGOs alone to solve. Working together, we can create a multiplier effect that helps build sustainable communities and addresses the issues of our planet.' He is a man with a mission going beyond the mere niggles of a few critics and now set to solve the problems of the world. 'All the efforts I have talked about are "nice" things to do, but we are not doing them just because they are nice. We've done them because they're the steps that we must take to earn a profit and to return a profit to you, our shareholders.'

And thus he has faced down his critics, mended the ways of the company, embraced social change, shouldered the burden of world leadership and wrapped it all into a corporate philosophy: you make money if you are seen to do good.

The board in front of Isdell lead the appreciation of their captain of industry. Behind me the woman has put down her knitting to join the applause. But the dad is holding his hands to his chest clapping wildly. He is a fan. Had he spare underwear to throw it would be in the air by now and Isdell would be whispering to his roadie 'That one to my dressing room.'

As the applause starts to dip B Wardlaw turns to me and says, 'Wow, that's the impact you folks have had, you wouldn't have heard that speech three years ago.' And I believe B, it has been the activists, union members, villagers, shopkeepers and students that have forced the Company to look at the issues. We would not have heard that three years ago, the speech was totally about Corporate Social Responsibility.

But it is also evident that the Company's old ways are resolutely at the helm. They remain wedded to their mantra that 'we only make and sell concentrate and are not responsible for the bottlers or suppliers' when it is clear that the 'Coca-Cola system' is controlled by The Coca-Cola Company, both in terms of the franchise and The Coca-Cola Company's share ownership. It is also evident that the company has not addressed the specific issues.

The story told here is the story of a company going through the growing pains of Corporate Social Responsibility and emerging a changed and mature business leader working for a better world. But any storyteller knows that what you leave out of a story is as important as what is kept in. And Coca-Cola's omissions are the uncomfortable specifics.

- Isdell talks of 'communities lack of public access to clean water,' but doesn't mention Kaladera, the farmers or the women from the *basti* fighting at the pumps.
- Isdell talks of 'creating economic empowerment everywhere we do business,' but blanks out the *fleteros* in Colombia working with no job protection, with long hours and low pay.
- Isdell talks of how creating jobs 'helps alleviate poverty in the communities we serve,' but skipped the children working the fields for Coke's sugar who are not alleviated but condemned to poverty.
- Isdell talks of a workplace 'free from violence, harassment, intimidation and other unsafe or disruptive conditions due to internal or external threats' but dropped the page that mentioned the Indian workers passing out in unsafe conditions and the Turkish deliverymen sacked for wanting to join a union and then gassed in a Coke plant with their children.
- Isdell says, 'If the communities we serve are in and of themselves not sustainable then we do not have a sustainable business' but didn't have time to mention the unpaid taxes to Nejapa and the slums where local people pay for water since Coke came.
- Isdell talks of the company being a 'functioning part of the local community,' but the name of Raquel Chavez has slipped his mind.

Campaigners have forced the company to respond and the company has responded with PR. It seems to be their pathological response. Ron Oswald, the leader of the International Union of Foodworkers, a man who regularly meets with the company, said 'When you build that whole thing around a product that nobody needs, that product is pure image...so the communications people inside Coca-Cola accumulate huge amounts of power over many years...they see issues of substance and they interpret them as issues of communication and then they try to communicate the solution, instead of dealing with the issue.'[9]

* * *

The shareholders' resolutions are next on the agenda and the outcome is predictably in favour of the company. Isdell's responses to questions are by now so prepared, prepacked and ready to go that you can practically hear the microwave bell ping before he opens his mouth. Polite and orderly, he controls the meeting like a teacher in a slightly rowdy class. Ray Rogers shouts 'Point of order' and jumps out of his chair at every possible opportunity. Amit tells Isdell he is insulting. B says 'I have worked out that with about 1,500,000 shares in the company and an hour to question the board that gives each share about 0.00024 seconds' worth of time, so I will be as quick as I can' before putting his idea of a board committee for human rights.

Isdell bats away the questions with his trusty PR shield and gets a few shareholders making supportive statements too, one shareholder compares Isdell to a 'gifted athlete', making leadership look so easy. Someone else congratulates the company on advertising on family-friendly TV like *American Idol*...But the meeting closes with a gentleman being called from the front executive enclave, he has thick glasses and is reasonably elderly.

'My name is Herbert Pinkus,' he says, looking as if he had been well named. 'I control around 10,000 shares, I personally own around 6,000 shares. I want to congratulate the board and thank them for the fine job.' Then he turns to face the rest of the room, 'And I also want to say a word or two to the naysayers here. The Coca-Cola Company is not the conscience of the world, The Coca-Cola Company is not the policeman of the world. The mission of The Coca-Cola Company is to enhance shareowner value and I think they do a terrific job in that.' He starts to get a round of applause but carries on over it raising his voice, ' and I have another personal message for the naysayers.' He pauses for good effect, 'Sell your shares and get out of the way. Thank you.'

The executive enclosure erupts and claps heartily and so do I. For all the talk of sustainable communities it is refreshing to hear an honest opinion, red in tooth and claw. B nudges me, 'I am glad you had an opportunity to see that attitude in action. America love it or leave it!' And he smiles, despite having had his proposal to set up a human rights committee within Coke defeated by 91 per cent of the shareholders.

The meeting closes and the lights are raised. The executives start to stand in their remarkably uniform bespoke suits, stretching their legs and slapping each other on the shoulder. A small group of big men assemble around Neville, and when the prerequisite number are fore and aft they set off down the side of the room, with Isdell in the middle, through the shareholders and the crowd. I remain seated, surrounded by the noise of scraping chairs and the litter of discarded order papers, thinking through what I've just heard.

This is the problem. You can call it sparkling beverages as many times as you want and you can talk of magic moments of refreshments but Coca-Cola is fizzy pop. You can talk of consumers inviting you into their lives and you can treasure secret formulas but all you are selling is essentially sugar and water: fizzy pop. No one actually needs Coca-Cola and no one would die if it disappeared off the planet tomorrow.

And that is my realisation. The brand is the most important thing the Company has because put aside the concentrate and that is all they have left to sell. The brand is what transforms fizzy pop into Coca-Cola, that intangible bundle of images and feelings held within people's minds and kept alive on a $2.4 billion advertising budget.[10] Coca-Cola is more image than product and as such exists as a mental construct within each and every one of us. Except my image of Coca-Cola is no longer linked to polar bears, Santa ads, iconic script and bottles. When I think of Coca-Cola now I think of Luis Eduardo in jail throwing notes wrapped around sweets out of the windows to his daughter on the street. On other days I think of a child disappearing into forest of sugar cane and sometimes I think of Raquel Chavez winning against the company or the protestors who shut down the plants in India.

There have been some significant successes in the struggles against the Company and there are campaigns and solidarity groups that anyone can take part in. Yet despite this there is an aching question of 'what can I do, they are one of the world's biggest companies?' But the one thing the Company has taught me is that stories matter. How much do they matter? The Coca-Cola Company does not want people seeing a bottle of Coke and not hearing the story they have spent US $2.4 billion telling. The last thing the Company wants is consumers thinking about their product rather than associating it with memories or feelings, things that do not sit well with awkward questions. The stories I have heard on these trips challenge the corporate narrative. The bundles of stories on scribbled notes and Edirol recordings matter, and they matter to the Company as much as to the people who told them. Each time they get told it is another chip away at the brand value. Sure, the Company will continue making profit, but they won't make as much as they could do...and believe me that really hurts them.

As epiphanies go this one lacks the dramatic gesture of being struck blind on the way to Damascus but it does mean I can make it out of the hall without stumbling for help.

It is time for me to go. I take leave of B Wardlaw, wave goodbye to Amit and search out Lew to try and get a lift back to Brooklyn. As I get to the top of the steps one of the Company staff stops me.

'Sir.'

'Pardon?'

'Have you got your shareholder's card?'

'Er...no...'

She tuts. 'Doesn't matter, you have one anyway. You should hand over your shareholder's card to receive one but it doesn't matter. There you go.'

Conspiratorially she hands me a thin cardboard box. 'Here you go, sir,' she says winking.

'Thank you.'

Heading to the hotel entrance I open the box. Inside is a slim silver metal commemorative Coca-Cola Company pen, a gift to the shareholders. 'Wow,' I think, 'they even give me the ink with which to write.'

POSTSCRIPT: BRAND LOYALTY

'Over the last thirty years, the employees in the Drogheda plant have made a very valuable contribution to the Coca-Cola business.'

Hugo Reidy, General Manager, Drogheda Concentrates, 29 August 2007[1]

Jerry Farrell is travelling to a football match with his brother and their children when his mobile rings. Jerry is in his early fifties and works as a line manager at Drogheda Concentrates where he oversees about eighteen workers. The plant, north of Dublin, is where The Coca-Cola Company makes the syrup and concentrates for their drinks. Jerry is a union official there for SIPTU (Services, Industrial, Professional and Technical Union). He is also the Co-Chair of the Coca-Cola Communications Forum. It is a grand title but essentially this is where managers and workers discuss how the company's long-term plans will affect employees. But today the business of work is relegated to its proper place and the matter in hand is football. Tomorrow Drogheda United will play against Helsingborg in the UEFA Cup in Sweden and the most important thing is to get to the hotel.

The mobile rings again, showing a number he isn't expecting. Not today leastways, today is holiday time. The voice on the end of the line is Coke's General Manager in Ireland.

'Jerry, sorry to disturb you, I know you are away at a football match, but I have to tell you there is an announcement being made in under an hour.'

'About what?'

'We are going to shut the plant in Drogheda.'

It is 29 August 2007, the day before Drogheda lost to Helsingborg 3–0. There are about 200 fans travelling to see the match, out of which fifty work at the plant. Jerry hangs up and goes to give them the news.

The plant employs 256 workers, probably 350 when you include the contract staff, the canteen, security and cleaners. As Jerry is the Co-Chair of the Coca-Cola Communications Forum the company informs him of the closure an hour before it is announced publicly; the call, says the General Manager, is out of respect.

Eleven months after that phone call and the plant is all but closed. 'Respect...' Jerry shakes his head as he tells the story. 'An hour before they make the announcement and they call it respect.' Most workers left for the last time on 27 June 2008, leaving the plant to be run down for good by the end of August. By the time you read this it will be shut.

I had phoned SIPTU a few weeks ago and they had put me in touch with Jerry, so this is the first time I have met him. Jerry is fifty-two, dresses well but not too flash, has a wife, two kids: he's a typical working-class guy. But the thing that defines him today is his anger and resignation, he exudes a kind of fuming fatalism. In his car he talks non-stop during the forty-five-minute drive from Dublin to Drogheda along the motorway, then on through the quieter lanes, following the lush riverbanks. 'This is where they fought the Battle of the Boyne' he says, pointing at a gateway, 'the tourist folk have done it really nicely.'

As we head through Drogheda he explains that they call it a 'Bed and Breakfast town, so many people work in Dublin and commute.' But driving through the industrial area is a different story. We seem to pass rows of disused warehouses and industrial units. Jerry nods at each and starts every sentence with the words, 'This was the place where the so and so factory used to be...' or 'This is the site of the old so and so place...' Row upon row of empty factories and businesses, the stillborn pups of the Celtic Tiger.

Sitting in a near-empty hotel bar just by the river we drink tea and natter for two hours while waiters in standard black shirts and white aprons glide around the room to the sound of discreet hotel tunes, 'lobby house music' or a compilation that is probably on sale at reception.

Jerry explains the significance of the plant, 'Seven out of every ten of Coca-Cola's drinks drunk around the world on any given day start in Ireland, the concentrate is made in Ireland.' Given that 1.5 billion servings of Coke's products are consumed every day – that's a lot of concentrate.[2] This is the hub of Coke's operations.

Different drinks require different types of 'beverage base' some are liquid concentrates, some are powder, the various mixes leave the plant in various forms and head off as far afield as Australia. 'The flavourings come over from Sidcup in the UK,' says Jerry explaining that The Coca-Cola Company's secret ingredient called '7X' is manufactured there. 'But the main ingredient that goes into Coke for concentrate is caramel. Then you have things like phosphoric acid and obviously the 7X and then you have all these little flavours. So in a batch of Coke there are probably ten ingredients.' As there is little automation in the plant Jerry says the process of making the concentrate is quite skilled. 'It tends to be people weighing out ingredients into tanks, it is very, very manual. So it is very hands on, and that is why they rely so much on experienced operators knowing what they are doing 'cause if you make a mistake in any of this and it is not picked up by the labs and it goes out to the fields...' He shakes his head.

I am curious about the concentrate business. 'How much did the plant make?' I ask.

'Drogheda would make about 8 million units of concentrate a year,' Jerry replies.

'And how big is a unit?'

'For Coca-Cola a unit is a US gallon.'

'How many drinks would you get out of a unit?'

'Depends what it is, it varies from drink to drink.'

'Coca-Cola...'

'I think about two units make 100,000 or somewhere around there.'

'How much does a unit cost to make?'

'Drogheda made it for about $3.67.'

'So roughly $3.67 is enough for about 50,000 drinks...'

'The $3.67 is for the ingredients and labour costs to make it.'

I believe my next word is 'Fuck...'

According to Jerry the cost of concentrate was even lower in Ballina, 'US $2.60 a unit,' he says. The differences in production costs was used by the company, 'so if Drogheda didn't get down to Ballina's level the company shift work from Drogheda to Ballina. What they have is an internal competition going on. The company create a very competitive internal environment.'

The company might say they had overcapacity in Drogheda but the lure of cheaper concentrate could have played a part in the decision to shut down the plant here.

Drogheda Concentrates is owned by Atlantic Industries, which is registered in the Cayman Islands and is a direct subsidiary of The Coca-Cola Company. There is a distinct whiff of 'tax efficiencies' in the air. And by a 'distinct whiff' I mean 'stink'. For most of its history, Ireland has been a predominantly agricultural economy but in the Seventies it made some radical changes to its tax system to encourage investment. Corporation Tax for some industries was slashed to 10 per cent and it now stands at 12.5 per cent, offering one 'of the most beneficial corporate tax environments in the world'.[3] It is not surprising therefore that Ireland was by 2004, the world's most profitable country for US corporations.[4] (Though for lovers of irony and gossip the anti-poverty campaigner and musician Bono moved his music publishing company to the Netherlands after Ireland scrapped a tax break on royalties.[5])

According to Jerry, 'Coca-Cola came here purely for the taxes. Nothing else.' And logically he has a point, why else would a company establish its operations in Ireland and send 'seven out of ten' of its concentrates around the world from there?

Coke Throat in Mexico had explained that the concentrate for Coca-Cola made in Mexico came from Ireland, 'Well, we have a huge manufacturing facility here in Mexico that used to supply all the concentrate, we have the capability, the problem was that producing it here, and paying taxes here was less attractive than the full incentive of bringing it from Ireland and shipping it on a ship, on a freight to Mexico...it's just accounting.' For the Company it is a way of ensuring large profits remain in low tax regimes. As Coke Throat said, 'that way you reduce jobs in the country your bottling plants operate and you reduce tax paying, and this transfers all the benefits to Coca-Cola.'

Indeed, The Coca-Cola Company's annual report for 2006 says, 'Our effective tax rate reflects tax benefits derived from significant operations outside the United States, which are generally taxed at rates lower than the US statutory rate of 35 per cent. Our effective tax rate of approximately 22.8 per cent for the year ended 31 December 2006.' That year the company profits were US $6,578 million. By putting their business in tax havens the Company's declared tax paid that year was US $1,498 million. Had they paid tax in the US at 35 per cent the Company would have contributed approximately another US $804 million. So Coke Throat is right in the sense that is does indeed 'benefit Coca-Cola'.

* * *

Back in Ireland there were three plants that made concentrates, Drogheda in the east, Ballina in the west and a small plant in Athy to the south of Dublin. According to the company, Athy and Ballina 'are sufficient to meet the current and future demand for concentrate and beverage base supply from Ireland'.[6] So Drogheda was shut because of overcapacity and Drogheda's work was moved to Ballina. But according to Jerry there is another agenda going on here, Drogheda is totally unionised and Ballina is totally non-union.

The reason for Ballina being non-union is historic. 'In the Seventies they had a Japanese plant there and the union there had a strike,' Jerry tells me. 'Now the company said "If you don't report for work on Monday we will shut the plant down." And everyone said "Oh yeah, that's what they always say." But come Monday the plant shut and the company left...'

'And because of that the community is anti-union...'

'They blame the union for losing the jobs.'

'So is SIPTU going to try and form a branch in Ballina?'

'It is very difficult to get into Ballina...I have spoken to managers and supervisors, the normal people you would expect to talk to about it. They tell you the same thing. "Not interested, Jerry, not interested, Jerry..."'

When I talked to Ron Oswald from the International Union of Foodworkers, a man who deals with Coca-Cola a lot, he was quite blunt about Coke's operations in Ireland. 'We think there are sophisticated human resource practices inside these operations which essentially are designed to squeeze the space out from where unions can operate.'

The feeling that the company's moves were motivated by a degree of antipathy towards the union was compounded by what happened next. The workers from Drogheda finished their final shift on Friday 27 June 2008. On the following Monday morning, 30 June, it was announced that Coca-Cola was to open a new plant in Wexford in the south.[7] 'By which stage it was too late to try and negotiate moving the Drogheda workers to Wexford.' That chance had gone, and you wouldn't need to be a cynic to think that the timing of the announcement about the Wexford plant was deliberately chosen to come after Drogheda had closed. Jerry says, 'There is one reason and one reason only why they do not want Drogheda people there, they do not want a union over there.'

In their defence Coca-Cola point to the fact that the new plant in Wexford is a flavourings plant, which is different from a concentrate plant. But Jerry says 'Well, if you are trained in one side of the business it won't be too difficult to train for flavourings.' Surely retraining experienced Drogheda workers would be preferable to starting with people with no knowledge at all.

There are rumours that the Wexford plant will make 7X, the company's secret ingredient and Coca-Cola management are reported to have said that the company never allows a union into a 7X plant, apparently fearful that if they have a dispute in the flavour plant the worldwide system goes down. So with Drogheda gone the only union members are in Athy. 'You have about fifty union members, and that is about it for the concentrates side of it, for the whole of Ireland.'

When the closure of Drogheda was announced SIPTU organised demonstrations, Ireland's national media covered the issue and the union even developed its own rescue package that would save the company some 10 million euros in voluntary redundancies and changes in overtime patterns. None of which had any effect. But as Jerry points out 'We failed to get the local community on our side, the local community sees Coca-Cola workers as extremely well paid... So was there a lot of sympathy for them? Probably not.' According to Jerry folk around here have not yet grasped the implications of the plant going, 'This town does not realise the devastation. That plant brought about 30–40 million euros into the local economy. That is gone.'

Jerry comes from a trade-union family, his father was a union man, his brother Ollie is a shop steward. So, during a family holiday when the three of them were sitting up talking late one night, it came as a surprise when his father questioned him. Jerry's father had asked, 'Do you think the company shut the plant down or is it the union that shut the plant?'

'It took me a while to realise what he was getting at,' says Jerry, 'he is a well-known fella about the town, he knows what is going on.' His father's question was not so much a question at all but a gentle nudge as to what the town was thinking.

After taking advantage of the tax regime – and it is a fair bet to say that should the tax rate increase to an unfavourable level the company would shift its operations quicker than you could say 'Is Bono here too?', after 'assistance' from the Irish Development Agency to set up its plants, after reducing the trade union to the margins and after making nearly $6 billion in profit The Coca-Cola Company leaves Drogheda with the community wondering if it was the union that lost the jobs.

Welcome to the World of Coca-Cola.

Acknowledgements

A heartfelt salute goes to Susan McNicholas who agreed to research this book. She was an inspiration to work with and a loyal friend.

Thanks also must go to Conor McNicholas, and Rian too, who put up with my endless calls to Susan at all hours of the night and day.

Martin Herring – who went above and beyond the call of duty, came to India, filmed it, never got paid and remains a true friend.

Thanks to:
Nicky Branch who was transcript queen, Jess Hurd the comrade photographer, Emilio Rodriguez, Alpkan Birelma. Amit Srivasvta, who has been an enlightening presence and friend, Andy Higginbottom at Colombia Solidarity Campaign, Geoff Atkinson who oversaw the *Dispatches* documentary on Coca-Cola for Channel 4, Joan, Phoebe, Carrie, Amber, Sally Friedman, Kathy Haywood, Sarah McDonald at Uproar, David Lom, Armando, Eduardo, Sophie, Saroj Dosh and Alice Wynn Wilson at Action Aid, Peter Hirst and the Red Shed, Karen at Travel Matters, Olaf Christiansen, Kerim Yildiz, Mustafa Gundogu, Mel Alfonso, Tracey Moberley, Helen Waghorn, Bipasha Ahmet, Claudia, Lynn Sardinha, Sumita Joseph, Amanda Jordan. Lew Freidman and Nancy Romero – special thanks for looking after my family in Brooklyn, Ray Rogers, Jerad, Bernardo, Liam and Jaime for extended Brooklyn support, the Polaris Institute, Mariela Kohon at Justice for Colombia, Arife and Ronnie, Bijoy, Sandeep Panday, Nandlal Master, Santosh, Anita Komanduri, Kavaljit Singh, Nick Hildyard at the Corner House for advice and late-night support, Pablo Leal without whom stuff would not have happened, Alejandro Calvillo, Octavio, Joy and Damaso, Antonino García, Laura Jordan, Jason Parkinson, Guy Smallville, Tony Pletts, Ed Smith, Matthew Harvey, Amy Hopwood, Jeff and the list, Wendy, Andrea, Catherine Strauss and Michael Cummins who are bound to have helped somewhere along the line, Steve Mather and Charlie Allen at Hands Off Venezuela. Claire McMullen. Hannah MacDonald and Ken Barlow at Ebury Press, Justine Taylor for patient copyediting, Amanda Telfer for smoothing out the legal wrinkles and Sarah Bennie for waving at me on the M5.

As always CB, IJ and Gan Gan xxx

Appendix A: Endnotes

Prologue

1   Manifesto for Growth, The Coca-Cola Company website, www.thecoca-colacompany.com/ourcompany/manifesto_for_growth.html
2   Obesity Report, House of Commons Health Committee, www.publications.parliament.uk/pa/cm200304/cmselect/cmhealth/23/23.pdf
3   The Coca-Cola Company Press Center, www.thecoca-colacompany.com/presscenter/viewpoints_india_situation.html

Chapter 1: The Happiness Factory

1   'Another Trim In Spending', *New York Times*, 27 June 2007
2   Global Policy Forum
3   US Congressional Budget Office, Testimony before the Committee on the Budget, US House of Representatives, 24 October 2007
4   www.cia.gov/library/publications/the-world-factbook/print/li.html
5   Best Global Brands 2007, Interbrand/*Business Week*
6   The song was later re-recorded and the brand name removed to create 'I'd Like to Teach the World to Sing'
7   Atlanta Development Authority Quarterly Report, 18 May 2005, www.atlantada.com/media/1Q2005.pdf
8   'Business As Usual, Unfortunately', *The Atlanta Journal-Constitution*, 29 March 2005
9   'City Oks Bond Issue', *The Atlanta Journal-Constitution*, 9 June 2005
10 www.coca-cola.co.uk/Company_History/
11 Mark Pendergrast, *For God, Country, and Coca-Cola*, London: Weidenfeld & Nicolson, 1994
12 Martin Luther King, 'I've been to the Mountaintop', 3 April 1968, Mason Temple, Memphis
13 'Coke Settles Bias Lawsuit for $192.5 million', *USA Today*, 17 November 2000
14 www.gettherealfacts.co.uk/docs/gmbh.pdf
15 ibid
16 www.globalwaterchallenge.org/partners/partners.php
17 ibid
18 Best Global Brands 2007, Interbrand/*Business Week*
19 Best Global Brands 2006, Interbrand/*Business Week*
20 Best Global Brands 2005, Interbrand/*Business Week*

Chapter 2: Give 'Em Enough Coke

1   www.alertnet.org/printable.htm?URL=/db/crisisprofiles/CO_DIS.htm

2   'Colombia Paramilitary Chief Says Businesses Back Him', *New York Times*, 7 September 2000

3   www.amicustheunion.org/default.aspx?page=8139

4   www.hrw.org/reports/2001/colombia/1.htm669C8B63. Readers should note that the Colombian army now has created a 6th Division, so if the report were written today I would imagine it would now be entitled the 7th Division

5   'Colombia Paramilitary Chief Says Businesses Back Him', *New York Times*, 7 September 2000

6   Congressional Testimony on Violence against Trade Unionists and Human Rights in Colombia, Human Rights Watch, 28 June 2007

7   www.tuc.org.uk/international/tuc-13722-fo.cfm

8   'Colombia's Uribe ends Washington visit with fate of free trade agreement still uncertain', *International Herald Tribune*, 4 May 2007, www.iht.com/articles/ap/2007/05/04/america/NA-GEN-US-Colombia.php

9   www.amicustheunion.org/default.aspx?page=8139

10 Distorted perceptions of Colombia's conflict, Garry Leech, *Colombia Journal*, 1 June 2008, referencing Adam Isacson, 'CINEP: Colombia's Conflict Is Far from Over,' Center for International Policy, 10 April 2008, www.reliefweb.int/rw/RWB.NSF/db900SID/KKAA-7F89EE? OpenDocument

Chapter 3: Serious Charges

1   *Workplace Assessment in Colombia*, Cal Safety Compliance Corporation 2005, www.cokefacts.com/citizenship/cit_co_assessmentReport.pdf

2   ibid

3   ibid

4   'Coca-Cola sued over bottling plant "terror campaign"', *Guardian*, 21 July 2001, www.guardian.co.uk/world/2001/jul/21/julianborger

5   SINALTRAINAL v THE COCA-COLA COMPANY, news.lp.findlaw.com/ hdocs/docs/cocacola/clmbiacocacola72001.pdf

6   Coca-Cola FEMSA is the Mexican multinational that bought Panamco in December 2002 creating the world's second- largest Coke bottling company, behind Atlanta-based Coca-Cola Enterprises

7   'An Investigation of Allegations of Murder and Violence in Coca-Cola's Columbian plants', The New York City Fact-Finding Delegation on Coca-Cola in Colombia, January 2004 killercoke.org/pdf/ monsfinal.pdf

8   ibid

9   ibid

10 'Energy giant agrees settlement with Burmese villagers', *Guardian*, 15 December 2004

11 'Yahoo Settles With Chinese Journalists', *New York Times*, 14 November 2007

12 www.socialfunds.com/news/article.cgi/2353.html

13 'Feinstein Fights McCain on Burma Tax Break for Big Oil', *New York Sun*, 6 June 2008, www.nysun.com/foreign/feinstein-fights-mccain-on-tax- break-for-big-oil/79452/

14 www.earthrights.org/campaignfeature/senator_feinstein_puts_breaks_on_anti-atca_bill_s._1874.html

15 'Coca-Cola sued over bottling plant "terror campaign"', *Guardian*, 21 July 2001, www.guardian.co.uk/world/2001/jul/21/julianborger

16 fl1.findlaw.com/news.findlaw.com/hdocs/docs/cocacola/clmbiacocacola72001.pdf p. 14

17 ibid, p. 15

18 news.bbc.co.uk/1/hi/business/2909141.stm

19 www.cokefacts.com/facts/facts_co_court_new.pdf

20 'Dismissal Of Coke Lawsuit To Be Appealed', *International Business Times*, 3 November 2006, www.ibtimes.com/articles/20061103/apfn-colombia- coca-cola-lawsuit.htm

Chapter 3.5: The Hush Money That Didn't Stay Quiet

1 www.thecoca-colacompany.com/citizenship/strategic_vision.html

2 The New York City Fact-Finding Delegation on Coca-Cola in Colombia, January 2004, killercoke.org/pdf/monsfinal.pdf

3 www.thecoca-colacompany.com/ourcompany/ar/financial overview.html

4 www.guardian.co.uk/media/2006/aug/18/marketingandpr.business

5 www.newsdesk.org/archives/004005.html

6 www.gettherealfacts.co.uk/index.html

7 Ed Potter interview with author

8 Email from The Coca-Cola Company to author

9 ibid

10 Interview conducted by author

11 Email from The Coca-Cola Company to author

Chapter 4: 'Chile'

1 fl1.findlaw.com/news.findlaw.com/hdocs/docs/cocacola/clmbiacocacola72001.pdf p. 26

2 ibid

3 The defendant is listed as Panamco Colombia (d/b/a Embottellador de Santander, S.A.). Panamco was bought by Coca-Cola FEMSA in 2003. In turn, The Coca-Cola Company owns 31.6 per cent of Coca-Cola FEMSA, www.b2i.us/profiles/investor/fullpage.asp?f=1&BzID=994&to=cp&Nav =o&LangID=1&s=o&ID=1940#COCACOMPANY) although it 'indirectly owns 39.6% of our capital stock, representing 46.4% of our capital stock with full voting rights.' www.b2i.us/profiles/investor/fullpage.asp?f=1&BzID=994&to=cp&Nav= o&LangID=1&s=o&ID=1940#COCACOMPANY

4 fl1.findlaw.com/news.findlaw.com/hdocs/docs/cocacola/clmbiacocacola72001.pdf, p. 28

5   Email from The Coca-Cola Company to author
6   Coca-Cola's Global Workplace Rights Policy, www.thecoca-cola company.com/citizenship/workplace_rights_policy.html
7   Coca-Cola's Global Workplace Rights Homepage, www.thecoca-cola company.com/citizenship/workplace_rights.html
8   www.cokefacts.com/Colombia/facts_co_keyfacts.shtml
9   'The Political Economy of Labor Reform in Colombia', Background paper prepared for the World Development Report 2005, www-wds.worldbank.org/external/default/WDSContentServer/ WDSP/IB/2005/01/31/000090341_20050131101310/Original/314340 Echeverr14WDR050bkgd01public1.doc
10 Interview conducted by author
11 *Labour Rights and Freedom of Association in Colombia*, Colombian Trade Union Federations, October 2007
12 I asked the Company what was the ratio of permanent to casual labour but they ignored my question completely. However, the figures Sinaltrainal give do reflect a nationwide trend in Colombia to put an increasingly large number of workers into casual or temporary employment
13 www.scottish.parliament.uk/business/businessbulletin/bb-06/ bb-12-22f.htm
14 Get The Real Facts, The Coca-Cola Company website, www.gettherealfacts.co.uk/workplace/workplace.html

Chapter 5: The Days of the Great Coke Pledge
1   The Facts: Coca-Cola and Colombia, Coca-Cola website www.cokefacts.com/Colombia/facts_co_colombia_fact_sheet.pdf
2   ibid
3   www.cci.com.tr/en/index.asp
4   Coke Facts: The Truth About The Coca-Cola Company Around the Globe, Coca-Cola website, www.cokefacts.com/facts/facts_aw_ keyfacts.shtml
5   lrights.igc.org/projects/corporate/coke/turkeycoke_complaint_ part_1.pdf page 10
6   lrights.igc.org/projects/corporate/coke/turkeycoke_complaint_ part_1.pdf
7   Kurdish Human Rights Project
8   Coke Facts: The Truth About The Coca-Cola Company Around The Globe, Coca-Cola website, www.cokefacts.com/facts/facts_aw_ keyfacts.shtml
9   ibid
10 ibid
11 lrights.igc.org/projects/corporate/coke/turkeycoke_complaint_ part_1.pdf page 13
12 ibid

13 Coke Facts: The Truth About The Coca-Cola Company Around the Globe, Coca-Cola website, www.cokefacts.com/facts/facts_aw_keyfacts.shtml

Chapter 6: May Contain Traces of Child Labour

1   Coca-Cola website, www.gettherealfacts.co.uk/workplace/workplace.html
2   Coca-Cola website, www.letsgettogether.co.uk/ListQuestionsOfTopic/TopicId=24/
3   El Salvador Turning a Blind Eye, Hazardous Child Labor in El Salvador's Sugarcane Cultivation, June 2004, hrw.org/reports/2004/elsalvadoro604/elsalvadoro604simple.pdf
4   Coca-Cola website, www.gettherealfacts.co.uk/workplace/workplace.html
5   'El Salvador Scarred by Child Labor', *Washington Post*, 10 June 2004
6   *Children for Hire: The Perils of Child Labor in the United States*, Marvin J. Levine, Greenwood Publishing Group, 2003
7   El Salvador Turning a Blind Eye, Hazardous Child Labor in El Salvador's Sugarcane Cultivation June 2004, hrw.org/reports/2004/elsalvadoro604/elsalvadoro604simple.pdf
8   The Coca-Cola Company Response to the Human Rights Watch Report on Child Labor in El Salvador, 13 June 2005, Coca-Cola website, www.thecoca-colacompany.com/presscenter/viewpoints hrw report.html
9   El Salvador Turning a Blind Eye, Hazardous Child Labor in El Salvador's Sugarcane Cultivation, June 2004, hrw.org/reports/2004/elsalvadoro604/elsalvadoro604simple.pdf
10 Email from The Coca-Cola Company to author
11 El Salvador Turning a Blind Eye, Hazardous Child Labor in El Salvador's Sugarcane Cultivation, June 2004, hrw.org/reports/2004/elsalvadoro604/elsalvadoro604simple.pdf
12 Coke Facts: Supplier Guiding Principles, Coca-Cola website, www.cokefacts.com/AroundTheWorld/cit_aw_supplier.shtml
13 El Salvador Turning a Blind Eye, Hazardous Child Labor in El Salvador's Sugarcane Cultivation June 2004, hrw.org/reports/2004/elsalvadoro604/elsalvadoro604simple.pdf
14 Get The Real Facts, Coca-Cola website, www.gettherealfacts.co.uk/workplace/workplace.html
15 El Salvador Turning a Blind Eye, Hazardous Child Labor in El Salvador's Sugarcane Cultivation, June 2004, hrw.org/reports/2004/elsalvadoro604/elsalvadoro604simple.pdf
16 Get The Real facts, Coca-Cola website, www.gettherealfacts.co.uk/workplace/workplace.html
17 El Salvador Turning a Blind Eye, Hazardous Child Labor in El Salvador's Sugarcane Cultivation, June 2004, hrw.org/reports/2004/elsalvadoro604/elsalvadoro604simple.pdf

18 Get The Real facts, Coca-Cola website, www.gettherealfacts.co.uk/
    workplace/workplace.html
19 Email from The Coca-Cola Company to author
20 Get The Real facts, Coca-Cola website, www.gettherealfacts.co.uk/
    workplace/workplace.html
21 ibid
22 Global Workplace Rights Policy, Coca-Cola website, www.thecoca-
    colacompany.com/citizenship/workplace_rights_policy.html
23 Coke Facts: Supplier Guiding Principles, Coca-Cola website,
    www.cokefacts.com/AroundTheWorld/cit_aw_supplier.shtml
24 El Salvador Turning a Blind Eye, Hazardous Child Labor in El
    Salvador's Sugarcane Cultivation, June 2004, hrw.org/reports/
    2004/elsalvador0604/elsalvador0604simple.pdf
25 Get The Real facts, Coca-Cola website, www.gettherealfacts.co.uk/
    workplace/workplace.html
26 ibid
27 ibid
28 ibid
29 Email to author

Chapter 7: Dodge City
1 www.thecoca-colacompany.com/citizenship
2 Centre for Science and the Environment website, www.cseindia.org/
    misc/cola-indepth/cola2006/cola-index.htm
3 'Coke, Pepsi Pay Himalayan Fines', BBC News Online, 17 September
    2002, news.bbc.co.uk/1/hi/world/south_asia/2263917.stm
4 Best Practices in Adult Video website, bpav.org/bp.html
5 'Watch out, Sarge! It's environmentally friendly fire', *Sunday Times*,
    17 September 2006, www.timesonline.co.uk/tol/news/uk/
    article641494.ece
6 BP 2006 Environmental Statement, www.bp.com/liveassets/
    bp_internet/globalbp/STAGING/global_assets/downloads/V/
    verfied_site_reports/N_Amer ica/Whiting_2006.pdf

Chapter 8: Let Them Dig Wells
1 Our Economic Impact, The Coca-Cola Company website,
    www.thecoca-colacompany.com/citizenship/economic_impact.html
2 CIA Factbook: El Salvador, www.cia.gov/library/publications/
    the-world-factbook/geos/es.html
3 Speech by Neville Isdell, Coca-Cola Annual Meeting 2008,
    www.thecoca-colacompany.com/presscenter/viewpoints_
    isdell_annual_meeting_2008.html
4 ibid
5 FMLN – Farabundo Marti Liberation Front (*Frente Farabundo para la
    Liberation*)
6 Ashveille Global Report 2003, www.theglobalreport.org/issues/212/
    environment.html

7   Get the Real Facts, The Coca-Cola Company, www.gettherealfacts. co.uk/environment/environment.html

8   www.thecoca-colacompany.com/citizenship/pdf/cwp_011608.pdf

India: A Prequel

1   'To deny voting rights to Indian shareholders – Coke knocks at FIPB doors', 30 January 2003, www.thehindubusinessline.com/2003/01/ 30/stories/2003013002590100.htm

2   Multilateral Investment Agreement in the WTO, Kavaljit Singh, July 2003, www.wto.org/english/forums_e/ngo_e/multi_invest_agree_ july03_e.pdf

3   To deny voting rights to Indian shareholders – Coke knocks at FIPB doors, The Hindu BusinessLine, 30 January 2003, www.thehindu businessline.com/2003/01/30/stories/2003013002590100.htm

4   'Kerala's Plachimada Struggle', *Economic and Political Weekly*, 14 October 2006, C R Bijoy

5   Poison Vs Nutrition, Centre for Science and Environment, www.cseindia.org/misc/cola-indepth/poison.pdf

6   Minister of Water Resources reply to Lok Sabha (lower House of Indian Parliament) starred question No.2 on 5 July 2004 as cited in Poison Vs Nutrition, Centre for Science and Environment, www.cseindia.org/misc/cola-indepth/poison.pdf

7   www.coca-colaindia.com/water_management/approach-to-water.asp

8   'Coke may wreak havoc in Plachimada: KSSP', *The Hindu* 9 February 2003, www.hinduonnet.com/2003/02/09/stories/ 2003020905340400.htm

9   Letter to Shri. V.K Ebrahim Kunju, The Minister for Industry in Kerala from the Hindustan Coca-Cola Beverages Pvt Ltd, 28 November 2005

10   *Face the Facts* Coca-Cola Update Transcript transmitted 2 January 2004, www.bbc.co.uk/radio4/youandyours/yy_20040102.shtml

11   '*Face The Facts* investigates Coca-Cola plant in India', BBC Press Release, 24 July 2003, www.bbc.co.uk/pressofficepressreleases/ stories/2003/07_july/24/face_facts.shtml

12   ibid

13   ibid

14   Letter to Shri. V.K Ebrahim Kunju, The Minister for Industry in Kerala from the Hindustan Coca-Cola Beverages Pvt Ltd, 28 November 2005

15   'Coca-Cola Don't Poison My Well', *Outlook* 16 May 2005, cited in 'Kerala's Plachimada Struggle', *Economic and Political Weekly*, C R Bijoy, 14 October 2006

16   Letter to Shri. V.K Ebrahim Kunju, The Minister for Industry in Kerala from the Hindustan Coca-Cola Beverages Pvt Ltd, 28 November 2005

17   Email to author

18   Analysis of Pesticides in Soft Drinks, Centre for Science and Environment, 5 August 2003, www.cseindia.org/misc/cola-indepth/ cola2006/pdf/labreport2003.pdf

19   ibid
20   'HC orders govt to test Pepsi products', *The Tribune India*, 11 August
      2003, www.tribuneindia.com/2003/20030812/nation.htm#1
21   'The Street Fight', *Down to Earth*, 15 August 2006, www.downto
      earth.org.in/cover.asp?foldername=20060815&filename=
      news&sid=70&page=1&sec_id=9&p=1
22   Interview conducted by author
23   'JPC report upholds CSE findings', *Hindu Business Line*, 5 February
      2004
24   One Indian crore is a unit of measurement equivalent to 10 million.
      So the soft drink industry turnover is Rs60,000 million (or US$1.4
      billion)
25   Report of Joint Committee on Pesticide Residues in and Safety
      Standards for Soft Drinks, Fruit Juice and Other Beverages,
      parliamentofindia.nic.in/ls/jpc/jpc-prsfb.htm
26   www.cseindia.org/misc/cola-indepth/cola2006/cola_
      press2006.htm

Chapter 9: Kuriji
1   Coca-Cola website, www.gettherealfacts.co.uk
2   Author interview with Professor Rathore, Institute of Development
      Studies, Jaipur
3   'Independent, Third Party Assessment of Coca-Cola Facilities in
      India', TERI Report, www.teriin.org/coke_files/FReport.pdf, page 123
4   Email sent to the author
5   www.vpcomm.umich.edu/pa/key/coke_qa.html
6   'Independent, Third Party Assessment of Coca-Cola Facilities in
      India', TERI Report, www.teriin.org/coke_files/FReport.pdf
7   ibid, p. 124
8   Letter to the University of Michigan from The Coca-Cola Company,
      11 January 2008, www.cokefacts.com/PressCenter/TERI_
      Michigan_Letter.pdf
9   Independent, Third Party Assessment of Coca-Cola Facilities in India',
      TERI Report, www.teriin.org/coke_files/FReport.pdf, page 22
10   Coke Gets CSR Award Amidst Protests, Business Standard, 19
      February 2008, www.indiaresource.org/news/2008/1013.html
11   Deepak Jolly Conferred Communicator of the Year Award, Company
      News, 21 March 2006, www.afaqs.com/news/company_news/
      Corporate/13108.html

Chapter 10: Gas
1   Coke Facts: The Truth About The Coca-Cola Company Around the
      Globe, www.cokefacts.com/India/facts_in_keyfacts.shtml
2   Email from The Coca-Cola Company to author
3   Interview conducted by author

4   'Independent, Third Party Assessment of Coca-Cola Facilities in India', TERI Report, www.teriin.org/coke_files/FReport.pdf, page 128
5   ibid, p. 128
6   ibid, p. 128

Chapter 11: The Fizz Man's Burden

1   Letter to the University of Michigan from The Coca-Cola Company, 11 January 2008, www.cokefacts.com/PressCenter/TERI_Michigan_Letter.pdf
2   ibid
3   ibid
4   Email sent to author
5   ibid
6   Interview conducted by author
7   'Independent, Third Party Assessment of Coca-Cola Facilities in India', TERI Report, www.teriin.org/coke_files/FReport.pdf
8   ibid
9   Letter to the University of Michigan from The Coca-Cola Company, 11 January 2008, www.cokefacts.com/PressCenter/TERI_Michigan_Letter.pdf
10   TERI report

Chapter 12: Second Fattest in the Infants

1   'Mexicans living fat, almost like Americans', *Oakland Tribune*, 24 March 2008
2   World Health Organisation, www.who.int/infobase/report.aspx?rid=114&iso=MEX&ind=BMI
3   'Mexicans living fat, almost like Americans', *Oakland Tribune*, 24 March 2008
4   www.ustr.gov/assets/Trade_Agreements/Monitoring_Enforcement/Dispute_Settlement/WTO/Dispute_Settlement_Listings/asset_upload_file565_6449.pdf
5   'In Mexico, Taking Fizz Out of the Cola Giants', *Los Angeles Times*, 28 December 2005
6   'Pepsi tackles childhood obesity with videogames in Mexico', *Guardian*, 2 January 2008
7   www.thecoca-colacompany.com/ourcompany/ar/percapitaconsumption_latin_america.html#mexico
8   Controversial Sweetener Dropped from Mexican Coke Zero, Cox News Service, 18 March 2008
9   fox.presidencia.gob.mx/en/cabinet/?contenido=18150
10   Coca-Cola Refuses To Cut Advertising Spending In Mexico, Internet Securities, April 2001
11   Interview conducted by author with Big Cola lawyer

Chapter 13: Belching Out the Devil

1   *Huitepec, the Mayan Hill of Water*, Coca-Cola's Raid on a Sacred
    Mountain, John Ross 7 September 2007, www.counterpunch.org/
    ross09072007.html,
2   Author interview with Antonino García
3   Cola Wars in Mexico, Beverly Bell, In These Times, 6 October 2006,
    www.inthesetimes.com/article/2840/
4   fox.presidencia.gob.mx/en/cabinet/development/?contenido=18150

Chapter 14: We're On a Road to Delaware

1   www.thecoca-colacompany.com/presscenter/viewpoints_isdell_
    annual_meeting_2008.html
2   Information on Ray's campaign can be found at: www.killercoke.org
3   Coca-Cola Annual Report SEC Filing 2007, www.secinfo.com/
    d14D5a.t18P7.b.htm
4   www.ilo.org/global/lang—en/index.htm
5   University of Michigan, Press and Media Relations Department,
    Questions and Answers re: Coca-Cola, Updated 11 April 2006,
    www.vpcomm.umich.edu/pa/key/coke_qa.html
6   'The Facts: Coca-Cola and Columbia', The Coca-Cola Company
7   events.streamlogics.com/pmtv/coke/apr19-06/auditorium/
    index.asp at 29:56
8   www.thecoca-colacompany.com/ourcompany/bios/ bio_76.html
9   Interview conducted by the author
10 'Make Your Mark With Branding', *Ocala Business Journal*, 21 April
    2008, www.ocala.com/article/20080421/OBIZ/
    117317226/1357/obiz&title=Make_your_mark_with_branding

Postscript

1   'Coca-Cola to cut 256 jobs in Drogheda', *The Irish Times*, 29 August
    2007
2   The Coca-Cola Company Press Release, 2 April 2008, www.thecoca-
    colacompany.com/presscenter/nr_20080402_timing_of_first_qtr_
    earnings.html
3   www.idaireland.com/home/index.aspx?id=659
4   www.finfacts.ie/irelandeconomy/usmultinationalprofitsireland.htm
5   'Bono, Preacher on Poverty Tarnishes Halo with Irish Tax move,'
    6 Oct 2006, Fergal O'Brien, Bloomberg,
    www.bloomberg.com/apps/news?pid=20601109&sid=aef6sR6o.
    DgM&refer=home
6   'Coca-Cola to move production to non-unionised plant',
    www.eurofound.europa.eu/euro/2007/09/articles/ie0709079i/htm
7   'Shock over Coca-Cola investment in Wexford', 2 July 2008, *Drogheda
    Independent*, www.drogheda-independent.ie/news/shock-over-
    cocacola-investment-in-wexford-1431032.html

Appendix B: Coke Q&A

Initially I expected the company not to respond to any of the questions I put to them. I had chased Ed Potter, The Coca-Cola Company's Global Workplace Rights Director. I had even negotiated with company personnel about 'potentially answering questions' but all of this faded to nothing and they returned to silent mode. However, Coke did resurface responding to a critical comment piece [by the NGO War on Want] in the *Guardian* newspaper by way of the letters page. As all other avenues of communication with them had been closed to me, I decided to write to the *Guardian* too.

> *Guardian*, Saturday 10 May 2008
> Interesting to see Lauren Branston defending Coca-Cola against 'alleged misdeeds in the past' (Letters, May 8). Especially as I visited India last month to research the current accusations levelled at the company. Lauren and Coca-Cola have not been able to reply to these serious questions about their business practices. So here are a few of them, in the hope that I can get a reply now. 1) Didn't Coca-Cola formally sponsor the TERI foundation, which carried out the 'independent report' Lauren refers to? 2) Despite this potential conflict, the report noted the company's refusal to give crucial documents and data needed for a proper assessment of the company; are you going to make this data available? 3) The report says the company's efforts to deal with the water crisis in Kaladera rely on rainwater harvesting – the company's much-vaunted solution to its water consumption problems. However, the report also notes that rainwater harvesting relies on rainfall, so can you tell me where this rainfall comes from in a drought-prone area, ie, a place with not much rainfall? Even the report concludes the company's efforts are 'unlikely to be meaningful'. 4) The report lists possible options to address the water crisis in Kaladera – one of those is to shut the Coke plant down. Any chance you will follow the report's advice? 5) Should I send other questions for Lauren to answer via the *Guardian* letters page?
> **Mark Thomas**
> London

The company did not respond to the *Guardian* letter, however, after a series of emails to the company detailing questions for them, they agreed to provide some answers. You can get a flavour of the correspondence between us from the two emails below.

Dear Mark,

Thanks for your email with another set of questions, which I would like to reassure you that we are working on. I am happy to come back to you once, to all your questions and will endeavour to meet your deadline of the 8th of July, however, I hope you understand that this involves a lot of work, pulling together answers from questions directed to our operations in many different countries around the world on important, and complex issues.

Moreover, I have to tell you that when you say 'these are all the questions I have at the moment', I have to say to you – we will not continue to answer your questions ad nauseam. I would suggest that if you have any further questions you submit them now (and we will let you know how quickly we can come back to you with answers, which will most likely be later than the 8th of July, at this stage).

Best wishes,

Lauren

Dear Lauren

Thanks for your mail. I understand you're very busy and that you will need to contact your colleagues abroad for some of the answers. I appreciate your efforts to find these answers. If I do have any other questions I will send them to you in the hope that you will be able to do your best with them.

Moreover, I should remind you that the Company has responded to precisely none of the questions for the book, some of which were submitted well over a month ago. Thus the use of the term ad nauseam, meaning a sickening or excessive degree, might be more appropriate for example in a phrase like, 'The Company prevaricated ad nauseam'.

Kindest Regards

Mark

Eventually the Company sent over their responses. Here are their answers reproduced word for word with my questions included. There is one unexpected bonus: when the Company sent over their replies to the allegations about Colombia, they accidentally included their lawyers' strikethroughs and comments – so you get a chance to see how they finessed their answers and spot the odd line the company deemed unfit for public consumption. Enjoy...and a hearty thank you to whoever left them in.

Colombia

~~CONFIDENTIAL ATTORNEY-CLIENT PRIVILEGED WORK PRODUCT AND COMMUNICATION~~

Note: Since our bottlers are separate companies that are not controlled by The Coca-Cola Company, the responses below are necessarily based on information available to The Coca-Cola Company and our subsidiary in Colombia. W~~and we~~ do not purport to speak for the independent bottlers.~~:~~

1) Has The Coca-Cola Company *itself* ever issued any public statements or taken out any advertising defending the right to unionizse and/or to denounce the violence directed against SINALTRAINAL? If so, may we see a copy of these statements? Representatives of The Coca-Cola Company in Colombia meet regularly with Vice President Francisco Santos and members of the Human Rights Office of the Vice Presidency, to keep them informed of our challenges and initiatives, to reiterate the Company's strong support of efforts to eradicate violence of any kind, including vio~~oi~~lence directed at union organizers, and to request ~~their~~ the Government's assistance in ~~the~~ protecting~~protection of~~ union leaders in ~~the Coca-Cola~~ bottling plants and ~~, as well as~~ the timely and thorough investigation of any incidents of violence reported by the trade unions. Company representatives ~~have~~ also have met regularly with the Minister of Social Protection (Labor) and the Defensor del Pueblo (Ombudsman) on similar topics, and with the Minister of the Interior, who manages the government's protection program for union leaders (with funds from Plan Colombia).

The Coca-Cola Company~~[I understand that TCCC~~, in conjunction with setting-up the Colombia Foundation, itself specifically advertised its support for union rights an opposition to violence. ~~(PL would know the answer to this I assume.) I also believe that the press release advertising the existence of the now defunct settlement talks specifically referenced TCCC's strong opposition to trade union violence. JNH will check my records and revert. These examples would more directly answer the question.]~~

2) Has The Coca-Cola Company's bottlers in Colombia ever issued any public statements or taken out any advertising defending the right to unionizse and/or to denounce the violence directed against SINALTRAINAL? If so, may we see a copy of these statements?

Throughout the years the independent bottlers of Coca-Cola ® brand products in Colombia ~~The independent Coca-Cola bottlers in Colombia~~ have frequently and publicly denounced violence against union members in Colombia. See attached advertisement for example.

The largest of such bottling enterprises, Coca-Cola FEMSA, ~~has~~ also has informed us that it is their practice immediately to notify the appropriate authorities as soon as management is made aware of threats against union members. Coca-Cola FEMSA supplies notification and information to, among others, the Minister of Social Protection (Labor) and the Defensor del Pueblo (Ombudsman), as well as the Minister of the Interior, who manages the government's protection program for union leaders.

3) Has The Coca-Cola Company *itself* ever investigated or engaged an independent third party to conduct a comprehensive investigation into the allegations of ties between bottler management and paramilitaries? And if so, what were the conclusions?

In the spring of 2005, The Company commissioned an independent assessment of bottling plants in Colombia by the internationally respected and certified social compliance auditor Cal Safety Compliance Corporation to look into current workplace rights practices of the bottlers in Colombia. The assessment, which included interviews of hundreds of employees throughout Colombia, confirmed that workers in ~~Coca-Cola~~such plants enjoy freedom of association, collective bargaining rights, and a work atmosphere free of anti-union intimidation.

Assessments by other unions in Colombia and elsewhere have likewise found no evidence of wrongdoing by the Company or its independent bottlers. In an open letter to the National Union of Students, the UK trade unions explained the Company's lack culpability as follows:

Since the first call to boycott Coca-Cola over Colombia was issued in 2003, the UK trade union movement has investigated and monitored the situation closely. We have sent delegations to Colombia to speak to workers' representatives there. We have kept in close contact with trade unions in Colombia and have continued to raise issues of importance to them by taking up their cause with workers, politicians and the media here in the UK. We have taken the lead from the CUT [Colombia's United Workers Confederation] . . . the democratic umbrella organization for Colombian trade unions, as well as from the IUF (the International Union of Foodworkers), the relevant global union federation. ~~Since 2003, no evidence has been provided to link Coca-Cola to the assassination of its workers in Colombia.~~

(March 21, 2006 joint letter to the National Union of Students from three UK trade unions, Amicus, T & G and GMB). (emphasis added).

In addition, the Company and its independent bottlers welcome efforts by other international organizations, including the International Labor Organization, to verify the Company's internal assessments.

4) When did The Coca-Cola Company become aware of the murder of Isidero Gil in the Carepa plant? And what was the Company's immediate response?

[JNH: Will need Ben Garren or Ed Potter to opine. My understanding is that Wwithin days of the murder, the Company was alerted to the situation and gave its full support to all staff and employees of the Carepa facility, the vast majority of whom (employees and managers alike) were forced to relocate from the territory.]

5) What is the current status of the promised ILO investigation and evaluation of Coca-Cola bottling operations in Colombia and what is the new timetable?

The political situation in Colombia has become more complicated since the assessment requests were made to the ILO. In particular, the ILO has placed a priority on addressing the issue of impunity, resolving the inconsistencies between the ILO standards that the Colombian Government has ratified and existing labor and employment law, and assuring that the historic tripartite agreement reached in June 2006 under the auspices of the ILO is fully implemented. To address these political complexities, in particular to be certain that there is overall government, business and union support for the procedures and methods of the ILO assessment, the Director General of the ILO, has required that each of these constituencies sign off of the assessment protocol before it begins.

For its part, The Coca-Cola Company fully supports the ILO initiative and investigation and remains willing and ready to cooperate in whatever reasonable form the ILO requests.

6) What is the remit scope of the promised ILO investigation?

This is an independent investigation that will be conducted by the ILO, therefore we do not know the full remit scope and process of the assessment. They The ILO has have informed us the Company that the assessment will include a scope will be primarily a review of current workers' rights at in the workplace, including conditions of work, health and safety, labor relations and social security.

7) Can The Coca-Cola Company confirm its claims that if the ILO investigation does get underway, it will investigate both past and present labour rights abuses in the Coke bottling plants in Colombia?

~~The ILO assessment is of current workplace rights at independent Coca-Cola bottling facilities in Colombia.~~

~~[FC: Suggest we attempt to address the ILO's non-investigation of past incidents this way:~~ "By mandate, the ILO assessment team is concerned with ensuring the implementation and maintenance of progressive labor practices in member countries. Accordingly, the assessment function traditionally does not investigate specific allegations of past labor abuse, which is a task performed by a separate arm of the ILO charged with evaluating formal complaints made by union members. In fact, SINALTRAINAL recently has filed complaints with the ILO, who is considering the charges and whether to conduct a further inquiry into the allegations."

8) If that is the case, can The Coca-Cola Company explain how the ILO can investigate past labour rights abuses within a company (in this case The Coca-Cola Company bottlers – Panamco and Bebidas y Alimentos) when the ILO has a remit to investigate only on a countrywide rather than company specific basis and can only investigate current labour rights abuse?
As noted immediately above, t~~T~~he ILO assessment ~~is~~ concerns~~of~~ current workplace ~~rights~~ practices at the independent ~~Coca-Cola~~ bottling facilities in Colombia. The ILO has relevant experience monitoring labor practices in the garment industry which we believe will be helpful in this investigation. And as set forth above, the ILO has a separate arm to investigate complaints by union members.

9) Will The Coca-Cola Company publish or show the contents of the letter/agreement Neville Isdell claims the company has from the ILO stating the organization will investigate past and present labour rights abuses in the Coke bottling plants in Colombia?
The ILO assessment is of current workplace rights at independent ~~Coca-Cola~~ bottling facilities in Colombia. As set forth above, the ILO has a well-established procedure for investigating formal complaints by union members.

10) Has The Coca-Cola Company taken any action against its bottler for the false allegation made by a bottler security manager in Bucaramanga that lead to the wrongful imprisonment of Luis Eduardo García and Domingo Flores amongst others?
The Coca-Cola Company does not own or have the right to unilaterally punish or sanction the employees of the independent bottlers within its system. The Company does, however, seek to promote progressive labor rights within its bottling system and supply chain, and has established an office within the Company headed by Ed Potter that is charged with liaising with local bottlers to resolve any issue that may arise.

In the case of Messrs. Garcia and Flores, TCCC has discussed the matter with the bottler and understands that the bottler employees gave truthful statements to the Colombian government investigators. This was the extent of the involvement of the bottler involvement in the case. The Company understands that following the Government's investigation, Messrs. Garcia and Flores were compensated for their time away from work, provided additional security and protection and have remained employed by the bottler.

11) Does The Coca-Cola Company share the view of its bottlers that in bringing legal action against the Company, SINALTRAINAL had libelled and defamed the company? And did the Company agree with the defamation suit brought against SINALTRAINAL?

~~TCCC~~ The Company has not~~never~~ filed any official action against SINALTRAINAL in the case. ~~Coca-Cola~~ Local bottlers in Colombia ~~Panamco~~ have denounced the ~~defendants'~~ certain actions – including incidents such as the painting of graffiti on bottling plant walls and barricading of plant entrances – to authorities based on ~~its~~ reasonable concerns for the safety of the Company and its ability to continue operations. In particular, the union's careless accusations that the bottlers somehow conspire with or support paramlitaries endangers the lives of the bottlers' management and personnel, who themselves are targets for violence, including at the direction Colombia's notorious guerila insurgency. T~~Regardless, regarding the circumstance of the incident, but~~to our knowledge, the bottlers have not ~~did not~~ filed any separate official action against SINALTRAINAL or its leaders.~~; rather, the company relied on the government's investigation of the crime, which resulted in the arrest and later release of some of the union members.~~

~~For its part, The Coca-Cola Company believes that the allegations in the law suits – and the law suits themselves – not only are intentionally false, but are part of a well-funded effort by U.S. labor interests, including the United Steelworkers (whose counsel assisted in bringing the lawsuits), to use the Coca-Cola ® brand to undermine free trade and the interests of foreign employers. [FG: I assume that we would prefer not to take potshots at the Steealworkers not sound like we are favoring foreigners of any stripe over the U.S. I wouldn't push this beyond saying that the lawsuits are intentionally false and part of a coordinated effort to use the Coca-Cola brand for their own political purposes.]~~

12) Did any Coca-Cola ~~Femsa~~ FEMSA bottling plants pay money for SINALTRAINAL members to give up their trade-union membership? If so how any many trade union members did the Coca-Cola FEMSA bottling plants pay to the trade-union members? How many trade-union members were given money to give up their membership? Over what period of time did this occur?

We ~~cannot respond on behalf of Coca-Cola FEMSA, however it is the case that in any company, some employees are are terminated forbeen fired with legal cause (such as absenteeism, non- or under-performance, or violation of workplace rules). During an economic downturn or restructuring, other employees – some union members, some not – also may seek to retire and accept due to different reasons- and accept early retirement packages as part of restructuring of the bottlers' operations. The presence of unions in the local bottling plants of Coca-Cola ® brand products in Colombia remains strong.~~ have no information to indicate that Coca-Cola FEMSA has ever paid money for SINALTRAINAL members to give up their trade union membership. The independent bottler guarantees the right to freedom of association and collective bargaining and has multiple agreements with multiple unions- and in a country where 4 percent of workers from unionizing, 31 percent of Coca-Cola bottler employees belong to unions.

13) Why did negotiations between The Coca-Cola Company and the plaintiffs in the ATCA suit break down earlier this year? What conditions did The Coca-Company put on any settlement?
In 2001, SINALTRAINAL, with the assistance of U.S. labor interests, filed ~~The ATCA~~ Alient Torts Statute lawsuits ~~were filed in 2001 by the Colombian union Sinaltrainal~~ against The Coca-Cola Company and ~~two~~ several entities affiliated with independent bottlers of Coca-Cola ® brand products in Colombia~~bottlers~~. The Coca-Cola Company was dismissed by the United States District Court for the Southern District of Florida from the case in 2003, which held that the Company possessed no control over or liability for the alleged conduct of third parties in rural Colombia. In October 2006, ~~the two~~ the remaining defendants ~~Coca-Cola bottlers in Colombia~~ also were dismissed from the case. ~~Sinaltrainal's motion to bring The Coca-Cola Company back into the lawsuit was denied and the judge has ordered that the cases be closed. Sinaltrainal has appealed the dismissal of the case and the appeal is pending.~~

Despite having secured its dismissal from the lawsuits, the Company ~~TCCC~~ sought - as it has throughout this dispute - to engage~~d~~ in ~~extended direct~~ constructive dialogue with the plaintiffs — both to better understand their concerns and also to assess whether a mediated resolution of the parties' differences could be achieved.~~in the litigation and the plaintiffs' representatives but the dialogue reached an impasse.~~ The parties' talks were fruitful and informative, although no final resolution was possible. An impasse was reached and no further discussions are anticipated at this time. ~~No further dialogue is anticipated related to the allegations of the lawsuit.~~

The Coca-Cola Company wishes to underscore that it is innocent of the charges brought by the plaintiffs in the dismissed litigation. However, ~~TCCC~~ the Company is sympathetic to the underlying concerns about violence against any member of Colombian society, including union members – which is one of the reasons why the Company helped fund and sponsor the Colombia Foundation, whose work continues to remediate the effects of violence in the country.

El Salvador

14. Is it still the case that Central Izalco is the sole supplier for Coke bottlers in El Salvador? If not, who are the other suppliers?
El Salvador is a controlled market and as such we buy from a marketing agency, who in turn assigns the volume to a qualified source. Central Izalco and El Angel are the two mills (out of 8) that meet our quality requirements and have been approved for use by our system in that country.

15. Your website states, '*We only buy from sugar mills that adhere to our standards and we constantly monitor for compliance. If we find a supplier is not meeting our standards, we take immediate action. We care about the plight of these children and are serious about helping them*' – could you explain how often and what form the constant monitoring takes place for Central Izalco and/or any other suppliers?
Our Company TCCC routinely utilizes independent third-parties to assess suppliers' compliance with our Company's Supplier Guiding Principles (SGP). The SGP are a vital pillar of TCCC's workplace accountability programs. They contain requirements that our direct suppliers must comply with regarding freedom of association and collective bargaining; prohibition of child labor; prohibition of forced labor and abuse of labor; elimination of discrimination; work hours and wages; provision of a safe and healthy workplace; and protection of the environment. If a supplier fails to uphold any aspect of the SGP requirements, the supplier is expected to implement corrective actions. The Company reserves the right to terminate an agreement with any supplier that cannot demonstrate that they are upholding the SGP requirements and has done so.

16. Your website states that you are '*working towards hiring a monitoring system for plantations*' – has the multi-stakeholder initiative yet hired a monitoring system? And if so, what is its remit, how often does it report, how is it funded and what results have been found so far?
The multi-stakeholder initiative, led by the Ministry of Labor and the El Salvadoran Sugar Association, has put into place several social monitoring systems for the plantations.

Ministry of Labor Work:

- During the harvest the Ministry of Labor has labor inspectors whose only task is to detect child labor.
- Those cooperatives found to have child labor are subject to economic sanctions.

El Salvadoran Sugar Association Work:
- The Sugar Association employs 10 social workers who implement the industry's social responsibility programs.
- Every morning during the harvest those 10 social workers visit the cane farms looking for evidence of child labor.
- If a child is found cutting cane he or she is immediately removed.

In addition, every engineer from the sugar mills who works at the sugar cane farms has the obligation to report child labor. Failure to report child labor, would result in the termination of the engineer's contract.

17. Your website refers to *'Nine thousand children have been removed from the sugarcane fields in El Salvador over the last three years through our efforts with the UN and the Sugar Association.'*
a) Can you explain how the figure of 9,000 was calculated and by whom? How many of those 9,000 were removed from plantations that provide cane for Central Izalco?
All figures quoted have been determined by the International Labour Organizations' International Programme on the Elimination of Child Labor. More information about IPEC can be found at: http://www.ilo.org/ipec
b) What is the nature of the work that The Coca-Cola Company has undertaken through the UN that has led to this? Has the company sponsored or paid for practical programmes or are you referring to company support / lobbying for the establishment of UN norms and standards?
Our Company has publicly supported a proposal, authored by the World Bank and Business for Social Responsibility, to help position El Salvador as a responsible-sourcing country in conjunction with UN norms and standards. And we have funded the multi-stakeholder initiative working towards hiring social monitors to work with the co-ops to monitor and address child labor, led by the Ministry of Labor and the El Salvadoran Sugar Association.

We have also participated in multi-stakeholder dialogues that have included the International Labor Organization of the UN to understand and address the root causes of this serious issue in El Salvador.

18. Your website states, *'On Coca-Cola's recommendation, Fundazucar (the Salvadoran Sugar Association) engaged a social compliance auditing firm that helped the Association determine how to detect and control child labour and associated issues.'* **What is the name of the social auditing firm? How often have they reported**

and what were their recommendations?
The social auditing firm is the internationally respected and certified
social compliance auditor, Cal Safety Compliance Corporation. The
audits have taken place during the 2004–2007 harvests.

**19. Your website states, 'Coca-Cola has partnered with TechnoServe,
a local NGO working with targeted co-ops to find alternative sources
of income for youth 14–18 years of age'. What is the nature of the
partnering of TechnoServe? Was there any financial assistance
involved? Have there been any assessments made of the results
of the partnering and if so, by whom?**
Techno Serve is an NGO dedicated to the development of businesses
who work in the agricultural field. We partnered with Techo Serve to
financially support the programs that aid children through educational
opportunities in El Salvador.

**20. The Human Rights Watch report, Turning a Blind Eye,
recommends, 'In particular, it [Coca-Cola] should incorporate the
UN Norms in its contractual arrangements with suppliers and should
require its suppliers to do the same throughout their supply chains'.
Are there any plans to do this and if so, what is your timetable?**
Our Company's Supplier Guiding Principles (SGP) communicate to
direct suppliers our values and expectations and emphasize the
importance of responsible environmental and workplace policies and
practices that comply, at a minimum, with applicable local laws and
regulations. Our SGP is consistent with the key elements of the
International Labor Organization of the UN's core labor standards
(freedom of association and collective bargaining, forced or compulsory
labor, child labor and discrimination).

India

**21. According to the Company website, 'indirectly, our business in
India creates employment to more than 150,000 people'. a) Of this
figure, how many is casual or outsourced labour working within
the plants? b) Can you break down this figure into categories?
Does this figure include street vendors, outsourced workers,
delivery drivers etc?**
The Company and its bottling partners provide direct employment to
more than 10,000 people in India. In addition, soft drinks being a
seasonal business in India, the Company and its bottling partners also
employ nearly 10,000 contractor's workmen during the peak season
(summer season). This positive economic impact is multiplied by the
employment generated through our chain of distributors and retailers,

through our vendors and suppliers, through the transporters, signage painters, point of purchase and other marketing material designers and manufacturers etc. As per an estimate by National Council of Applied Economic Research (NCAER) the soft drink industry generates an overall employment of 1,300 for every 1 million cases sold.

22. What financial benefits – tax incentives/subsidies/ infrastructure payments etc – were given to Coca-Cola for building their plant in Kaladera?

In order to fuel economic development in remote areas, the governments of all states set up Industrial areas to encourage industries to invest in economically undeveloped/underdeveloped areas. The government gives financial incentives such as tax exemptions of 5–7 years etc. as per the policy. The Coca-Cola plant at Kaladera was given sales tax exemption as per the Industrial policy of the Rajasthan State government.

23. How much ground water has Coca-Cola extracted each year for its plant in Kaladera for the last five years?

Year	Water Extraction in Kilo litres
2003	139156
2004	211173
2005	90660
2006	84074
2007	87977

24. What on-going relationship regarding rainwater harvesting do Coca-Cola and the Rajasthan Ground Water Board have?

Coca-Cola in India has undertaken a range of water conservation and awareness programs across the country. These programs are undertaken in partnership with Central Ground Water Authority, State Ground Water Boards, Resident Welfare Associations, Market Welfare Associations, Schools and Colleges, Industry Associations, NGOs and local communities. In Rajasthan also the Company has undertaken a range of water conservation initiatives like revival of traditional water bodies, installation of rainwater recharge shafts, rooftop rainwater harvesting projects etc. These projects have been undertaken under the guidance of Rajasthan State Ground Water Board. Thus, while there is formal relationship that exists between Rajasthan State Ground Water Board (RSGWB) and the Company, RSGWB focuses on initiatives that could enhance groundwater levels and hence have provided guidance to our rainwater harvesting initiatives in the state and have also assessed them periodically.

25. Specifically, how many rainwater harvesting shafts does Coca-Cola have in its rainwater harvesting scheme in Kaladera? And over what area?

The Company has installed 143 recharge shafts in Kaladera and surrounding areas spread over an area of 17 sq. KMS

26. How does Coca-Cola monitor its rainwater harvesting scheme?
The RWH schemes are monitored through defined protocols. For any location, before establishing any Rainwater Harvesting (RWH) system, studies are done with respect to area available for recharge, average annual rainfall, the type water harvesting area (to determine the coefficient of recharge) and any assumptions/considerations made in site selection. The site selection would depend on ground water situation, infiltration capacity of the local hydrogeology, and need for RWH intervention, including the ownership of such intervention. The established technical feasibility is vetted by local government or research agency involved with water resource management and the designs are finalized. The structures are executed by expert agencies and its completeness is verified by the competent technical experts. Usually, the executing agency is a local NGO group and would have responsibility to maintain the developed structure for period of three years initially. We have also developed a monitoring protocol to maintain the structures on annual basis to understand its full functionality and usefulness. Each year the incident rainfall data is obtained from nearest government meteorological observatory at the end of the year and the estimated recharge potential is revalidated by inserting the appropriate value of rainfall.

In addition, the Company undertakes regular maintenance of most of the structures with help of NGOs/ environmental groups. The Company, along with community/NGO, tries to take water table readings before and after monsoon, keeps historical data, conduct community interviews, facilitate media visits to understand the efficacy and impact of such projects besides site visits by its own high-ranking officials.

Besides the above, rising water level, non requirement to re-drill the borewells, functioning of defunct borewells, higher agriculture yield etc have been reported by communities across the country which serves as the community's own assessment of the impact of RWH.

27. What size are the rainwater harvesting shafts? And from what area (measurement) of land do they collect from?
The recharge shafts provide a pathway to the collected rainwater to flow into the ground through a reverse filter system and recharge the ground water. Each shaft has a diameter of 2 feet and average depth of about 105 feet. While the catchment area is different for different locations, each shaft receives water from approximately 10-15 hectares. Each shaft goes to a depth of over 100 feet below the ground and is filled with filter media to enable quick recharge of the ground water.

28. How much rainwater does the Coca-Cola Company estimate

has been recharged by its rainwater harvesting shafts in Kaladera annually for the last five years? How is this monitored? Is it independently verified?

Our rainwater harvesting through recharge shafts started in 2004. In Kaladera, the rainwater harvesting systems that the Company has installed have the potential to recharge about 15 times the amount of water the plant uses currently, assuming normal rainfall (560 mm/year). Even in recent years when rainfall has been below average, actual recharge has been more than 5 times the amount of water used for production of our beverages. (See attached report by the former Chief Engineer of Rajasthan State Ground water Department)

Besides the Company's efforts at monitoring the RWH projects in partnership with NGOs etc as mentioned above, senior hydrogeologists of State Ground water department have been independently monitoring the RWH initiatives. A former chief engineer of Rajasthan State Ground Water Board had independently assessed potential of the same (copy attached). Need this report [sic] Most recently TERI has assessed our water management practices including RWH projects in Kaladera area.

29. How much rainwater does The Coca-Cola Company estimate has been recharged by its rainwater harvesting scheme on the two school roofs in Kaladera annually for the last five years? How is this monitored? Is it independently verified? What is the coverage area (measurement) of the roofs?

In fact there are four educational institutions are covered under roof water harvesting in Kaladera locations. The total roof area covered is about 6,400 square metres and the design RWH potential at average annual rain fall is about 3,400 cubic metres.

The monitoring activity is detailed under question 8 [sic] above.

30. What are the specific calculations that led Coca-Cola to claim its rainwater harvesting structures in Kaladera recharge five times more water than it uses even in drought years, and furthermore has the potential to recharge over 50 core litres of ground water annually at average rainfall?

There are accepted norms as adhered by Central Ground Water Board, UN agencies, Govt. bodies for estimating RWH potential from different surfaces. While for roof top a coefficient between 80-85% is well accepted (given that recharge pit/well/shaft is designed to receive that quantity of water) and for surface water coefficients between 10-20% are accepted, depending on land use/topography, intensity of rainfall, nature of soil etc.

Even with most conservative estimate for catchment of 0.1 sq KM for each shaft and a coefficient of 10%, these shafts would receive over 850 million litres of water.

31. What is the Company's response to the TERI report assertion in its plant specific recommendations for Kaladera, regarding Coca-Cola's rainwater harvesting structures, that 'since the rainfall is scanty, the recharge achieved through such structures is unlikely to be meaningful'?

The TERI report notes that the Company is a relatively small user of water in Kaladera, tapping far less than one percent the area's available water. In Kaladera, the rainwater harvesting systems Coca-Cola has installed have the potential to recharge about 15 times the amount of water the plant uses currently, assuming normal rainfall (560 mm/year). Even in recent years when rainfall has been below average, actual recharge has been more than 5 times the amount of water used for production of our beverages. Coca-Cola has reduced its water use ratio within the plant by more than 40% over the last five years. The Confederation of Indian Industries (CII) has recognized the Hindustan Coca-Cola Kaladera plant as a 'Water Efficient Unit' across industries at the National Awards for Excellence in Water Management. The Kaladera plant also has won the 'Innovative Project Award' for its contribution towards reduction in specific water consumption.

32. What controls and monitoring have been put in place regarding treated wastewater through land application at Coca-Cola's Kaladera plant?

The wastewater is treated at the wastewater treatment plant at the manufacturing facility prior to use of treated wastewater for irrigating developed greenbelt at the plant premises. The treated wastewater complies with both the company and local standard on the wastewater treatment and disposal. The wastewater treatment plant is designed to treat 1000 m3/day wastewater, while average wastewater generation does not exceed more than 120 m3/day on an average. The overcapacity of the wastewater plant, resultant of the water conservation measures taken by the plant over the period ensures the consistent quality of the wastewater from the treatment plant.

The treated wastewater is monitored in-house as well as external laboratory as per below mentioned frequency

- Routine monitoring of about 8 parameters at in-house laboratory (Biological Oxygen Demand (BOD), Chemical Oxygen Demand (COD), Total Dissolved Solids (TDS), Oil and Grease (O & G), TSS (Total suspended solids),PH, Sulfates and Chlorides.)
- Monthly check of 9 parameters required by pollution control board from Ministry of Environment and Forest (MOEF), India approved laboratory.
- Quarterly monitoring of wastewater as per Coca-Cola standards.
- The monthly monitoring of wastewater report is submitted to state pollution control board for their records.

33. What controls and monitoring are there of the groundwater within the application area of treated wastewater at Coca-Cola's Kaladera plant?

The Company's bottling plant at Kaladera plant uses groundwater (borewells located inside the plant) as source of water. The groundwater within the plant is monitored on annual basis which has hardly shown any deterioration in quality over the period of time. External borewells at upstream and downstream are being monitored (since last 2 years) pre monsoon and post monsoon for quality of groundwater which has shown hardly any deterioration in the quality.

34. What controls and monitoring have been put in place to ensure that the soil's carrying capacity should not be exceeded within the application area of treated wastewater at Coca-Cola's Kaladera plant?

An area of about 40,000 sq. metres has been developed as greenbelt in the plant. This consists of about 10,000 sq. metres of lawn area and about 1,600 numbers of trees. The greenbelt is irrigated by the treated wastewater by means of sprinkler system. This prevents any run off and water-logging in the greenbelt. On an average about 120 cu. metre/day wastewater is used to maintain greenbelt of 40,000 sq. metre (4 hectare) which is well within the standard of 134 to 180 m3 of water / hectare prescribed by the state pollution control board for sandy loamy soil.

35. When did the Coca-Cola bottling plant in Ballia last produce beverages? What is its current operational status?

Ballia plant was a co-packing facility owned by a franchise bottler. As part of business restructuring and consolidation, the production at Ballia was discontinued from June 26, 2007.

36. When did the Coca-Cola bottling plant in Plachimada Kerala last produce beverages? What is its current operational status?

The bottling plant at Plachimada in Kerala has not been operational since March 9, 2004.

37. What is the current status of negotiations regarding the relocation of the plant in Kerala?

We are continuously engaging with all stakeholders to ensure a win-win solution for all.

Appendix C:
The Non-Answers of
Ed Potter

Ed Potter is the Coca-Cola Global Workplace Rights Director and is in charge of labour issues. After the company blocked my formal attempts to communicate with him I managed to secure an interview from the time-honoured method of 'bumrushing', namely, I spotted him in the street and ran at him with a recorder [Chapter 14: The Road to Delaware]. He assured me that allegation of misconduct and labour issues would be investigated seriously, so alongside other questions that arose from our chat, I emailed him. This is the summation of our all too brief exchange.

Sent: 05/01/2008 06:54 PM CET
To: Ed Potter
Subject: From Mark Thomas in the UK
Dear Ed

Good to see you at the AGM in Delaware the other month and I hope you are keeping well. I was wondering about some of the statements you made and wanted to follow up a few points.

Firstly, on Colombia, I asked if the union that replaced Sinaltrainal (SICO I believe) negotiated a pay cut following the events in Carepa where Sinaltrainal was driven out of town and had their offices burnt down. You said you didn't know, but would it be possible to find out?

Secondly, you said there was good relations with twelve other unions, what is the number of members in each of these unions and what percentage of the workforce does this represent?

Thirdly, you have said previously that CUT do not support the boycott call from Sinaltrainal. I was under the impression that CUT did support the boycott call, could you clarify this and provide the source for this statement?

Fourthly, you said that casual workers in Colombia were not allowed to join an industrial trade union, I wonder if you might point out the law which you refer to?

Fifthly, you said 31 per cent of the workers at Coca-Cola bottlers in Colombia were unionised, does this include casual labour? If it does not, what percentage of Coke workers are unionised if you were to include the casual workers into the equation?

On the subject of India, I was reading in the *Nation*'s letter pages that you said that The Coca-Cola Company and its bottlers 'indirectly create employment for 125,000 more [workers] in related procurement supply and distribution roles'. I wonder if you might break down the 125,000 figure for me? Does this figure include panawallahs and juicewallahs (people who sell Coca-Cola products from their stalls)?

On the issue of passing on claims to you regarding the treatment of workers in developing nations, I wonder if you might spell out to me what measures would be taken to investigate the matters or indeed if you have initiated any measures? I look forward to hearing from you.

Best Wishes

Mark Thomas

Subject: response to the email

Ed Potter has referred your email to me. You can find information about our workplace practices on both cokefacts.com and on www.GetTheRealFacts.co.uk.

Sincerely,

Kari Bjorhus

Director, Public Affairs

The Coca-Cola Company

Appendix D:
Death Threat

This is a copy of a death threat sent by the Black Eagles, naming Luis Eduardo aka Chile [Chapter 4: 'Chile']. This death threat was sent in February 2007.

> The Black Eagles call on the terrorists in the trade union of Coca-Cola – Javier Correa, Luis Garcia AKA El Chile, Domingo Flores AKA El Gordo, Nelson Perez – to stop the backlash against the Coca-Cola company – You have already caused enough damage – Stop this campaign against the employers of Santander who are supporting the downtrodden of this country – We declare that the military objective of the Black Eagles – how do you prefer death – torture – cutting up into pieces – coup de grace – in the style of Magdalena Medio and this is how you terrorists define it – So stop your campaign, the backlash – Remember Commander Mancuso doesn't like a fuss.
>
> This isn't just a threat, we will carry it out. We will do it. The day will arrive.